Finding Life Beyond Trauma

Using Acceptance and Commitment Therapy to Heal from Post-Traumatic Stress and Trauma-Related Problems

By
Victoria M. Follette, Ph.D.
Jacqueline Pistorello, Ph.D.

16
EasyRead Large

Copyright Page from the Original Book

Publisher's Note

Permission to use the image *La condition humaine* granted by the National Gallery of Art.

Permission to use the image "Regular Division of the Plane IV (Horsemen)" granted by the M.C. Escher Company.

Distributed in Canada by Raincoast Books

Acquired by Tesilya Hanauer; Cover design by Amy Shoup;
Edited by Carole Honeychurch; Text design by Tracy Carlson

Library of Congress Cataloging-in-Publication Data

Follette, Victoria M.
   Finding life beyond trauma : using acceptance and commitment therapy to heal from post-traumatic stress and trauma-related problems / Victoria M. Follette and Jacqueline Pistorello.
      p. cm.
   ISBN-13: 978-1-57224-497-9
   ISBN-10: 1-57224-497-6
   1. Post-traumatic stress disorder—Treatment. 2. Psychic trauma—Treatment. 3. Acceptance and commitment therapy. I. Pistorello, Jacqueline. II. Title.
   RC552.P67F65 2007
   616.85'21—dc22

                                    2007013041

09 08 07

10 9 8 7 6 5 4 3 2 1   First printing

ReadHowYouWant partners with publishers to provide books for ALL Kinds of Readers. For more information about Becoming A RHYW Registered Reader and to find more titles in your preferred format, visit:
www.readhowyouwant.com

TABLE OF CONTENTS

To my students and my clients, who teach me about life beyond trauma every day.

—VF

To my mother, Maria Formolo Pistorello, whose lifelong commitment to following one's values served as the beacon of light in times of uncertainty in my life.

—JP

Finding a New Way Forward

In the developed world, dying of starvation or thirst is rare enough to make national news. If you think about it, that fact is a small indication of a larger human reality. We have learned a great deal about how to control our external world, and in parts of the world where we have resources to apply, we've come to expect it as a matter of course.

When pain intrudes unexpectedly, that assumption is disrupted. Violent attacks, tragic accidents, natural disasters, wars, sexual and emotional abuse, and dozens of other such events show that the external world is not always controllable, regardless of our knowledge and resources. These painful challenges can suddenly shift the apparent arena of control from the external to the internal world. The pain may have begun on the outside, but it lives on in the inside, in the form of painful memories, difficult emotions, negative thoughts, or unpleasant urges. Once there, people do what people do with painful memories, difficult emotions, negative thoughts, or unpleasant urges. And that's often a problem.

Humans' relative skill in controlling their external world often fails them when applied to the world within. It is hard to get rid of painful memories, reduce difficult emotions, or eliminate negative thoughts and urges. Indeed, modern psychological research is showing us that part of what often turns pain into trauma is the misapplication of some of the very skills we most trust in controlling the world outside the skin—judging, planning, problem solving, and controlling—to the world inside the skin.

The human mind is a problem-solving organ—it cannot help but do what it does. When we look at our own pain, we initially cannot help but judge it, anticipate it, reason with it, and try to get it to go away. And sometimes that may even be useful—but for those picking up this book wanting help, I suspect it is not. It is very likely you've already tried that. And if it produced everything you want, you would not be picking up this book. You are looking for a new way forward.

You have found one.

Until the secret of how the human mind works is revealed, it tends to do what it has always done—like a pony who knows only one trick endlessly performing it. But modern psychological research is also revealing that it is possible to do truly new things with our memories, emotions, thoughts, and urges than what problem-solving minds normally do. These mindfulness and acceptance methods seem to allow us to move quickly in the direction of a life we value without first waiting for the war inside us to be won.

This book will show you how to take that alternative path.

What you will find in these pages is an approach—Acceptance and Commitment Therapy (ACT, said as a single word, not initials)—that takes the view that your life is not a problem to be solved. A life is to be lived, *with* the past exactly as it has been but with a future as broad as your most deeply held values. Moving in that direction requires learning how to let go of some kinds of problem solving. It means learning how to feel feelings as feelings, and thinking thoughts as thoughts. This is a workbook, because it takes work to learn an alternative path. Mere understanding is not enough. Minds cannot fully grasp how to solve problems in a nonjudgmental way because solving problems planfully and judgmentally is what minds *do.*

ACT allows us a new way forward when some of our most trusted skills are no longer very effective. It offers suggestions for what to do when little we can think of is very likely to be helpful. It gently points toward exciting alternatives when seemingly nothing we can do will do.

The scientific evidence base for ACT in the areas of trauma, pain, anxiety, and depression—areas most readers of this book will likely know something about in personal terms—is growing rapidly. The body of evidence is not as large as for some other more traditional approaches, so people who have never worked on these problems with traditional cognitive behavioral or other more fully empirically supported methods may wish to consider that. Nevertheless, there is enough solid evidence that it seemed time to put this new way forward into the hands of those who may benefit, especially those who need a fresh approach.

I am one of the originators of ACT, but I have also known these two authors for many years. Victoria Follette is a valued colleague and friend, and Jacque Pistorello is not only one of the best ACT therapists I know—she is also my dear wife. I suppose that means I am not objective, but I did watch how this book came together and I know how much care, compassion, and concern have gone into it. I am excited by the possibility that many thousands will be helped.

You are in a unique position. If you are willing to be guided by your own pain, it has purchased the openness to learning a new way forward. I'd like to believe that is part of why fate and happenstance have placed this book in front of you. You would have no reason to learn a new way if the old ways had continued to work adequately. Two people I respect and trust a great deal will walk with you through this learning process.

When you are ready, turn the page. It is time to begin to learn a new way.

—Steven C. Hayes, *University of Nevada*

Acknowledgments

We would like to thank a number of individuals who have contributed to this book. Several authors have allowed us to either reproduce some of their original exercises in this volume or to adapt them to the specific aims of this book. These are Steven C. Hayes and Spencer Smith, James Pennebaker, Michael Addis and Chris Martell, J.T. Blackledge, and Joseph Ciarrochi. Robyn Walser, Kelly Wilson, and Sonja Batten have helped hone our thinking about the application of ACT to trauma treatment. We would also like to acknowledge others whose work has either inspired us or provided the foundation for some of the elements in this book. Many trauma researchers have had an important influence over the years. Pam Alexander, John Briere, Christine Courtois, Chris Brewin, Judith Herman, Patricia Resick, Edna Foa, Terry Keane, and Josef Ruzek are just a few of the people who paved the way for us and helped us to find our own path. The teachings of individuals from the mindfulness traditions, such as Kabat-Zinn, Pema Chodron, and Thich Nhat Hahn, along with other local resources, have been valuable in many ways. Marsha Linehan, Robert Kohlenberg, and Neil Jacobson also were essential teachers who helped define the new wave in behavior therapy. Our appreciation and gratitude also go to our students Adria Pearson, Jennifer Plumb, and Karen Murphy for their assistance in developing some of the chapters in this book. Special thanks goes to another one of our students, Kate M. Iverson, who wrote for this book and also provided encouragement and support when deadlines were looming. Emily Neilan was wonderful in helping us with formatting and a number of technical tasks.

We could not have written this book without the support of two groups of people. First, we are indebted to the international network of ACT researchers and therapists who have helped us along this path and whose work provided the foundation for this book. Second, we will always remain grateful to our clients who have been willing to share their lives with us and who have taught us so much.

Finally, we would like to thank New Harbinger for giving us this opportunity and Tesilya Hanauer and Carole Honeychurch for all of their efforts and support in making this book happen.

I am grateful to Steve Hayes for his mentorship and for allowing me to be part of the ACT work. Thank you to Jacque—I would not have attempted this book without you. Thank you to all the students who taught me so much along the way and continue to influence my work. I appreciate the ongoing advice and support of William Follette. Most especially I am thankful to the many clients and research participants who informed this work. This book is meant to share what you have taught me with other survivors. Special thanks go to my friends Sandy, Alyson, Anne, and Patty for all their support over the years.

—V.F.

I would like to thank Victoria Follette for inviting me to cowrite this book and for teaching me to treat the impact of trauma and to bear witness to my clients' pain with compassion and respect. Many, many thanks go to my husband, Steven C. Hayes, for his unwavering support and patience, for taking care of our child during many weekends and evenings so that I could write, and for introducing me to ACT seventeen years ago—an experience that changed my life in many different ways. I would also like to thank a number of friends and family who, through their emotional or instrumental support, allowed me to write this book: Neiva Pistorello, Inge Skeans, Laura Vargas, Elza Major, Catherine Armstrong, Erin Oksol, Nancy Taylor, and Duane Varble.

x

—J.P.

Introduction

The mystery of life is not a problem to be solved, but a reality to be experienced.

—Zen saying

While the pain and suffering of trauma can seem unbearable, every day we see examples of people who have found a way not only to survive their experiences but also to really live their life to the fullest. This book is about finding your way back to your valued life. In *Finding Life Beyond Trauma* we hope to help you to move toward living a vital, rich, and awake life.

What Is Trauma?

Trauma is defined as a serious physical or emotional injury or shock that can cause significant damage or distress and disruption. Experiencing trauma can be the result of common life experiences such as accidents or involvement in personal relationships. However, trauma can also result from extraordinary experiences such as war, natural disasters, or terrorist events. No matter how careful we are, it is fairly likely that we will experience one or more traumatic experiences in our lifetime. You probably picked out this book because you, or someone you know, are hurting and have not been able to find the cure to help the pain go away.

Many people wonder why the hurt and fear from trauma do not fade on their own and why they often seem to be getting worse. Some people feel empty, out of control, scared, hopeless, or even "dead." These are common reactions in people who have experienced trauma. But, along with these feelings, you can also feel proud that you are a survivor. You are alive and have persevered despite the trauma you have experienced. No matter how hard it has been, you are here and you are reading this book. We assume that you are looking for ways to enhance your life, and that is what this book is about. This book is based on acceptance and commitment therapy (ACT), an approach we have been using for over fifteen years to treat individuals in the aftermath of trauma.

Acceptance and Commitment Therapy

ACT (pronounced as the word "act" and not as three separate letters) is an approach to psychotherapy that relies on a combination of behavioral and cognitive therapies, values clarification, and mindfulness (Hayes, Strosahl, and Wilson, 1999; Hayes and Smith 2005). ACT is a form of therapy that will invite you to observe and describe your deepest inner experiences, taking a new look at what you are doing in response to your trauma—what is working for you and what isn't. Using this approach, we will ask you to let go of strategies that might be keeping you from having your most valued life. ACT is based on the assumption that as we try to suppress or escape pain, we often generate more suffering in our lives. The "solution" we sometimes cling to for dear life, such as "I must not feel pain," becomes part of the problem. Getting unstuck then involves looking at things from a fresh perspective. In order to do that, ACT relies on counterintuitive and sometimes surprising strategies. All of these ACT concepts will be explained more fully later on in the book through our writing and exercises you will be asked to complete.

For now, we would like to summarize some basic assumptions underlying ACT, to give you a sample of what is to follow. ACT can be described as encompassing three areas: accept, choose, and take action (Hayes, Strosahl, and Wilson 1999).

Accept Your Reactions and Be Present

Pain is inevitable in life; suffering is not. Unnecessary suffering comes from trying to push away or eliminate the original pain. This is called *experiential avoidance.*

We try to eliminate, control, or suppress thoughts, feelings, memories, and bodily sensations when we forget that these are just private experiences that cannot harm us directly. Feelings of sadness or a thought of "I'm bad" cannot by themselves hurt us—unless we let them.

The reason we may lose sight of the fact that a thought is just a thought is because of language. Language, albeit extremely helpful, has a dark side that allows our minds to construct scary futures, compare ourselves to unmet ideals, and create realities that only exist in our mind's eye.

Mindfulness, a way of focusing our attention on the present moment, whatever it brings, without judgment, can help us develop the ongoing awareness that a thought is just a thought, a feeling is just a feeling, a bodily reaction is just a bodily reaction, a memory is just a memory.

This awareness, which has been taught through sitting and guided meditations for hundred of years, allows us to be more open to our own experiences.

Choose a Valued Direction

Instead of looking backward to the unchangeable past, ACT guides us to aim toward what we want now and in the future. Life opens up when we turn our attention to what we really want to be about—what we value.

Through values clarification, we can choose a life direction, even with the difficult histories we have. The values that most liberate us are not embraced to avoid guilt or to please others but rather because of their intrinsic worth and the vitality they bring to our lives.

Take Action

Through a continuous process of bringing acceptance, mindfulness, and values into the present moment, we can reorient our own behavior toward what really works. Creating a vital life is done step-by-step by building larger and larger patterns of committed action. It is a process never completed, but it does not need to be. Life is a process, not an outcome. Life will be asking you the same question over and over again across different situations and times: Are you willing to do what needs to be done, often sitting with some type of internal discomfort, in order to have a vital life?

ACT is about taking a loving stance with oneself and living life as a compassionate expression of your own wholeness. ACT has been shown scientifically to be helpful with a wide variety of problems, including depression, anxiety, substance abuse, chronic pain, and even psychotic disorders (Hayes and Strosahl 2004). The underlying theory of ACT, which is based on the idea that language leads to experiential avoidance and is responsible for most forms of human psychological problems, has received support in laboratory studies (Hayes, Barnes-Holmes, and Roche 2001; Hayes et al. 2006).

How Can ACT Help Trauma Survivors?

ACT has much to offer those in recovery from trauma. We believe that the pain you are experiencing, which may be present in the form of depression, post-traumatic stress disorder, feeling numb, excessive alcohol use, or pushing others away, is at least partially the result of your efforts to try to get rid of, escape from, suppress, or avoid any reminders of your trauma or other painful life experiences. ACT provides guidance on how to live a meaningful life without disowning a big part of who you are: your past experiences, both positive and negative.

Although we can't promise that the process will be easy, we think that there is a way to accept your painful past, heal from it, and lead a more fulfilling life. Judith Herman has stated in the introduction of her book *Trauma and Recovery*, "The conflict between the will to deny horrible events and the will to proclaim them aloud is the central dialectic of psychological trauma" (1992, 1). Living through trauma involves surviving an experience that is often filled with shame, humiliation, and fear, which in turn, as the quote suggests, leads to a constant ambivalence between sharing the pain or hiding it, or even hiding *from* it. We live in a society that has difficulty tolerating other people's discomfort and actually promotes secrecy, thus reinforcing the idea that we should not talk about what we have experienced and perpetuating a society of avoidance. For example, how many times have you turned the channel when you saw something painful on TV? Maybe you were watching the news and saw a story on war, famine, or some other suffering that you were unable to ease. Because you felt pain and felt helpless to ameliorate it, you chose to click to another channel. Similarly, many survivors learn to avoid uncomfortable memories, thoughts, and feelings by pushing them away, focusing on a distraction, or using some other method of turning the channel. We believe this is a significant disservice to survivors of trauma.

Even though most of us will try using avoidance with some success in the short run, it just doesn't work in the long haul, particularly when it's the only or the main tool in our bag. Many of us will try to employ avoidance as our main coping strategy, and usually it only makes things worse. However, if we can look inside ourselves and see what is going on, then and only then do we claim the power to do something different. This *awareness* of what is going on for yourself is the opposite of experiential avoidance, and we will teach you how to look at your experience throughout the chapters in this book.

In *Finding Life Beyond Trauma,* we hope to show you how to reclaim your experience while also helping you to understand that *you are not just what has happened to you.* You are not your traumatic memories, your thoughts, or your feelings. Instead, you are the person who holds all of these things. You may not have created your problems, and you certainly did not choose to experience trauma. Yet, in order to take hold of your life, you will have to deal with these problems. Although there will likely be some pain that accompanies self-awareness, you will also gain a tremendous amount of freedom to choose where to go from here. We hope that the chapters in this book will help you to:

- Be awake and present for your life now *with* (and not in spite of) your trauma history, your memories, your fears, and your sadness and grief

- Find freedom in choosing new and vital life directions

- Be able to "walk the talk" in terms of what you would like your life to be about

How to Use This Book

This section provides some guidance to you on how to make the best use of this book from an ACT perspective. This is an important part of the work, and we encourage you not to skip it. If you frequently find yourself setting self-help books aside, feeling disheartened after an initial phase of excitement, these words of advice and encouragement may be of help to you. There is an Eastern saying that goes, "When the student is ready, the teacher appears." The few guidelines that follow are intended to help prepare you to be ready to take in whatever teachings could prove useful to you in this book.

Intend for This Book to Work

Would you be willing to intend for this book to work? Would you be willing to start from the premise that there is something between the front and back covers of this book that can be useful to you in a meaningful way? We are not asking you to blindly believe, rather to consider that this book offers something here that could be life changing for you. Would you be willing to start reading this book with that approach? It is easy to fall prey to cynicism or hopelessness right off the bat, particularly if you have tried many other approaches and nothing seems to help. Actually, ACT seems to be particularly relevant to those who have experienced multiple failures before. Therefore, we would like to ask you to make a commitment right here, right now, to intend for this book to work for you.

Check Back with Your Experience

We are not trying to sell you on an idea or a belief system. We are trying to help you get into direct contact with your own experience. It is your experience, and not the words on these pages, that will ultimately tell you how useful some of these concepts are. Only your experience can inform you as to what is working for you, what your values are, and what feels meaningful and vital for you. Your mind and your experience are two different things, though. For example, your mind may say that keeping yourself closed off from others is good, but your experience of loneliness may say otherwise. Throughout this book, we invite you to go back to your experience. This means that actually doing the exercises, as opposed to simply reading them, will be far more helpful for you, because it will bring you in contact with your actual experience and not its intellectual equivalent.

Cultivate Acceptance and Compassion for Yourself

If you are going to do this work, you need to bring compassion toward yourself into the process. If you find yourself having self-blaming or judgmental thoughts, guilt, or shame while reading this book or completing exercises, just gently notice these reactions nonjudgmentally. Encountering areas in need of work is a given in this book. See if you can bring loving kindness toward yourself as you begin this journey. If you do find yourself judging yourself, "don't judge your judging," (Linehan 1993b, 208). Judging may be natural and habitual for you at this point, but that doesn't mean you need to pay attention to them or blame yourself for them.

Psychological Flexibility

In ACT, we believe that psychological flexibility is the key to psychological health. We don't have a recipe for how you should be at the end of this book, except that having increased flexibility can lead you to a wider range of choices in how you live your life. Flexibility may come in handy in two ways as you work on this book. First, "trauma survivors" is a very large category of people. You are a unique individual with unique circumstances and unique values. Not all examples and stories will pertain to you or feel relevant. Take what is useful and leave the rest. Second, as you progress through this workbook, you may find yourself changing your view about yourself and the world. See if you can make room for that and let go of being right or wrong or being consistent. This approach is about finding a very new way of being in the world. In ACT we view life as an ongoing journey of growth and change.

Your Safety Comes First

Your safety is very important. You have survived your trauma, and it's important that you take very good care of yourself while you do this work. Therefore, in chapter 2 we will go over some basic skills, particularly mindfulness, that may help you recognize your limits and do something healthy with your own struggles. In the final chapter of the book we provide some resources for professional help, which you may consult at any point.

The Structure of the Book

This is a workbook; therefore, as mentioned earlier, exercises are a crucial aspect of the book and there will be several in each chapter. Most, but not all, of the exercises involve some writing component. Because there might be some very personal content written into the book, where you keep it may be important if you don't live alone. After you start completing the exercises, we suggest that you consider this book like a personal journal and take steps to preserve its privacy accordingly.

To help you navigate through the book, we'll now discuss some unique aspects of its structure.

Strategies to Undermine the Dark Side of Language

Because ACT comes from the perspective that language, a friend in many ways, can also be a psychological foe, several aspects of the work in this book will involve teaching you to undermine the impact of language or to hold its power lightly. Therefore, we will use a lot of new language conventions, metaphors, stories, and hands-on exercises, some of which may seem silly to you on occasion. For instance, you will see right away that we use the conjunction "AND" in capital letters where you might expect the word "but." As explained later in the book, we do so for a reason—to emphasize that both sides of a coin can exist together. Instead of "I went to work, but I was depressed," we say "I went to work, AND I was depressed." Both conditions can be true. You do not have to get rid of depression or anxiety or even your trauma history to live your life fully.

The Mindfulness Bell

The ability to develop awareness of your thoughts, emotions, bodily reactions, judgments, and memories is a key aspect of ACT and other related treatments. In some mindfulness traditions, when a bell is rung, participants are invited to check and see where their minds are as a way of enhancing inner awareness. We will utilize a similar strategy in this book, except that instead of ringing the bell, we will introduce a picture of a bell. Throughout the book, at various points, we will introduce a small bell that looks like this: 🔔. When you see this symbol, the invitation is for you to come back to the present moment—to notice your breath, your thoughts and feelings, sensations within your body, images and memories, or where your mind was taking you. In addition to being a good way to practice mindfulness, this convention might help you notice if you are becoming distressed or dissociated while reading this book. Please allow it to be useful to you. If you notice yourself having a difficult reaction when you see the bell, turn to the journaling section at the end of each chapter and make a note of it.

Personal Journaling Page

At the end of each chapter, we will provide you with a space to write down any reactions you were having to the reading and exercises: thoughts, feelings or emotions, self-judgments, physical sensations, and action urges (what you felt or feel like doing). You may complete this page whenever you encounter the bell sign during your reading. Conversely, you may wait until the end of the chapter and then note your reactions to the reading. Research shows that writing about emotional topics can have a very helpful impact on individuals (Pennebaker 2004; see chapter 7). Therefore, we wanted to include a component of written expression throughout the book. If you need more space, feel free to use the back side of the page or a separate sheet of paper.

Case Stories

To illustrate points, we will sometimes rely on stories about different individuals. These are not specific clients. Rather, they are a compilation of many people we have encountered over the years in a variety of settings. Names, demographic characteristics, and other identifying information have been deliberately changed or distorted, and details about different people have been combined. No case story presented in this book is that of an actual individual we know. However, the examples we use come from the truth of what people have told us over the years.

Our Message to You

We have been doing this work for a number of years with people who have survived a wide range of traumas. Both of us have had the opportunity to work with survivors of rape, child abuse, combat, natural disasters, and terrorist events. We have worked in hospitals, outpatient clinics, and community agencies. In all of this work we have remained impressed with the tremendous strength of the human spirit. We know that barriers to therapy sometimes get in the way—issues of access, affordability, willingness, and so on. We have written this book to share what we have learned with you in the service of helping you to regain your own sense of strength and identity in order to live your valued life.

CHAPTER 1

Understanding Trauma

With Kate M. Iverson

Although the world is full of suffering, it is full also of the overcoming of it.

—Helen Keller

What Is Trauma?

Human beings have reported painful traumatic events in one way or the other since the earliest written records. Men and women have lived through natural disasters, fought wars, experienced loss, and been the victims of other forms of violence by other human beings.

Traumatic experiences can happen to anyone. The word "trauma" generally refers to a wide range of intensely stressful situations that involve high levels of danger, fear, helplessness, or horror that evoke high levels of distress for most people in such situations (American Psychiatric Association [APA] 1994). The range of events that can be labeled as traumas may include, but certainly isn't limited to, the following experiences:

- Childhood sexual or physical abuse

- Partner abuse (emotional, sexual, and/or physical)

- Sexual assault

- Rape

- Physical attacks or assaults

- Serious car accidents

- Torture

- War combat

- Fire

- Natural disasters, such as hurricanes, tornadoes, and earthquakes

- Witnessing or hearing about something horrible that has happened to another person

The effects of trauma are diverse and range far beyond post-traumatic stress symptoms (Follette and Ruzek 2006; Herman 1992). In many cases, a survivor of trauma may experience problems after the traumatic event that he or she had not experienced before the trauma occurred. The symptoms or problems people experience after trauma can be thought of as falling within a spectrum or continuum ranging from limited effects to very severe effects. Furthermore, we know that the effects of trauma can be cumulative. In other words, the more traumas you have experienced, the more problems you may experience as a result. So, even if you've experienced many traumas, you're not likely to just get used to it.

The psychological impacts after trauma can vary from one individual to another. 🔔 [Pay attention to your breathing at this moment. As noted in the introduction, this bell sign in the text is an invitation to take a moment to notice what is happening inside your own skin. You can either silently notice these reactions, be it your breathing, thoughts, feelings, or other reactions, or else you may take a little time to write about it at the end of the chapter.] However, there are some common factors that have emerged. Some people may experience some slight adjustment issues immediately following a trauma but then achieve a full recovery in which they never experience any additional problems related to the trauma. Other people may have re-curring episodes of psychological difficulties, especially during times of other life stressors. Some people may experience symptoms that begin immediately after the trauma and get worse and worse over time for many years, resulting in complex and long-lasting outcomes.

Those in the field of traumatic stress have learned a lot about trauma in the past thirty years, yet we have not always done a very good job in making our knowledge available for those who most need it. As you likely know from your own experience, it is hard to acknowl-edge when you are experiencing difficulties or problems in your life. Having difficulties admitting and talking about psychological problems is a very common response, particu-larly when it seems that many people will not be able to relate to the trauma you have experienced. Most trauma survivors are afraid that other people won't be able to understand what they've been through or that they just won't get it. If traumatic experiences are so much more common than people think, then why is it that people rarely talk openly about their experiences with trauma? It can feel very invalidating, or minimizing, of your experience if you are telling yourself (and/or others are telling you) to "just get over it" or "try not to think about it." If only recovering from trauma were so easy! Additionally, some people will let you know directly or indirectly that they don't really want to hear about your experience.

Despite more media coverage in recent times of traumatic events and their effects, there is still considerable stigma associated with talking about trauma. As a result, many survivors may feel that they are going crazy or that they are somehow inadequate or broken because they appear to be dealing with the trauma less successfully than other people seem to be dealing with similar stressful situations. Unfortunately, many people, including mental health professionals, are afraid, unwilling, or too uncomfortable to talk about traumatic events. For this reason, it's possible that you may not have had a good experience sharing or talking about your traumatic experiences with even the most well-intentioned people. For example, sometimes partners, parents, therapists, family members, or even your best friends may have trouble understanding what you have been through. However, it is very important for you to understand that you are not going crazy, you are not weak, and you are not broken. The problems you are having are common reactions to trauma.

You Are Not the Only One: The Truth About Trauma

Trauma has been covered in a veil of myths over the years. Often, people do not want to believe that trauma happens as frequently as it does, and many people do not want to believe what a large impact it has on individuals, families, and society at large. Let's take a look at some common myths surrounding trauma.

Myth 1: Traumatic Experiences Are Uncommon

The reported prevalence of trauma is startling, with over 70 percent of the adult population experiencing trauma at some point in their lives (Breslau 2002). The methods and definitions used in the research on the prevalence of trauma vary widely and can be controversial. However, it's clear that traumatic experiences occur at a very high rate. Trauma used to be viewed as isolated events that are not typical of the normal human experience. We now know that trauma impacts many people every year.

🔔 [Any thoughts or feelings coming up for you at this moment?]

Myth 2: If People Were Just Stronger, They Could Get Over Trauma

Although the severity of problems or symptoms can vary from individual to individual, no one can completely avoid trauma or completely protect himself or herself from the consequences of traumatic experiences. The normal response is to experience some problems coping after a traumatic experience. These common responses are discussed in greater detail later on in this chapter. How serious these problems are after trauma depends on a variety of factors, including previous traumatic experiences, a person's own natural abilities to cope with stress, the perceived severity of the trauma, and, importantly, what kind of support a person gets from family members, friends, and professionals following the trauma (Herman 1992). The issue of recovery from trauma is a complex one that continues to be an active focus of research.

Myth 3: Every Trauma Survivor Will Need Therapy

Why are some people, despite experiencing trauma, stress, and hardship, still able to overcome life's difficulties and thrive after trauma? What skills or qualities do these people possess? The answers to this question are being researched every day. This is one of many topics we will face where two seemingly opposite ideas can be true. Despite the many common consequences of trauma, the bottom line is that trauma does not have to ruin your life. This doesn't mean you are to blame for the problems you have encountered in dealing with your stressful life experiences. The idea of recovery is a personal one and will mean something different for each person who picks up this book.

We believe that you have the power to make your life meaningful and satisfying through the choices you make. "Resilience" is a term often used to denote bouncing or springing back into shape, and it's often used to describe those who seemingly bounce back from trauma. But the word doesn't seem to accurately describe the human process of gradually returning to your previous level of functioning through a process of healing. Being resilient does not mean that the trauma is not difficult and upsetting or that it doesn't impact you in many of the ways mentioned above; it simply means that despite these obstacles, you are willing and able to move forward in your life. In fact, we believe you can move beyond your previous experience to an even more satisfying stage of life. 🔔 [Any thoughts or feelings coming up right now? What about changes in heart rate or breathing?]

You already are exhibiting characteristics that indicate your ability to recover from your experiences as evidenced by the fact that you have picked up this book and are willing to work on changing your life. You were able to recognize that you were struggling and took steps to get help.

Exercise 1.1: Recognizing Your Own Strength

In your recovery, it will be important for you to notice and acknowledge all of the positive steps you are making. List some other steps you have been taking to move forward (for instance, taking the time to learn about the consequences of trauma).

1. _Learning + reading_

2. _Started to jog again_

3. _Took mindfulness course_

---

4. _Contacted_ Mullin, Rena, Centre S.A.T

5. _Doing_ "being present" exercise

6. _____

7. _____

Myth 4: Traumatic Experiences Mainly Happen to Women

A common myth is that noncombat trauma only happens to women. We know that this is not the case. According to the National Comorbidity Study (NCS), over 60 percent of the males surveyed reported at least one potential trauma, with many of them reporting experiencing two or more types of trauma (Kessler et al. 1995). According to the NCS results and other studies, men were more likely than women to report witnessing someone being injured or killed, involvement in a life-threatening accident or natural disaster, or involvement in a physical attack or combat exposure (Breslau et al. 1998; Kessler et al. 1995).

Myth 5: Men Are Rarely Victims of Sexual Trauma

Our society repeatedly fails to recognize that men and boys can be victims of sexual assault. Rates of sexual abuse of young boys or adolescents vary from 4 percent to 16 percent depending on the population studied, data collected, and the definitions of sexual assault or abuse (Dong et al. 2003). One study found that nearly 12 percent of new navy recruits reported a history of childhood sexual abuse (Merrill et al. 2001). Males are most often sexually assaulted by other men (although women can sexually assault men too), and the perpetrators are often authority figures or strangers. Furthermore, many men do not disclose their sexual trauma to anyone, which can fuel shame and isolation.

Myth 6: The Media Exaggerate the Frequency of Trauma

In the context of more frequent discussions about traumatic experiences in the news, reality TV, and talk shows, some of our clients report experiencing a backlash of sorts, with individuals in their environment now assuming that this increased media exposure has led to an unwarranted and exaggerated public perception of the frequency and impact of trauma. However, data on prevalence rates about interpersonal violence against women alone proves otherwise.

A national survey of adult women in the United States pointed out that nearly 13 percent of participants had experienced a completed rape, and approximately 14 percent had experienced molestation or attempted sexual assault (Resnick et al. 1993). Studies have indicated that approximately one out of six women is raped in her lifetime (Brenner, McMahon, and Douglas 1999; Tjaden and Thoennes 1998). Additionally, according to the National Violence Against Women Survey, approximately 25 percent of American women experience partner abuse in their lifetime (Tjaden and Thoennes 2000).

🔔 [Notice where your mind is right now. Is it on this page or elsewhere?]

Myth 7: Abuse Only Happens in Poor Families

The concept that abuse only occurs among the disadvantaged is typically applied in interpersonal violence situations such as rape, child sexual and physical abuse, and domestic violence.

Somehow, people find it easier to believe that an unemployed alcoholic is hitting his wife than a well-dressed doctor. Yet, the evidence is that trauma happens across a variety of social and economic dimensions. Although the very experience of poverty, particularly living in crime-infested areas, can be similar to other forms of trauma (Kiser and Black 2005), traumatic events can happen to anyone at any time in his or her life, regardless of gender, ethnicity, education, or financial stability.

Myth 8: Post-traumatic Stress Disorder Is Rare Among Military Men and Women

Military men and women often experience psychological difficulties as a result of the trauma they experience in combat zones. Approximately 30 percent of Vietnam veterans experience post-traumatic stress disorder (see description below) in their lifetime (Kulka et al. 1988). A recent study has demonstrated that rates of post-traumatic stress disorder, depression, and anxiety disorders are elevated among American troops who have been stationed in Iraq and Afghanistan. Rates of post-traumatic stress disorder were as high as 17 percent of military returnees from Iraq. Furthermore, military personnel who experienced the most symptoms were less likely to seek psychological services (Hoge et al. 2004). Although many military personnel will return from combat and adjust well, a significant number of combatants will experience post-traumatic stress disorder (Friedman 2006).

Myth 9: Only Really Severely Distressed People Would Benefit from Help

There is no one truth that will be accurate for everyone. The question of whether only severely distressed people benefit from help remains one that is highly debated in the trauma literature. Traumatic experiences and the effects of trauma can happen to all of us, no matter how healthy, strong, and resourceful we may be. When people are still experiencing problems weeks and months after a trauma has occurred, there are many specialized treatments, such as this self-help book, that can help. Some people will find that the symptoms tend to resolve over time, while others will decide to seek treatment immediately. Part of our goal in this book is to help you to look at what is true for you and to choose a direction that fits your unique needs and goals.

Myth 10: We Have Become a Society of Victims

The idea that we've become a society of victims is related to the second myth we listed. Unfortunately, it's not unusual to hear people say that individuals who claim to be traumatized are "just creating a mountain out of a molehill. If they really wanted to, they could pull themselves out of it. I personally or others I know have been through a lot, and we are doing just fine."

You may have heard such comments from others in your life or may have said this to yourself privately. It makes sense that such thoughts would pop into your head; it makes less sense to actually believe the thought. It is human nature to compare our experiences to those of others. Although this natural tendency, which is possible because of language (see chapter 6), may help us not feel so alone, it also has a very unhelpful side. We want to tell you at least three reasons why you may be better off not getting too caught up in comparing your experience with someone else's.

First, research shows that human beings tend to make some errors while making these comparisons. 🔔[Pay attention to your thoughts or judgments.] Some people may blame others' problems on some internal flaws while attributing their own to external factors (Kelley 1973). For example, "My trauma was really severe, that's why I'm struggling; so-and-so is making a big deal out of nothing because he or she doesn't want life to work." On the other hand, when people are depressed or have low self-esteem, it may go the other way: They attribute their own behavior to internal, global, and stable features of their character, such as "I'm just a failure," while others' tends to be attributed to external, temporary, and specific features, such as "Well, her perpetrator was her dad, so I understand why she would be struggling." Alcoholics Anonymous (AA) has a helpful saying to keep in mind here: "We often compare our insides to other people's outsides." We will come back to this topic in chapter 3.

Second, sometimes the impact of trauma is delayed. Someone who was abused as a child may not even regularly think of the abuse for years and then something happens that triggers flashbacks. For example, the birth of a child, a child reaching a certain age, or the release of a new war movie may trigger trauma symptoms for the first time, unexpectedly. Recent accounts showed, for example, that some male war veterans functioned well throughout their lives until they retired and then had a resurgence of symptoms (Friedman 2006). So, you may be comparing yourself to someone who may appear to be unaffected by his or her trauma; however, we are not always aware of the pain and suffering of others.

Third, and probably the major problem with comparing yourself to others, is that everyone has a different history, and therefore what looks like the same experience isn't. For example, someone who comes from a loving, protective family and goes to war may have a different experience of combat than someone who comes from an abusive family—even if at war they were in the same troop and experienced the same type of combat. But what differentiates two people's experience of a similar event is difficult to know, and even if we do know, it's nearly impossible to predict the effect. In general, in the above scenario, the person coming from an abusive family is more likely to experience traumatic symptoms. However, on an individual basis it may go the other way around: The person who came from a loving family may have his or her experience of the world as basically a safe place shattered and now be suffering from a significantly altered world view, whereas the person who came from an abusive environment may respond to war with tough skin. The latter scenario is less likely but still possible, because each person is different and experiences the world in different ways. So, comparing experiences across people doesn't always work. The suggestions we will make later in the book are to hold such comparisons lightly and focus on what you want your life to be about as opposed to gauging the validity of your own pain based on someone else's appearance.

Exercise 1.2: Demystifying Your Own Myths

What are your thoughts about each of these myths? How have these myths impacted your life, either through your own thoughts and actions or through those of other people in your life? What other myths have you encountered? What myths have you made up about your own experiences with trauma?

[space left intentionally blank in the original book]

How Do Traumatic Experiences Affect People?

Responses to trauma can be considered quite ordinary reactions to extraordinary situations. The bottom line is that your reaction to trauma, no matter how confusing it may seem to you, is not unusual. Although the human response to trauma is complex, it includes common reactions of the body and the mind.

A word of caution: Do not assume that because something is described below as an effect of trauma and you are a trauma survivor, that you must have it and just don't know it. That's not the case. These are potential effects, but as we noted above under myths, we are all different and respond differently to trauma.

Acute Stress Disorder

Acute stress disorder, or ASD (APA 1994), is a diagnostic label that is given to stress reactions of individuals within the first month of experiencing a trauma. The symptoms of ASD overlap with those of post-traumatic stress disorder (PTSD, see below). ASD can occur after experiencing or witnessing a threatening event and the response involves intense fear, helplessness, or horror. The symptoms of ASD include:

- *Numbness or detachment:* After trauma, some people have the sense that they do not feel their emotions very strongly or no longer have loving feelings toward other people.

- *Reduced awareness of your surroundings:* Some people report that they feel out of it or in a daze in certain situations.

- *Derealization:* After trauma, the world around you may feel different or unfamiliar, or you may have a sense of detachment from your surroundings.

- *Depersonalization:* Trauma survivors sometimes experience a sense of change in their self-awareness, feeling detached from themselves, their experience, or their body.

- *Dissociative amnesia:* Sometimes people are unable to remember parts of or important details of the traumatic event.

People who develop ASD within the month after the trauma are also more likely to later meet criteria for PTSD. However, it is also possible that someone may experience very few ASD symptoms and still later develop PTSD. 🔔[Notice what shows up for you right now, as you read the above.]

Post-traumatic Stress Disorder

Not everyone will develop post-traumatic stress disorder (APA 1994), the label for a cluster of distressing problems or symptoms that may continue to occur for at least a month following a traumatic experience. However, it is one of the most well-known problems associated with experiencing a traumatic event. For some people, these symptoms may not get better on their own or may even get worse over time.

Re-experiencing Symptoms
People who develop PTSD will tend to re-experience the ordeal in the form of:

- Upsetting memories or recollections of the event, such as images or thoughts about the traumatic event

- Recurrent and distressing dreams or nightmares related to the event

- Flashback episodes (acting as if the events were reoccurring in the present moment) and frightening thoughts

- Feeling upset by certain scents, sounds, places, or people that can trigger these intrusive experiences

- Physiological reactivity, such as increased heart rate, or the danger or survival response, which typically is the experience of needing to defend oneself even when there is no imminent danger, triggered by reminders of the traumatic experience

A common response is to experience more of these symptoms around anniversaries of the event (even decades after the traumatic event occurred).

Avoidance Symptoms
People with PTSD also tend to avoid reminders, places (for example, the scene of the trauma), or people (for instance, individuals who know about the trauma) that are associated with the traumatic event and may thus trigger responses to the trauma. Usually trauma sur-

vivors avoid these things in order to avoid experiencing general distress or emotional numbness. It is not uncommon for people to experience:

- Efforts to avoid thoughts, feelings, or memories about the event

- Efforts to avoid activities, places, or conversations about the traumatic event

- Difficulties and inabilities recalling important pieces of the trauma

- A noticeable loss of interest in formerly important or pleasurable activities

- Feelings of detachment or estrangement from other people

- Restricted range of emotions, such as blunted emotions or difficulties having loving feelings toward other people or things

- A sense of shortened future and changes in the way they might think about or plan for the future

🔔 [Notice any thoughts, feelings, or bodily reactions coming up.]

Symptoms of Increased Anxious Arousal
People with PTSD will experience physiological symptoms of arousal that were not present before the traumatic experience. Increased arousal symptoms can include:

- Difficulties falling or staying asleep

- Increased physiological responses, such as increased heart rate and feeling shaky or sweaty

- Difficulties concentrating or thinking clearly

- Hypervigilance, or feeling particularly agitated and on the lookout for danger

- Exaggerated startle response, such as getting startled by sudden noises or by people unexpectedly coming up from behind

It may be the case that you are experiencing some of these symptoms from time to time. The above symptoms are very common after people experience trauma because the mind and body are trying to cope with the previous traumatic experience and help keep you safe in the future. These symptoms become automatic responses to reminders of the trauma, even when you aren't in any real danger. Studies suggest that about 8 percent of the general population will develop PTSD (Kessler et al. 1995). Therefore, it is very important to note that many people who experience trauma will not develop PTSD. In fact, the majority of individuals who experience trauma will not develop severe psychological problems at all (Breslau and Kessler 2001; Resnick et al. 1993).

Trauma and Memory: Issues and Controversy

The issue of trauma and memory is a controversial topic in the field of traumatic stress. The memory system is very complex and we continue to learn more about the strength and fallibility of our brain processes. Generally speaking, *memory* refers to the process by which people draw on previous experience in order to use such knowledge in the present moment. Some prominent theorists have suggested that our minds may prevent us from thinking about unpleasant or traumatic experiences as a way of helping us cope after trauma. In other words, we unknowingly exclude or block traumatic memories, such as experience of childhood sexual abuse or violent combat situations, so that we can go on with our daily lives.

As discussed later in this chapter, some people *dissociate* during traumatic events. This means that they become so emotionally and physically overwhelmed by the experience that the body and mind shut down or disconnect from the situation. This process of dissociation is often automatic and is very helpful for survivors in coping with the present moment. However, memory difficulties can be a side effect of being in a dissociative state. Some survivors have difficulty remembering parts of or even entire traumatic events. This is often the case in motor vehicle accidents. For example, someone who gets into a serious car accident and experiences physical injury as a result may have a hard time remembering the entire accident.

One of the interesting things about trauma and memory is that our memories of trauma are not concrete. 🔔[Pay attention to your breathing at this moment.] Memory is not recorded like a videotape that makes a perfect record of what has happened. Our memories about experiences, including trauma, can change over time. You have probably heard about people "recovering memories" of a traumatic event. There has been some debate over whether recovered memories may sometimes be inaccurate or false. *False memories* refer to experiences of "remembering" a relatively complete version of an event that did not, in fact, actually occur. Some evidence for this phenomenon comes from reports from people who say that they have been falsely accused of sexual abuse and from others who have at one time reported having memories of sexual abuse but then later report that they believe that these memories were false (Loftus 1993). Furthermore, researchers have been able to create false memories in experimental situations. In other words, when people who witness an event are later exposed to new and misleading information about it, their later recollections of the event often become distorted by the misleading information. Such research has led therapists to be more careful to avoid accidentally creating false memories when working with clients.

There is no clear evidence or way of knowing if a recovered memory is accurate or inaccurate. Researchers and clinicians working in the area of traumatic stress tend to agree that blocked, recovered, or repressed memories do indeed exist (DePrince and Freyd 2004). In other words, it is possible that someone blocks out or does not have conscious access to a particular traumatic memory. Of course, not remembering parts or all of what has happened to you can be very distressing. Some trauma survivors remember what happened to them during the trauma but can not remember how they felt at the time it occurred.

We continue to learn more about how trauma and memory work. While we want you to know something about these issues, we don't want you to feel invalidated by this information. The truth is that most trauma survivors do remember something about the experience, even if it's only a partial memory. Many clients have told us that all the controversy about memory has been one more example of making them feel that they are making up the trauma. We believe that this type of invalidation is a part of our cultural response to dealing with trauma and represents avoidance on a broader level. However, if you have concerns about this topic, we support you in reading more and talking to professionals who have expertise in the area. Brewin's 2003 text, *Posttraumatic Stress Disorder: Malady or Myth?* provides a comprehensive review of the data in regard to many of these issues, including memory.

Depression: I Feel Sad All the Time

Many people who have been traumatized experience depression, sadness, or a loss of meaning in life. People who experience depression feel down or sad much of the time or find that they lose interest or pleasure in things they used to enjoy. Additionally, someone who is depressed may notice changes in their eating, sleeping, and concentration, and may feel worthless and hopeless. When people are depressed, they may isolate themselves from other people because they have little energy or because they feel bad about themselves. When people have experienced trauma, they also may avoid other people, which leads to less opportunity for pleasant experiences, which may lead to depression. Sometimes when people feel depressed, they may also experience suicidal thoughts, like "I don't want to go on anymore," or "I want to be dead." If you think that you might act on these thoughts, please seek professional counseling or call the local crisis call line in your area. They will be able to help you to contact a trained professional to help you through this period. Remember, like other thoughts, *this will pass.*

Traumatic experiences put people at much higher risk for developing depression because they often result in a sense of great loss. Many people have difficulty coping with painful experiences and loss associated with trauma. Some people will feel like they lost part of themselves during the trauma ("I'm not the same person I was" or "I'm damaged goods"). People returning from combat experiences may have painful memories or feelings of guilt. Some people may have difficulty believing that they will be able to cope or that life will get better again. With time, and sometimes with the help of friends or books such as this one, you can regain your sense of who you are and begin again to live a life that is important to you.

Common Symptoms of Depression

- Persistent sad, anxious, or empty mood

- Feelings of hopelessness or pessimism

- Loss of interest or pleasure in hobbies and activities that were once enjoyed, including hanging out with friends, exercising, reading, and so forth

- Feelings of guilt, worthlessness, or helplessness

- Decreased energy or feelings of fatigue

- Difficulty concentrating, remembering, or making decisions

- Difficulty sleeping, early morning awakening, or sleeping too much

- Weight loss or loss of appetite, or overeating and weight gain

- Restlessness, irritability, or agitation

- Persistent physical symptoms that do not respond to treatment, such as headaches, digestive disorders, muscle tension, and chronic pain

- Low self-esteem

- Thoughts of death or suicide, or suicide attempts

Anger: Why Do I Feel So Angry with Myself and Others?

Have you been finding that you are angrier and more irritable with people? Maybe you snap more at your kids or your partner? If you consider the context of trauma, it is not hard to understand why anger might be a common reaction after surviving trauma. Human beings have incredible survival responses that allow them to protect themselves from trauma. Many traumatic stress researchers agree that the emotion of anger is a common feature of our natural survival response to trauma. In fact, it makes a lot of sense that people would feel angry if they have been physically attacked or been in a bad accident or other trauma—because something is happening to you (or someone else) that is beyond your control and that "shouldn't" happen to you. Most of us will feel angry when we are being emotionally or physically attacked or witness someone else being violated, such as witnessing a burglary or murder or seeing your father beat up your mother. Anger functions to give people increased physical energy to survive in the face of danger or trauma. However, anger does not always go away when the trauma is over. When someone experiences trauma, the resulting anger response that it kindles can be so intense that it becomes etched in the brain and may become activated when the person doesn't necessarily want or intend to be angry. Thus, anger can be adaptive in certain circumstances, but anger without self-awareness and resulting in impulsive actions may occasion more misery and suffering in safe situations, such as in daily interactions within relationships or in the workplace.

Some research (Orth and Wieland 2006) has shown that experiencing trauma, particularly ongoing trauma, can interfere with a person's ability to manage emotions effectively—often leading to extreme outbursts of emotions, such as anger or rage. Additionally, you may have problems feeling in general and thus are likely to have difficulty expressing personal experiences to other people. Many people report feeling much more irritable and tense after experiencing trauma, which sets the stage for them to experience anger more easily because they are much more vulnerable to that emotional state.

And, it may also seem easier to feel anger than to feel other emotions, such as sadness, pain, or fear, after trauma. 🔔[Notice what feelings or thoughts show up for you right now, as you read this.]

Exercise 1.3: Examining Anger

When have you felt angry?

[space left intentionally blank in the original book]

How do you typically express your anger?

[space left intentionally blank in the original book]

In what ways has acting on your anger helped you?

[space left intentionally blank in the original book]

In what ways has acting on your anger interfered with the way you have wanted to live your life?

[space left intentionally blank in the original book]

Interpersonal Difficulties: Why Can't I Get Along with Others?

Difficulties interacting with or getting along with others is very common after trauma. There is research that suggests that trauma is associated with short- and long-term disruptions in intimacy and connection with others. For instance, women with a history of early abuse often experience increased fear and distrust of others and experience dissatisfaction in their romantic relationships (Herman 1981). Problems with connecting, closeness, and intimacy are more likely to happen when the trauma was caused or worsened by other people (as opposed to a car accident or a natural disaster). Furthermore, combat veterans have been shown to have high rates of family and marital problems, as well as general difficulties getting along with and trusting others (Stretch 1991). The many changes that individuals experience as a result of trauma are bound to impact their relationships with other people. 🔔[Any thoughts or judgments coming up?] For example, someone who has experienced an interpersonal trauma, such as sexual assault, may have a hard time trusting other people.

Exercise 1.4: Awareness of Your Relationship Patterns

Do you find it difficult to trust other people? If so, given what you've been through, why might it make sense that it is hard for you to trust others?

[space left intentionally blank in the original book]

Do you have any close friends or family that you can count on?

[space left intentionally blank in the original book]

What is difficult for you in romantic relationships? In other words, what are the parts of romantic relationships that you struggle with (trust, intimacy, sexuality, sharing, etc.)?

[space left intentionally blank in the original book]

Do you find yourself attracted to a certain type of person? For example, many women who have experienced abuse from a parent may report that they find themselves in relationships with people who are similar to that parent, either physically or psychologically.

[space left intentionally blank in the original book]

Do you have a hard time letting others get close to you? For example, many combat veterans have reported that they have a hard time sharing with others, and their partners may feel that they are shut out or kept at a distance.

[space left intentionally blank in the original book]

What are the things you do to attempt to get close to people, and what are the things you do to keep others at a distance?

[space left intentionally blank in the original book]

Self or Identity Issues: What Happened to Me?

At times it seems that the pain associated with experiencing trauma hurts more than other painful experiences because of the impact it can have on the self. The most extreme result is the feeling that you no longer have a sense of self—that something or someone took it away from you. This can be a very lonely and scary place to be, and it can leave you confused about who you are and what you want out of your life. Many people may be left feeling damaged, broken, or tainted by the things that have happened to them. Have you ever felt like that? If so, you are not alone. After experiencing trauma, some are left wondering who they are and what they want in their lives.

Another common consequence of trauma that some people experience long after the trauma has ended is feeling detached from one's experience or feeling numb or *dissociated* (having difficulty feeling emotions, or the experience of being detached from one's self or body). When people are overcome by strong emotions in a traumatic situation, the mind and body may react to this by shutting down or becoming numb. This may be very protective and adaptive for people during and immediately after trauma, but may become maladaptive when continued over time.

It's not uncommon to experience some amount of dissociation or disconnect from yourself or the world around you related to traumatic events or even everyday life experiences. If you think about dissociation as being on a continuum, ranging from none (being completely aware of what is going on in your body and in your immediate environment) to complete dissociation (being completely checked out and unaware of yourself or your surroundings), how much one shifts in awareness level depends on a variety of circumstances. Many people can relate to the experience of driving along a very familiar route, such as from work to home, and not being fully aware of what happened during the drive. On the other hand, we may witness a beautiful sunset and be very aware of every aspect of our experience in that moment. This variability is typical for most people. However, when you have experienced a very stressful event and you are vividly reminded of your trauma, you may feel as if you or the world around you is not real. When you are experiencing high levels of dissociation, you may have the experience of "I am physically here but not *really* here." In such cases, you may have the experience of physically being in a situation, such as talking to a therapist, but you may feel as if you are not really in your body. Many survivors of trauma will report that they felt outside of their body when the trauma occurred. For example, in the case of childhood sexual abuse, some survivors report that they emotionally left their body during the acts.

Exercise 1.5: It's Hard to Be In My Skin When...

Take a minute and list some situations when you are more likely to dissociate or disconnect from your experience:

> [space left intentionally blank in the original book]
>
> 🔔 [Notice what shows up for you right now, after writing about this.]

Shame and Guilt: Two Common Accomplices

Some people are overcome with feelings of self-blame, shame, and guilt after surviving trauma. Shame experienced without awareness can be a very debilitating emotion, particularly if it is the primary emotion you experience. We know how well it works when people try to ignore their feelings—these feelings end up silently building over time. Sometimes you might even feel ashamed about feeling shame.

It is a common response for people to second-guess things they did or did not do during the trauma. Many people end up blaming themselves for not doing things differently before, during, or after the trauma. For instance, you may have thoughts such as "I should have fought more," "I shouldn't have ever joined the military," "I shouldn't have been drinking that night," "Why did I have to live through it when so many other people died?" Guilt is closely related to these responses as well. In an attempt to make sense of why we might be feeling shame or guilt, we may end up blaming ourselves for what has happened. Self-blame is often completely unwarranted in trauma situations and ends up blocking progress on your road to recovery. For example, getting stuck in feelings of shame and blaming yourself for what has happened is a little like sitting alone in a room without any lights on. You may feel paralyzed and stuck in that dark room. On the one hand, part of you knows that there is a door nearby. On the other hand, part of you may feel paralyzed by shame and thus have difficulty getting up and looking for the light switch. The thing is, if you could turn on the light and take a clear look at the situation without judging yourself, then you could see the truth of the situation—that the trauma experience was not your fault—and find the doorknob and move outside of the room when you are ready. In order to turn the light on, you need to put your arms out in front of you and start looking for that light. Start exploring and noticing these experiences of shame and guilt, and consider the possibility that these experiences do not have to keep you paralyzed.

Dissociation: Where Do I Go?

People who have survived a serious trauma may feel distant and not connected to a variety of aspects of everyday life. There are a lot of ways to describe this feeling of not being in touch with either your external or internal life experiences. Not all survivors will experience dissociation as a result of the trauma. However, we do know that if the traumatic situation required the survivor to dissociate, which is often the case in combat and sexual assaults, then the survivor is likely to have more problems with dissociation after the trauma is over. 🔔[Notice your breathing right now. Breathing in ... Breathing out...]

There may be specific situations from which a person is more likely to dissociate. For example, those who were sexually assaulted or molested may find that they have a hard time staying in their body when they are sexual in their current intimate relationships, even when these relationships are satisfying. Dissociation can also feel much like feeling numb or detached from emotions. For example, it's not unusual for trauma survivors to talk about a very personal trauma in a very matter-of-fact manner, disconnected from their actual experience and feeling or expressing little emotion. The problem with being cut off or distancing yourself from the moment is that you are not only disconnected from yourself, but you are also distancing yourself from other people and the possibility of connecting deeply with another person.

Exercise 1.6: How Present Are You?

Using a scale of 0 to 10, with 0 being really checked out and 10 being very aware of the present moment, rate yourself in terms of where you are right now in regard to being in contact with life experiences: (Image 1.1)

0   10
not at —————————————————————— very
all aware   aware

Image 1.1

Now use this same scale to rate where you want to be: (Image 1.2)

0   10
not at —————————————————————— very
all aware   aware

Image 1.2

We'll look at this issue of awareness, or mindfulness, again in chapter 2.

Drugs and Alcohol: Risky Business

Turning to drugs or alcohol is a very common way for people to manage stress in their lives. This seems to be a particularly common thing to do if you have experienced trauma.

Who wouldn't want to escape from the uncomfortable or bad feelings associated with experiencing trauma? Many people turn to substances as a way to cope with their negative memories and feelings in the short run. Maybe you've found that drinking alcohol helps keep the bad feelings away and helps you numb yourself from the pain of trauma. Initially, using drugs or drinking alcohol may seem to make things better. However, most of the time addiction to or reliance on substances only exacerbates the problems people experience. Even if you are not addicted, you may still find that you turn to drugs or alcohol to avoid feeling uncomfortable things. Some survivors have said that they drink or use drugs to avoid the chronic emptiness they may experience when they are not using. It may be the case that you already know this to be true—part of you is probably exhausted from turning to drugs or alcohol to manage the uncomfortable feelings. Furthermore, many people may turn to drugs or alco-

hol to help manage some of the other symptoms they may be experiencing, such as depression or PTSD, as described above. For example,
many military personnel have reported that
they drink not only to reduce anxiety and other
negative feelings, but also to help manage the
severe symptoms that they experience as a
result of their combat experiences. Researchers
working with war veterans (Walser 2004) have
found that alcohol and drugs can serve a multi-
tude of functions for trauma survivors, as illustrated by the list below.

- Helping you fall asleep

- Unwinding or relaxing

- Dulling emotional pain and suffering

- Reducing worry and anxiety

- Managing emotions

- Escaping present difficulties

- Keeping upsetting memories from coming to
  mind

- Decreasing sadness and disappointment

- Reducing shame

- Making it easier to be around other people or helping get along with others

- Increasing positive experiences, such as laughter

- Avoiding feeling empty

- Numbing out

Exercise 1.7: What Are Some of the Reasons You Use Drugs or Alcohol?

Positive effects:

relaxing
[space left intentionally blank in the original book]

Negative effects:

wei
[space left intentionally blank in the original book]

Drug and alcohol abuse can cause serious problems in other aspects of your life. For example, when a trauma survivor experiences alcohol or drug problems, the negative effects of that drug or alcohol use also impact partners, children, other family members, and friends. It is very difficult to create or maintain close intimate relationships when you are drunk or high. Drugs and alcohol interfere with effective communication and closeness. Many partners may take a survivor's drinking to mean that he or she does not want to be close to the partner. Or, some partners may start drinking or using drugs in order to keep the person company. Finally, one of the clearest demonstrations of how alcohol and drug use negatively affects the family is the widely documented association between addiction and child abuse and domestic violence (Roberts, Roberts, and Leonard 1999). Most people do not intend to develop a dependency on drugs or alcohol. It usually begins gradually, as a way to escape, and develops into abuse or dependency over time.

Exercise 1.8: Are Alcohol or Other Drugs Affecting Your Life?

Do you believe that you need to be under the influence of drugs or alcohol to get along with other people?

48

[space left intentionally blank in the original book]

Is it hard for you to relax or enjoy yourself when you are not using drugs or alcohol?

[space left intentionally blank in the original book]

Do you tend to use drugs or alcohol to get relief from anxiety or other uncomfortable feelings?

yes

[space left intentionally blank in the original book]

Have other people commented on your drinking or drug use?

[space left intentionally blank in the original book]

Exercise 1.9: Becoming Aware of the Impact of Your Trauma

Now that you've learned a bit about some of the common effects of trauma, we would like you to take a look at some of the ways that your history has affected you on an individual level (in your mind and body) and interpersonal level (how you think the experience has affected your relationships with other people). Some of you may have experienced numerous traumas, as in the case of childhood sexual abuse, domestic violence, or combat situations. We would like you to pick one traumatic event for this exercise and describe the event briefly here.

The stressful experience that I have survived:

[space left intentionally blank in the original book]

As we've discussed above, traumatic experiences affect everybody differently, and yet there are many common reactions amongst trauma survivors. When asked the question "How do you think this traumatic experience has impacted you?" it is a very natural response to feel overwhelmed by all of the ways it has affected your life. You may find that it's difficult to write about yourself, and you may have difficulties finding the words to describe what it feels like on the inside. That is okay and is very common. Just do the best you can. Get the words out on paper any way

Impacts of trauma	Rating
Distrust of other people.	8
I have anger outbursts that seem like they are out of the blue.	5

Table 1.1

you know how, even if it feels like it is not making sense. Please know that there is absolutely no right or wrong here in these spaces. Some people may even go blank when trying to answer this question. These are normal responses when discussing reactions to trauma.

We want to help you organize the impact of the trauma by helping you break down its effects into manageable pieces. Also, we want to rate how much each of the effects is currently interfering with or preventing you from

Do I have the right to live? Do I have the right to chose? To say yes/no?

living the life you want. Use a scale of 0 to 10, where 0 means not at all and 10 means completely interferes. We will help you work with each of these effects through remainder of the workbook.

On the left, write down the various ways your selected traumatic experience has impacted your life. Then rate each impact from 0 to 10. We've provided two examples: (Table 1.1)

Now, we want you to consider the idea that even though everything in your list above appears very different, some of the effects listed above actually serve a similar function. Is it possible that some of the items on your list serve to help you avoid some uncomfortable private experience that may be related to the trauma you've experienced?

Feeling Stuck

If you feel stuck, we assume that you have tried all kinds of things that anybody would try when faced with this amount of pain: attempting to hide, run away from, get rid of, or bury the trauma you have experienced. You may have pushed down the memories or shoved them into a deep part of your brain—that way, you think you don't have to look at those memories or feel anything related to them. Attempting to avoid is what most people would do in this situation.

🔔 [Notice any self-judgments coming up.]

Over time, however, attempts to suppress or avoid become a little like a pot of water put on to boil—though the feelings, like the cold water, are initially calmed by avoidance, eventually all of the painful and conflicting emotions, thoughts, and memories will build up and start getting hotter and hotter and may even boil over to the point where it feels like you have no control over the situation. Instead of helping you move forward in your life, your attempts to avoid, although well-intentioned, keep you stuck. The difficult thing with traumatic memories is that sometimes it feels that they are no longer a problem and you have gotten rid of them. However, our experience is that until you address the avoidance and pain associated with these experiences, they tend to turn up again and again when you least expect them.

Metaphor: Autopilot

Avoidance is a little like living your life on autopilot. You are sitting in the pilot's seat; however, when you are living in autopilot mode you may not have your hands on the wheel, and therefore you are not actively guiding the direction in which you'd like your life to head. So, part of this book will be helping you learn to take hold of that steering wheel again and become an active participant in your life. Part of this journey will include the acknowledgment of your trauma and the awareness of the impact it has had on your behaviors. For example, you may want to ask yourself: "How long have I been living in autopilot mode?"

Exercise 1.10: Identifying When You Are on Autopilot

Let's now take a look at how you may tend to avoid or go into autopilot in a few aspects of your life.

Family Life

What do you do that feels automatic and without much awareness?

[space left intentionally blank in the original book] *Everything*

How is this helpful? *Don't have to think, make decisions*
[space left intentionally blank in the original book]

How does this interfere with what you want in life? *Don't have to chose = Never chose / decide*
[space left intentionally blank in the original book]

Health

What do you do that feels automatic and without much awareness?
Eating, sleeping too much
[space left intentionally blank in the original book]

How is this helpful? *Don't have to challenge myself / make an effort*
[space left intentionally blank in the original book]

How does this interfere with what you want in life?

[space left intentionally blank in the original book]

Work

What do you do that feels automatic and without much awareness?

[space left intentionally blank in the original book]

How is this helpful?

[space left intentionally blank in the original book]

How does this interfere with what you want in life?

[space left intentionally blank in the original book]

Being constantly on autopilot can interfere with living a valued life. See if you can notice how being on autopilot is a way of avoiding really being in contact with your life. What follows is a discussion of avoidance, the most common feature associated with a wide variety of symptoms of trauma. In our view, experiential avoidance may be the theme that holds together the many difficulties discussed above, such as anxiety, depression, post-traumatic stress, and so on, which are often associated with traumatic experiences (Polusny and Follette 1995).

Experiential Avoidance

We want to reiterate that avoidance is a very common response to trauma. However, avoidance is a problem for a lot of reasons. One of the most basic reasons is that it slows down and even prohibits recovery and healing after a trauma is over. As mentioned above, it makes perfect sense that you might want to avoid thinking about or to push away uncomfortable feelings related to the traumatic event; however, we also know that what we call experiential avoidance leads people to feel disconnected and more distressed in the long run (Hayes et al. 1996).

Experiential avoidance refers to the steps you take to avoid your own experience, things that happen within your own skin. Given that trauma is associated with uncomfortable memories, thoughts, feelings, and bodily sensations, most people who have experienced trauma try to avoid (with or without awareness) experiencing these difficult internal experiences. For example, a woman who has been raped may find that she is reminded of the rape in various situations. These memories and thoughts are understandably uncomfortable to experience, and thus she may force herself to think about other things whenever the thoughts arise. This strategy, called *thought suppression/avoidance,* works in the short run in that you do not have to experience feeling uncomfortable in that given moment because you are thinking about something else that is not as painful. However, over time, as in the example above, avoiding these memories, thoughts, feelings, and bodily sensations may interfere with the woman's ability and willingness to experience emotions in general, which is very likely to interfere with the life she wants to live.

There is a lot of research on thought suppression and how it works (Wegner 1994). For example, if we were to instruct you that you *must not,* under any circumstance, think about freshly baked bread—not the way it smells, tastes, or feels, what do you think would happen? Inevitably, you will think about freshly baked bread! Research has shown that, despite our best intentions, efforts to control, ignore, or suppress thoughts or feelings have the exact opposite effect—they often cause those experiences to continue and even increase (Salkovskis and Campbell 1994; Wegner, Erber, and Zanakos 1993). For example, if the woman in the above example feels scared and sad whenever she is reminded of the rape, her attempts to ignore or change the thoughts, such as by attempting to distract herself by thinking of something else, will interfere with her ability to work through the traumatic experience and accept the resulting emotional responses. But working through the experience and its attending emotions is exactly what will help her to experience them as less overwhelming and allow her to incorporate the experience. Furthermore, if you can't allow yourself to experience negative emotions and end up blocking them, then you will most likely block many of your positive emotions, too. This removal from the true emotional experiences in your life tends to result in the problems in other areas of your life that we've been discussing—depression, relationship problems, living on autopilot, or substance abuse.

People will go to great lengths to physically do things that help them avoid painful thoughts and feelings associated with traumatic events. For example, consider a combat veteran who has been through numerous traumatic combat experiences. He may have many memories that he would like to avoid because they feel so uncomfortable. Perhaps drinking alcohol allows him to avoid feeling the negative emotions associated with these memories. Or, perhaps he avoids talking to people about his combat or war experience. Similarly, he may isolate himself from other people altogether in order to avoid any situation or conversation that may trigger trauma memories. All these tactics are ways he protects himself from feeling uncomfortable in a given moment, but these actions have other long-term consequences. For example, the former soldier may become isolated from family and friends in general or develop a drinking problem. These are all examples of *behavioral avoidance,* which generally refers to the steps we take on the outside to avoid feeling what we are feeling on the inside, such as shame or memories of a trauma. The rape survivor above may avoid going to places that could trigger memories of the rape, or she may avoid watching news shows that might remind her of the rape. Another example would be that she no longer dates men in order to prevent feeling scared or vulnerable.

Exercise 1.11: Things You Do to Avoid Feeling Uncomfortable

Things I do to avoid feeling uncomfortable	Short-term benefits	Long-term gain	Long-term loss
I don't go to parties.	*I don't embarrass myself ever?*	*People think of me as "together."*	*No friends*
I don't leave the house	People don't laugh at me.	I don't feel ashamed	No new experiences/fun
I don't go on dates	I don't feel sick		No intimate relationship
I don't answer emails	Avoid feeling angry		

Table 1.2

Let's now take a look at some of the things that you may do, with varying degrees of self-awareness, to avoid feeling uncomfortable. What are the things you do to attempt to avoid painful memories, thoughts, and emotions from your traumatic experience? Remember, you do these things because they seem helpful in some way, at least in the short run. See if you can identify your avoidance strategies and how they help you cope with unpleasant situations (memories,

> emotions, physical sensations) in the short run. Also, see if you can identify long-term gains or losses. The first row is an example. (Table 1.2)

Journaling

In the remainder of this book, we are going to help you to examine what you have avoided and to come to terms with that experience. 🔔[Notice any internal reactions to this comment.] In doing so, we hope you will be able to step forward and discover your true self, identifying values and goals that will help you move forward in your life. The first step in this process is to help you increase awareness of what is going on inside and outside of your skin. Therefore, as we mentioned in the introduction, the end of each chapter will provide you with some space to write down your reactions to that chapter. If you haven't done so already, please take a few minutes to write down what you have observed within yourself as you worked through chapter 1.

Journaling

Thoughts

[space left intentionally blank in the original book]

Feelings or Emotions

[space left intentionally blank in the original book]

Self-Judgments

[space left intentionally blank in the original book]

Physical Sensations

[space left intentionally blank in the original book]

Action Urges (What Do You Feel Like Doing?)

[space left intentionally blank in the original book] (Image 1.3)

Image 1.3: René Magritte, La condition humaine, 1933.
Gift of the Collectors Committee. Image © Board of
Trustees, National Gallery of Art, Washington.

CHAPTER 2

Building a Safe Foundation with Mindfulness

Right now a moment of time is passing by!
... We must become that moment.

—Paul Cezanne

The Present Moment

Can you tell what is going on in the painting on the previous page? At first you may not notice anything unusual as it may just look like a regular landscape painting. But it isn't. If you pay close attention, you will see that there are two distinct elements in this picture: a canvas being painted on an easel and, to the right of the canvas and above it, the actual scene being painted. If you haven't yet noticed that, go back now and see if you can see the easel and notice that there is a painting on it; the white border of the canvas with regularly spaced staples marks the distinction between the painting and the scene being painted. To the unsuspecting eye, however, they look like the same thing, don't they? Yet, they may be drastically different. For example, it's possible that there is a barn with a cow in the actual landscape, but the artist, for whatever reason, is only painting the trees, grass, and mountains. Were we to assume that the painting is an accurate representation, we'd be very mistaken. The most telling aspect of this painting by Magritte, in our opinion, is its title, which translates to: "The Human Condition." The painting and its title capture the fact that it is human nature to "fuse" our perceptions, thoughts, worries, predictions, feelings, bodily sensations, and memories about events (the painting) with the actual events (the actual scene), to the point that we cannot distinguish which is which. Yet, we know from research that this inability can result in significant suffering (Hayes, Strosahl, and Wilson 1999).

Mindfulness, the main topic of this chapter, is about focusing our attention in order to distinguish the painting from the scene, and vice versa. The aim of this chapter is to give you some skills to help you cope while you are doing the work of dealing with your trauma. We believe that mindfulness is the first crucial step in being able to step back from your reactions and do something healthy when trauma issues get stirred up. Mindfulness will also set the foundation for the rest of the book.

Exercise 2.1. Strategies You Are Using Right Now

Before we start looking at new skills, let's look at what you have been doing to cope with life since your trauma. In the first column, list some of your strategies for coping. In the second, indicate how long you have been using each strategy. In the third column, rate how useful each has been using a scale of 0 to 10, where 0 is not at all useful and 10 is entirely effective. (Table 2.1)

Coping strategy	How long you've used it	Effectiveness (0 to 10)

Table 2.1

Take a moment and review your list above and notice any similarities among the strategies that are not as helpful. What most people notice is that a lot of the strategies that are not working as well in the long term revolve around avoiding experiencing or coming into contact with painful emotions in their lives. These emotions might be related to old traumas or current life experiences. You are taking the first steps here by just noticing what you do and being willing to become aware of how these things work in your life. In fact, you might even be engaging in some avoidance behaviors that *do* work for you at some level, such as studying to get away from sadness about a relationship breakup and getting good grades as a result. We know people who are straight-A students or who have accomplished a great deal in their work life with this style of coping. We are not saying that you should be judging these strategies as bad things to do, but rather taking a look at how they function in your life. So, if instead of being about a true joy in your work, your work behavior is driven by the need to avoid feeling bad about yourself, to avoid thinking about painful experiences, or to always try to please other people, we invite you to check and see if this is what you really want your life to be about.

Other ineffective coping strategies that people commonly use include drinking, using drugs, or finding other ways to avoid difficult emotions. Some people do things to hurt themselves like cutting, burning, or hurting their body in other ways. No matter what you are doing, you can be pretty sure that a lot of other people are doing something similar in their attempts to cope. There isn't much new under the sun, but most of these coping behaviors are done with a lot of secrecy, and people feel a lot of shame about them. This book is not about judging yourself but about trying new things.

Avoid Avoidance

We have talked about the issue of avoidance as a response to traumatic experiences. Our point of view is that the way to deal with the pain and suffering is to work through these experiences, as opposed to pushing them away, just as we know that the way to get over a spider phobia is to undergo some form of exposure to or contact with spiders. However, exposure to spiders doesn't mean walking into a room and, without any warning, throwing a spider on top of the person who fears spiders. That approach, in fact, is bound to reinforce the fear of spiders instead of reducing it. Similarly here, as we will discuss in the next chapter, we know that the way to reduce suffering associated with one's trauma is to be able to work through the original pain of the trauma in a careful, gradual way, where you maintain control over the what, how, and, importantly, when (Riggs, Cahill, and Foa 2006). This book is *not* about throwing a spider on your lap!

Part of the process here is, therefore, to build a safe foundation, through increased awareness of what is going on inside and outside you, so that you can do this very difficult work. This increased awareness, or mindfulness, is the opposite of avoidance and can be the foundation for effectively living a life you truly value. In our work, we have found that some people with trauma histories either never learned some of these skills in their early years or got so involved in using other methods of coping, sometimes not very healthy ones, that they have forgotten the utility of other methods of coping. We want you to develop some more effective ways of caring for yourself as you do this work. So, as you read this chapter, we urge you to consider these ideas as tools that are part of reaching toward your valued life goals. Maybe you feel like these sorts of things won't work for you, or they may seem silly. As discussed in the introduction, we are just asking you to stay open and try some things out. In some sense, we all do the work of psychologists in our private lives. We try to understand our behavior and find better ways to deal with problems and life issues. Part of being a psychologist is experimenting with new ideas and finding out what works for you.

Mindfulness

One of the first steps in building a safe foundation, learning any new skills, or making any changes at all in your life is being more aware of what you are experiencing right now. As we mentioned in the introduction, suffering is a secondary problem that comes from trying to push away or avoid pain. Most suffering comes from projecting into the future or thinking (sometimes rethinking) about the past. It is rare that there is incredible pain in this very moment. Most of the time, it's about the past or the future. Think about it right this second: how much of the pain you're experiencing right now is about the future (Will I be able to get to work on time tomorrow?) or the past (I can't believe how stupid I looked at that presentation last week!)?

Because part of the goal of this work is to wake up and be present for what is going on in your life at this very moment, the first thing we are going to talk about is something we call being *mindful.* As we explained above, this is key to building a safe foundation and for being able to successfully apply other concepts in this book.

Think about this past week. Have you done any of the following?

- Talking on your cell phone while driving

- Listening to music while reading or talking

- Planning ahead or making lists while "listening" to your spouse or friend

- Doing the dishes or being in front of the computer while on the phone

- Watching TV while eating

- Watching TV while eating and talking on the phone

- Watching TV while eating, talking on the phone, and reading a magazine or paper!

If you said yes to one or more of the above, you can relate to how hard it is to bring our awareness to one thing at a time. So, in this era of multitasking, what will it take for us to become more mindful? Practice, practice, practice.

The idea of being mindful has been talked about in both psychology and spiritual traditions (for example, Brach 2003; Chodron 2001; Hayes and Smith 2005; Linehan 1993a; Linehan 1993b; Kabat-Zinn 2005; Nhat Hanh 1987; Zindel, Williams, and Teasdale 2002). There are many ways to talk about this idea, but the basic concept of mindfulness involves being aware of your body, your life, and your mind. The goals of mindfulness are:

- Being present in your life for the variety of internal and external experiences that you are having

- Controlling your attention but not what you see

- Staying in the present moment

- Noticing and being aware of your experience without judgment and avoidance

Becoming mindful is one step in moving away from trauma and back into your life, but it is relevant to everyone, whether or not they are survivors of some particular trauma. Modern life has pulled us into a state of not being present in our own lives! If you picked up this book, you have enough motivation and self-awareness to look at your role in making your life vital. To increase awareness, we have to slow down enough to notice all the different components that go into our behavior in life.

For example, imagine that you have always driven an automatic transmission car and then, all of a sudden, you need to learn to drive a stick shift. That beginning process requires all your attention to be focused on a few steps: pressing your left foot on the clutch and releasing it as you step with your right foot on the accelerator. Over time, this process may become automatic, but for a while, you have to bring all your attention to this task to be able to learn it. A similar process happens when you're learning any new skill or when you are trying to correct the way you do something, such as trying to improve your backhand in tennis, start using your pinkie finger when you type, or improve your performance of a particular musical passage on your musical instrument.

This learning process is no different when it comes to things that happen inside us. We still need to bring awareness to these experiences in order to do something different. If you find yourself snapping at a coworker, friend, or partner and want to stop doing that, first you have to notice what is going on inside and outside of you. You must be able to notice that you are *feeling* anger to be able to stop yourself from *acting* in anger. This is particularly the case with issues related to your own safety, because safety can be compromised by impulsivity and thoughtlessness, which are the ultimate enemies of awareness.

This chapter will guide you through exercises asking you to notice what is going on with you in various areas as a way of helping you practice self-awareness, so that in times of crisis you can engage in actions that are based on your values rather than fleeting emotions or thoughts.

Mindfulness and Trauma Survivors

As mentioned in chapter 1, survivors of trauma tend to cope with the experience in different ways. Different people have a variety of ways of coping with stressful experiences and even the same person might deal with traumas differently across his or her lifetime. Often, these coping styles may go from one extreme to another, both of which tend to block the trauma from being assimilated. This has been called the "dialectic of trauma" (Herman 1992). This may show up as numbness for some people or hypervigilance in others. Being mindful is about being fully present in this moment as described in the quote by Cezanne at the beginning of this chapter. 🔔[Where are your thoughts right now?]

Part of being mindful is about being aware of your environment in a new way. At times trauma survivors report being either unaware or extremely sensitive to their surroundings. Interestingly, this is another one of those seemingly opposite patterns that we can see in people who have experienced traumatic events: Some people may report that they feel really shut down and don't notice much at all anymore. It's as if life is no longer real, or they feel like they aren't in touch with their body anymore. Life feels at a distance, as if the person is traveling in a thick fog with no real connections. On the other hand, other people report being intensely aware of either internal or external experiences. This phenomenon can be called *hypervigilance.*

People who have survived dangerous environments have sometimes reported that they are hyper-aware of everything around them. This acute sensitivity to the environment may have served a useful function at some time. For example, combat veterans may have been very sensitive to small sounds in order to stay alert for danger. But now they might use this sort of vigilance in everyday, noncombat situations. If you have experienced significant family violence, you may have become extremely aware of small changes in people, constantly watching for signals that a violent episode may be imminent. Sometimes this hyperawareness may have even been useful in helping you to stay alive, such as hearing the enemy before others noticed anything at all. Even if this sensitivity did not function in that way, it may have given you a sense of control, a sense of being able to predict when bad things were going to happen. This can be an interesting sort of paradox in that many combat veterans we have talked with report that they never felt more alive than they did while in country. We want you to look at how that hyperawareness functions now in your life.

This acute awareness of everything is not what we mean by being mindful. In fact this is a kind of hyperarousal that happens in extreme stress and can be very hard on you, both psychologically and physically. Psychologically, it means that you are so aware of small details that you can miss the big picture. It functions not unlike the image we included at the beginning of the chapter. And this hypersensitivity can lead to a lot of misinterpretation. For instance, if you interpret every small creak your house makes at night as a sign of danger, you're not likely to get much sleep. Or if you find yourself extremely sensitive to every small change in the behavior of people around you, you might end up misinterpreting small events as meaning that people are upset or angry with you, when in fact they are just dealing with their own issues. Physically, we know that staying in a state of extreme stress and arousal can cause all types of health problems over time, including heart disease, high blood pressure, and other stress-related illness (Kabat-Zinn 2005). 🔔[Notice any thoughts, judgments, or feelings coming up for you.]

In our experience, people who are struggling with traumatic experiences often become especially good at finding ways to be out of contact with their thoughts and feelings. Even when you don't do this all the time, small triggers can send you off, pulling you away from contact with your present life. This is part of the trick of doing work around your trauma experiences. The act of doing the work is very likely to trigger old thoughts and feelings that you will want to avoid. One of the basic aspects of working through trauma is sticking with treatment (reading, in this case) even when your thoughts and feelings tell you to run away. So we are going to have you practice coming back to the present moment in lots of different ways, including inviting you to check in with your experience every time you encounter one of the bell signs scattered throughout the book.

Exercise 2.2: Rating Your Awareness This Week

On a scale of 0 to 10, with 0 being not at all numb and 10 being completely numb—unable to notice or care about anything—how numb would you rate yourself this last week?

_____

On a scale of 0 to 10, with 0 being not at all hypervigilant and 10 being completely hyper-vigilant—noticing everything you feel or others do—how hypervigilant have you been this week? _____

One of the first steps in changing your behavior is to become more observant of where you are in awareness at the present moment. Throughout the next week we want you to stop and take your "awareness temperature," on a scale of 0 to 10, noticing situations when you are more likely to go numb or to be hypervigilant. When you give yourself a low rating on the awareness scale, see if you can bring your attention back to the present moment, gently and without judgment.

We are going to give you a variety of different exercises to try, because in our experience people respond differently to different ways of doing this work. To help each exercise best serve you, start by reading through it once or twice first, and then complete it. After many of the exercises, we will have you write about your experience doing the exercise.

Being mindful is a delicate balance of noticing and being in contact with both your inner self and your environment. The goal of this contact is to be compassionate and wise with yourself, to be able to notice and appreciate and yet have the perspective to not be pulled fully into the experience in such a way that you lose yourself and your sense of identity. The ultimate goal of mindfulness is living your life more effectively. Bringing your attention back to the present moment over and over again is not awareness as some sort of navel-gazing for its own sake; but rather, it is the means to living your life in a valued direction. Being mindful or awake is central to this work, and so we will give you several exercises to practice various aspects of being mindful.

Exercise 2.3: Mindful Noticing

Let's start with a very basic idea of noticing this current moment. After you read these instructions, just sit quietly and notice things around you. Do so slowly.

• Notice the chair you are sitting in: What is its color, texture, and temperature? What materials is it made from?

• Notice the light in the room: How bright is it? Where does it hit the wall right now, if at all? What is the temperature that it generates, if any?

• Notice the colors in the other furniture in the room and on the floor and ceiling.

• Just take a moment to really look around at where you are right now. You may have been in this place a hundred times, and yet even in this familiar place you may not have really been aware of your surroundings. Look at it with new eyes, as if you were a stranger walking in for the first time.

What did you notice? Anything that you hadn't noticed before? Any judgments? Any emotional reactions? Any thoughts? Write a bit about this experience here.

[space left intentionally blank in the original book]

Were there things that got in the way of your doing this exercise? Were you having the thought "This is stupid" or "How can this ever help?" Were you distracted by thoughts of the future or the past? Did you see things that are always around that you don't really see anymore? All of these things are normal. Just notice these reactions, too. This is all part of being mindful. Remember, it's about controlling your attention and not what you see, which means that you may not necessarily like what you see (often, in times of stress that is exactly the case).

Being mindful is just a process of being where you are, but, surprisingly, it takes a lot of practice. This is not something that is just true for trauma survivors. We are all so busy with our lives that we often miss the most basic experiences. You have probably heard the expression about taking time to smell the roses. This is just an example of how common it is to run through our lives without really experiencing it in a meaningful way. Let's practice mindful awareness with an eating exercise.

Exercise 2.4: Mindful Eating

Select a piece of fruit that you can eat for this exercise. It can be anything—an orange, a raisin, a banana, anything that you would typically eat. Don't pick something unusual, because looking at something very familiar is a part of this exercise.

First just spend some time looking at this fruit. Pick it up and really look at its color and shape. Is it all one color, or are there subtle variations? Are there some soft spots or parts that are a bit brown? What is its shape? As you look at this one piece of fruit, can you see how it is unique and has its own qualities?

Now take some time to smell the fruit. Does it smell sweet or sour? Can you detect any fragrance at all?

Take some time to really touch and feel this piece of fruit. How does if feel in your hand? Is it rough or smooth? Does it have a sticky feeling?

If you need to peel this fruit to eat it, gently pull away the peel, noticing each new part of the fruit as it is revealed and what it feels like to pull at the parts of the fruit. If you do not need to peel it, proceed to the next step.

Now put a piece of the fruit in your mouth. Take a small piece and let it just sit in your mouth, noticing how it feels and tastes. Notice it as it touches your tongue and what that feels like.

Now chew the fruit, noticing its texture change and how the intensity of the flavor alters. As you swallow the fruit, notice what that feels like.

Take a few minutes to do this exercise. Afterward, write down what you notice and how it was different from what it usually feels like to eat this fruit.

The fruit I picked was a _____

What I noticed about its color and texture was _____

What I noticed about its fragrance was _____

What I noticed about its texture was _____

What I noticed about its taste was _____

Of course, being mindful is about more than how you eat. However, if you're struggling with issues related to eating, this can be an important first step in the process. If you are like most people, you probably noticed something about the fruit you ate that you'd never noticed before.

Our first mindfulness exercise was with raisins, and we both had the thoughts "This is dumb" and "Why should I take so much time to eat a raisin?" Today, we teach mindfulness to almost all of our clients in one way or another. So, if you are having moments of doubt or feel bored with doing tasks in a way that feels slow, thank your mind for those thoughts and emotions and keep on reading. It is not a coincidence that several cutting-edge Western psychotherapies of our time are relying on mindfulness as a technology to help people change (Hayes,

Follette, and Linehan 2004; Hayes and Smith 2005; Linehan 1993a; Linehan 1993b; Kabat-Zinn 2005; Zindel, Williams, and Teasdale 2002). The fruit exercise is just one way of teaching mindfulness. However, being mindful or awake to your life is about everything that you do and experience—thoughts, feelings, and bodily sensations.

Exercise 2.5: Mindful Walking

Some people report difficulty in just sitting quietly with themselves at the beginning of this work. For these people, and really for anyone, a great way to start practicing mindfulness is with mindful walking. This is not meant to be exercise or walking in the usual sense. It is just learning to be aware of your body moving on this earth in a new way.

Pick a quiet place. Oftentimes walking in a yard or other outdoor space is good, but you can do this walking indoors. Start with just standing still and noticing your body, your feet on the ground, your balance, where you are.

Next, just slowly take easy steps, noticing your feet as they touch the ground, sensing each part of your foot as it bends and moves and you take the next step.

Walk slowly with your eyes open. Just walk, noticing how your body feels as it's moving.

Thoughts and feelings may come up. Just notice these and continue to walk.

Remember, there is no way to do this incorrectly.

If your mind is busy and full of thoughts, notice that.

If you notice that you end up walking more quickly, slow your pace in order to be more aware of every aspect of the experience of taking a step. Just gently notice and be aware of things around you as you walk: the feel of the grass on your feet, or the cool floor; the gentle breeze against your skin, or the sense of warm, unmoving air.

There will be sounds that you notice and maybe even wonder about. Just notice that.

Practice walking for ten minutes every day for a week, and then write about your experience.

What changes did you notice from one day to the next? _____

What did you notice in your body? _____

Are your thoughts more or less active as you do this? _____

Does it matter whether you do it at the beginning or the end of the day? _____

Whatever your experience, we want you to just notice that. This is one step of gradually becoming more aware of your body in a quiet and peaceful way.

Exercise 2.6: Mindful Thinking

One important part of this work is gaining perspective in regard to your thoughts and feelings. Imagine yourself in a quiet, safe place, sitting by a gently running stream (Hayes, Strosahl, and Wilson 1999). Just close your eyes and imagine this stream, letting

Image 2.1: Photo by Inge Skeans

yourself get very quiet. As you sit, notice the thoughts that come up. Some of these may even be visual images, words, or voices.

Gently put each thought on a large leaf that is floating by in the stream. As each thought comes, just place it on a leaf and watch it flow on down the stream. The same thought may come again, and you can let this thought flow on by. An image may come up, and you can put that image on a leaf and let it go. You may have the thought that this is a silly exercise, and you can put that thought on a leaf. Thoughts come, but as you practice this exercise you can also notice that thoughts go. You can notice these thoughts and let them flow, not with control or effort but with just letting go. (Image 2.1)

What did you notice as you tried this exercise?

[space left intentionally blank in the original book]

Could you picture the stream and leaves? _____

[space left intentionally blank in the original book]

Were there some leaves that were harder to picture or to let go? _____

Please use the lines below to write down some of your thoughts that were harder to let go. You may have found yourself going off on the content of the thought: justifying, explaining, remembering, and planning about and around the thought.

[space left intentionally blank in the original book]

Exercise 2.7: Mindful Breathing

Close your eyes and just notice your breath. Notice the air as it comes into your nose and down to your lungs. Can you feel how it is slightly cooler as it first flows into your nostrils? Notice your lungs filling and your chest rising slightly. Then notice the exhalation as your lungs empty and the warmer air flows out of your nose and over the skin of your upper lip.

Just notice the gradual rise and fall of your breath, not trying to speed it up or slow it down, just letting your breath flow. Remember that when you feel distracted or pulled away from your experience (which is inevitable), coming back to the breath is a sort of centering or grounding exercise that is always available to you.

In fact, a good way to practice this exercise is to spend a few moments just noticing your breath whenever you sit down to read this book. This small time spent noticing can bring your attention back to this moment and help prepare you to do this work. Mindful breathing is an opportunity to be gentle with yourself, breathing in compassion for yourself and letting warmth and caring into your world as you exhale.

What did you notice as you tried this exercise?

[space left intentionally blank in the original book]

Could you notice the gap between the in breath and the out breath? _____

Did you notice any changes in temperature and path from the air going in and the air coming out?

[space left intentionally blank in the original book]

Exercise 2.8: Mindful Body Scanning

One type of awareness or mindfulness that can be especially important for survivors of trauma is learning to become aware of your body in new ways. Many people who have experienced traumatic events, especially if those experiences involved some sort of violation of their body, report that they feel numb or very disconnected from their physical self. On the other hand, some people report lots of *somatic* or physical, symptoms. That is, they have many types of physical problems that don't seem to have any medical cause. This is a bit tricky, because it turns out that sometimes trauma survivors really do have ailments that are the result of their past traumatic experience. So the caution here is not to be your own doctor. If you have questions about physical complaints, see a doctor and be honest about your concerns.

No matter which side of things you fall on in terms of body awareness, this can be an important exercise for you. We recommend that you read over the exercise a few times and then find an opportunity to practice it on your own without reading the text. You don't have to do it perfectly—just begin the process of getting to know your body.

Generally, the body scan is done lying down with your eyes closed. But this position is not essential. If, for some reason, you can't lie down or you feel unsafe with your eyes closed, you can adapt your position to fit your particular needs.

Find a comfortable, safe place to lie down where you won't be disturbed. You may even have to close your pets out of the room. As soon as you get on their level, they often think it's time to play. You may want to use some type of mat under you so that you don't end up just noticing how hard the floor is.

Close your eyes and begin by noticing your breath.

Now notice your head. Is there any tension there? Can you feel the hair on your head? Notice your face and all the sensations there. Bring all your attention to your head, and if there is any tension, see if you can let it go.

Now notice your neck and shoulders. Is there any tension there? If present, where and how much tension is there right now? See if you can let it go.

Now notice your torso area. Is there any tension there? If present, where and how much tension is there right now? See if you can let it go.

Now notice your arms and hands. Bring all your attention to your left arm first, then your left hand, then your right arm, and finally your right hand. Notice any sensations or urges as you scan your arms and hands.

Now notice the area of your abdomen and buttocks. Any sensations or tension in this area? If so, where and how much? Can you let it go?

Now notice your left leg and then your right leg. Any sensations, tension, or urges to move in this area? If so, where?

Now notice your left foot and then your right foot. Any sensations, tension, or urges to move in this area? If so, where?

Where, if any place at all, did you find tension in your body as you did this exercise?

[space left intentionally blank in the original book]

Could you let the tension go? _____

Which areas were harder for you to remain mindful of? _____

> Did any self-judgments come up as you did this exercise? If you answered yes, what were those judgments and were you able to let them go? _____

This can be a hard exercise to do without support and guidance. And we think it is an important part of mindfulness for anyone who has experienced traumatic experiences. If you find it difficult to do this on your own, there are some really great tapes you can purchase that will guide you through the process. Also, you can look at the Web site www.mindfulnes stapes.com for CDs on meditation and body scans. Jon Kabat-Zinn (2005) has written extensively on the body scan and provides additional examples and guidelines if you would like to learn more about this process.

Mindfulness of Basic Physical, Emotional, and Interpersonal Needs

As discussed in chapter 1, traumatic experiences may lead to, or be associated with, a disruption in basic physical, emotional, interpersonal, and safety needs, such as sleep disturbances, eating disturbances, substance abuse, exhaustion due to hypervigilance, and withdrawal and disconnection from others.

The extent to which these human needs are being met, or your awareness of it if they aren't, may dictate how well you cope with a given challenge. In a way, these factors can be thought of as vulnerabilities to becoming unmindful. In fact, the extent to which these basic needs are or aren't being met may render individuals more or less vulnerable to entertaining the possibility of suicide and actually engaging in life-threatening behaviors, both of which are also associated with a history of trauma.

Have you noticed that sometimes you can deal with a tough situation like a pro, and at other times, you just can't seem to cope with it at all? This may seem like a puzzle to you and those around you, but the fact is that our ability to cope with difficult experiences, including thoughts and feelings, has everything to do with how well we are taking care of ourselves, or our level of awareness if we aren't.

Sometimes, we simply cannot take care of these needs despite our best intentions, such as when working double shifts, having financial difficulties, or having to take care of a baby or a sick relative. Knowing the impact on you of not having these needs met can still serve as a deterrent for ineffective behavior.

In the exercise below, please take the time to become mindful of how you tend to be affected by these factors. When you are exhausted, for example, does it make it more likely that you will drive fast, snap at people, avoid dealing with things, withdraw and isolate, do a job poorly, become hopeless more quickly, or quit trying?

Exercise 2.9: How Full Is Your Tank?

Notice your energy level. On a scale of 0 to 10, how physically exhausted are you feeling right now?

[space left intentionally blank in the original book]

In your experience, how does low energy or physical exhaustion affect you?

[space left intentionally blank in the original book]

How many hours did you sleep last night? Did you have trouble falling asleep or staying asleep? Did you take a long nap or hide out in bed in the middle of the day? Did you have nightmares during your sleep?

[space left intentionally blank in the original book]

In your experience, how does too much or too little sleep affect you? How do nightmares, if you have them, affect you after you wake up? Some survivors report having leftover feelings from a nightmare, such as anger at particular people or guilt and shame.

[space left intentionally blank in the original book]

Are you coping with difficulties in your life by using alcohol and drugs? How much are you drinking or using and how often? Do you find yourself saying things like "I need to drink or use to relax or to hang around people"? Do you feel guilty after you drink or use? Do you get angry when others ask you about your drinking and using? Do you ever drink or use first thing in the morning or immediately after you wake up?

[space left intentionally blank in the original book]

In your experience, how does drinking or using affect you? Are there problem behaviors that you find yourself engaging in only after you drink or use? If this is an area of concern for you, see if you can become mindful of the impact alcohol and drugs have on you, even if you are not yet ready to do anything about it.

[space left intentionally blank in the original book]

How much have you eaten today, when, and what kinds of food? Is this more or less than you intended to have eaten? If you shared this information with others around you, would they have any concerns over the amount of food you ate today? Do you tend to get angry or feel guilty when others comment on your eating habits?

[space left intentionally blank in the original book]

In your experience, how does eating too little or too much affect your thoughts, feelings, and behaviors? If this is an area of concern for you, see if you can become mindful of the impact that eating or not eating has on you, even if you are not yet ready to do anything about it.

[space left intentionally blank in the original book]

Are there particular stresses going on in your life right now that may be taxing your attention? Some stresses are negative, such as divorce, financial problems, or death. Others may be positive events, such as marriage, graduation, or a promotion. Research shows that events that involve a significant change in the person's life, even desired ones, can also be stressful (Rahe 1978).

[space left intentionally blank in the original book]

In your experience, how do stressors, which can be either undesired or desired changes in your life, affect your ability to remain mindful?

[space left intentionally blank in the original book]

Factors that can render us even more vulnerable to getting fused with difficult thoughts and feelings include: lack of energy or exhaustion (when people are depressed, they often feel tired or low in energy even when getting enough sleep), lack of sleep (or too much sleep), lack of adequate nourishment (or too much food), using alcohol or drugs regularly, and a high level of current stressors. Being aware of these factors and reducing them as much as possible can help us cope more effectively in the moment (Linehan 1993b).

We all experience vulnerabilities that make it more likely that we will encounter problems. If we don't sleep well, we may be tired and distracted while driving, resulting in a traffic ticket. If we're under the influence of drugs, we may end up having an argument for a trivial reason and later regret it. In a sense, taking care of your basic physical needs is analogous to the idea of not letting your tank get too low on gas. Sometimes we let our fuel level get as low as possible, gambling that we'll be able to make it through the day all right. And it almost always works, right? However, if we are running low on gas and something happens, such as needing to be at work earlier and therefore not having time to go to the gas station on the way, or getting lost, or having to lend your car to your teenager, who has no money, things are more likely to go wrong. It's not to say that they always do go wrong, but they are more likely to. The same applies to the vulnerability factors described above (low energy, sleep, substances, eating, stressors). Allowing yourself to get "low on gas" in these areas may not necessarily always result in increased suffering, but it sure makes it more likely that unneeded suffering will be added. Below we provide some ideas for how to address these physical and emotional vulnerabilities, with increased mindfulness of what is, even if it can't be changed, being the primary suggestion.

• Low energy and physical exhaustion is one kind of vulnerability to observe and take steps to remedy. Is your work physically demanding? Do you find yourself low in energy even after sleeping? Are there physical ailments that need to be taken care of or addressed? For example, do you take an aspirin when you have a headache or do you take time to rest when tired? Are you exercising too little or too much?

• Sleep problems are pervasive among trauma survivors (Polusny and Follette 1995), and their impact can be dire. Sometimes, a lack of sleep can even lead to people seeing things that are not there. This is not something to take lightly. Are you getting enough rest? If not, what is interfering with that? Even if you're having difficulty sleeping, can you take time to rest quietly?

• A lack of proper nourishment can contribute to feelings of low energy. You may find that you don't eat on a regular schedule. This can turn up in all kinds of ways, from eating all the time to snacking on foods that aren't healthful or avoiding or forgetting to eat. A lot of people, especially women in our culture, have developed really complicated relationships with food. This is not a book about eating disorders, and if this is part of your struggle we would urge you to seek help in dealing with this problem. But for many of us the issue is just a matter of being more mindful of when and how we eat. Part of the larger project of this book is to encourage you to develop compassion for yourself in many ways, including taking care of your body. Eating healthy food and getting appropriate rest and exercise are all part of caring for your body and are often first steps in caring for yourself. Please see the ACT workbook for anorexia (Heffner and Eifert 2004) for additional exercises in this area. [Notice any thoughts, judgments, or feelings coming up for you.]

• Abuse and dependence on alcohol and other drugs can have a pervasive and sometimes life-threatening impact on individuals, and we know that this can be a frequent way of coping for trauma survivors (Walser 2004). Substance use will be discussed throughout the book and will be a frequent example, given its prominent role in trauma-related issues.

Becoming mindful of the number and severity of stressors in your life at a given time may be quite helpful, as it may explain why sometimes you may be able to handle a challenge, such as your teenager snapping at you, and at other times you may not. Of particular interest is the fact that even positive events may tax your ability to remain mindful and present in your life (Rahe 1978). If you are moving to a new city, taking on a new job, and getting your kids adjusted to a new school, and are not mindful of the impact these things are having on you, you may find yourself being impatient with a friend in need or forgetting to pay an important bill.

Another crucial vulnerability factor to become mindful of is the quality of your social connections and support. This is such an important aspect of recovery from trauma (Herman 1992), that it will be discussed separately here and in greater detail in chapter 10. Below, we ask you to complete the Personal Support Inventory. Numbers are not the issue. Quality and access are. The idea here is to help you be mindful of what you have available as support while you're doing this work so that you can enlist the support when you need it.

Exercise 2.10: Personal Support Inventory

• In the first column, list up to five people who are close to you.

• In the second column, rate how close you feel to each person on a scale of 0 to 10, with 0 being not at all and 10 being the closest you could ever be.

• In the third column, note what kind of support (emotional, financial) each person gives you and in what areas (work, personal, kids).

• If you needed to talk to someone late at night or early in the morning, how willing do you think each person would be to take your phone call or see you? Rate that willingness

---

on a scale of 0 to 10, with 0 being not at all and 10 being completely willing. (Table 2.2)

Person	Closeness (0 to 10)	Support type	Willingness (0 to 10)
My sister	7	Emotional	9, if really important
My boss	6	With work skills	0-2, depending on relevance

Table 2.2

[Notice any thoughts, judgments, or feelings coming up for you.]

Becoming mindful, in an accurate manner, of your social connections and support is crucial in your recovery. Sometimes doing so can be painful, as it may reveal that you don't have as much access to support as you would like or need. Again, being mindful of what is, regardless of how painful, is the best place to start, because it might help you do something about it. Please look at your answers to the exercise above as you bring awareness to the following issues.

- Social isolation is a frequent problem for trauma survivors, and it's not a simple issue. How much is the quality or quantity of social support you have a part of your struggle? Are there people around you who don't really feel safe to be around and who might be best for you to avoid?

- How much do you find yourself withdrawing from people or keeping yourself from sharing important aspects of yourself with significant others around you? How much is this based on your actual experience with these individuals?

- Look at things you can do to feel less isolated. Are there people you can talk to? Do you want to consider a support group of some type? Or maybe you would rather get together with people around some activity or shared interest. Whatever you choose, the literature is pretty clear that social support is often part of the process of recovery for trauma survivors. The numbers of people are not so important. But finding at least one person you trust who can support you in your process of growth, discovery, and acceptance is an important step. For more information about dealing with interpersonal relationships, see chapter 10.

Mindful Distraction: Beginning Steps

At times during the process of healing your trauma, you may find it helpful to use some type of distraction. Sometimes, the wise choice is to focus on things other than your trauma experience. 🔔[Where is your mind right now?] However, mindful distraction is one of the last skills we would like to discuss because, as you may recall, we know that exposure to spiders is the way to get through spider phobia. In other words, feeling difficult feelings and thinking painful thoughts is an important part of the process of working through them and healing. Therefore, we do not recommend pushing away or trying to eliminate or get rid of unpleasant emotions. In fact, as discussed earlier, individuals create a lot of unneeded suffering precisely by trying to eliminate emotions, thoughts, and memories. Therefore, we present this potential mindfulness skill last because of the danger that distraction might be used without any awareness and as a way to avoid. We are not suggesting that you try to just "forget about it" whatever "it" is. We *are* suggesting that you be very mindful of what is going on with you that you want to distract yourself from, and then, with a lot of awareness, choose to distract for a period of time. This strategy should be particularly considered if safety becomes a concern.

Exercise 2.11: Situations for Mindful Distraction

List some situations that might call for you to create some distance from your experience and list strategies you might try. For example, if you are finding yourself upset and fearful before going into an important business meeting, you might label your experience and sip a cup of tea while sitting in a restful spot before the meeting. We are just suggesting a way to step back a bit so that you can attend to your needs right now. Some people have reported being overwhelmed by memories and having trouble being present in the current moment. Holding some ice cubes or sitting and noticing the room around you can be a way to come back to the now (Linehan 1993b). Even having a warm glass of milk before bed can be a comfort. Taking care of yourself can be taking a warm bath, having some tea, or imagining yourself in a peaceful quiet place. The key is to notice your distress and decide what to do that is going to be in the service of taking care of you right now. We are not talking about avoiding but rather finding a simple way of quietly returning to the present moment.

Below, list all the possible forms of healthy distraction that you can think of. We've provided a couple of examples to help you get started.

Exercising when having urges to drink

Volunteering at the homeless shelter when feeling hopeless and suicidal

[space left intentionally blank in the original book]

Mindfully Walking Your Path

Mindfulness is a crucial first step in finding a way back into contact with your life. This is about doing something different with respect to your thoughts, feelings, and even your body. As a part of the process of choosing a valued direction in your life, you need to be able to notice where you are right now. These are probably new skills for you, and you may find them tricky at first. They don't come automatically for most of us. As with any skill, the more you practice, the more you'll find mindfulness becomes a natural part of your everyday life. As you begin taking a closer look at your trauma experiences you may find yourself becoming upset and wanting to engage in old coping behaviors. When you find yourself in this situation, the first step is to be mindful of these urges, just noticing them and what thoughts or feelings may have triggered them. Next, see if you can do something different than you have usually done when you have had these feelings. 🔔[Notice what shows up for you right now, as you read this.]

Can you notice how you feel about making a different choice?

The most important thing here is heading in a direction that will keep you safe. You have already done the hardest thing. You have survived the original painful experience. We will begin looking at ways to accept your history and what is going on inside you while also moving forward in your life. However, this is a process, and some people will feel some very old and powerful urges come up. As a part of this work, we are asking you to bring a mindful stance to these old thoughts and feelings so as not to engage in harmful behaviors. As we mentioned above, sometimes the effective thing may actually be to engage in mindful distraction—that is, focus on other value-driven actions that do not pertain to your trauma history. Developing a sense of compassion for yourself for being where you are in life is part of the process of moving forward in living your valued life.

Journaling

Thoughts

[space left intentionally blank in the original book]

Feelings or Emotions

[space left intentionally blank in the original book]

Self-Judgments

[space left intentionally blank in the original book]

Physical Sensations

[space left intentionally blank in the original book]

Action Urges (What Do You Feel Like Doing?)

[space left intentionally blank in the original book]

CHAPTER 3

Pain Versus Suffering

The only way out is through.

—Robert Frost

Pain Is Universal

Pain is inevitable in life, and we know that you would not be reading this book if you had not experienced some very difficult life events. Despite outward appearances, there is no such thing as a person who has never experienced pain in life. Most of us will experience one or more of the following:

- Divorce

- The death of a close significant other

- Significant financial or legal problems

- Loss of a job we wanted

- Physical assault

- Denial of a promotion or grade we were counting on

- Betrayal by someone we trusted

- A chronic illness that will require ongoing treatment

- A car accident

- Social exclusion resulting in feeling like an outsider

- A significant injury

- Loss of hearing or sight

- Struggles with anxiety, depression, or substance abuse

- Discrimination based on age, religion, gender, ethnicity, disability, or attractiveness

- Humiliation and embarrassment in a public setting

- Living with the knowledge that we have hurt others in painful ways

When you are suffering from depression or are feeling down, it's not unusual to feel that everyone else is happier than you are, is coping better than you are, is more deserving than you are. Conversely, when things are going very well and you're having multiple successes in a row, it's not unusual to feel like things will always be this way as long as you stay on your best behavior. These beliefs are in fact not based on reality. Nobody can avoid pain on a consistent basis. 🔔[Notice any thoughts, feelings, and judgments coming up for you right now.]

There is a parable about King Solomon, who beseeched his subordinates to bring him a ring that would "make a sad person happy and a happy person sad" (Forest 1996). Many of his followers traveled far and wide looking for such an object, to no avail. But one day, a particular person who was feeling dejected about disappointing his king was walking forlornly in a street bazaar when he came upon a ring. After examining the ring, he immediately smiled, bought the ring, and brought it back to King Solomon. The king at that moment was being regaled with a dance and an abundance of delicious dishes and was feeling uplifted and happy. The moment the man gave him the ring and he took it into his hands, he became pensive and serious. The ring had indeed made a sad person happy and a happy person sad. On the inside of the ring, the following words had been engraved: "This too shall pass."

The ring had brought with it an undeniable awareness of the impermanence of things, something which in itself can be painful. Although most people readily acknowledge that happiness is ephemeral, the inevitability of pain in all people seems harder to believe. Check and see if it isn't so in your experience: When you are in distress, it feels like you are the only one feeling bad, or "this" bad, or "this bad so often." Yet, as psychologists who treat a wide range of individuals from trauma survivors to those with milder complaints, we're here to tell you that no matter how lonely you might occasionally feel with your pain, all human beings, to one extent or another, are in the same boat. To help check this out in your personal life, let's do a quick exercise.

Exercise 3.1: Painful Events List

Step 1. Think about people around you, at work, in your family, and among your friends whom you know very well, and write down the names of five to ten of these people. If you are concerned about someone seeing this list, use abbreviations or symbols.

Below is a list of people I know very well:

[space left intentionally blank in the original book]

Step 2. Go back to the list above and cross out anyone from the list who has experienced any of the following: emotional, physical, or sexual child abuse; war trauma; rape; physical attack; domestic violence; a man-made or natural disaster; or some other significant trauma. Notice how many people get crossed off your list.

Step 3. Go back to the list above and cross out anyone from the list who has experienced the death of a family member or friend, who has been divorced, who has had a disabling physical or psychological illness, or who has had a parent, sibling, or child with serious problems. Notice how many people remain on your list.

Step 4. Go back to your list one last time and cross out anyone who has failed at something important, been betrayed by someone close, had financial problems, had an accident, was denied a promotion at work, or has been rejected, ridiculed, or embarrassed.

🔔 [Take a moment here to notice any bodily sensations you're experiencing right now.]

We Compare Our Insides to Other People's Outsides

If your list is typical, there is virtually no one who is not crossed out on your list. If you do have someone who has not been marked off, consider the following points:

• Many people feel a lot of shame about painful experiences and tend not to talk about them. It may be that they have experienced something and don't talk about it, even with people they know well.

• We often compare our insides to the outsides of other people. We don't always know the struggles of other people. Consider, for example, how many people among those who think they know you well would be able to mark you off their lists without hesitation at any of the steps above. Do they know all the different aspects of pain you have experienced in your life? For some of them, probably not, right? In fact, that's another painful experience we didn't even list above: isolation, keeping secrets, and feeling like nobody would love us if they really knew everything about us.

• Experiencing traumatic events is a fairly common experience (Kessler et al. 1995), and there are many other types of painful experiences in life. In the event that there is someone on your list who has truly not encountered the type of painful experiences we listed above, see if you can become aware that it is very likely that this person will experience one of these events at some point in time. This fact is probably the reason many spiritual traditions talk about pain as an inherent aspect of the human experience.

• A number of things will happen that you wish wouldn't happen or go wrong. There is no amount of being good that will keep that from happening in life. Take death as an example: We often walk around under the illusion that death only happens to other people. Yet, death is an inherent part of life and will happen to us all eventually; it's a matter of when, not if. 🧘 [Notice any bodily sensations arising at this moment.]

Pain Is Inevitable; Suffering Is Not

Why are we inviting you to notice how common pain is? Because we want to point out that although pain is inevitable, *suffering is not* (Chodron 2001; Hayes and Smith 2005; Linehan 1993b).

What we are saying is that there are two types of painful experiences in life:

- The painful events themselves. This is *pain,* and some amount of it, no matter how attentive, thoughtful, and well-behaved we are, is inevitable.

- The extra burdens we involuntarily add by trying to get away from, reduce, eliminate, or suppress the original pain. This is *suffering,* and it can be eliminated from your life.

The Difference Between Pain and Suffering: An Example

At this point, you might be wondering about the difference between pain and suffering. It can be a confusing distinction, but we can use a minor daily event to convey it. One of the authors (JP) sometimes is late driving to work, and then she has to park in time-limited metered parking, hoping to feed the meter before the time runs out. Although this works most of the time, at other times it doesn't. A ticket for meter violation costs $15. That's the pain in this example, represented by the inner circle in the following illustration.

In some less skillful moments, when she gets a parking ticket, she gets mad at herself and may feel embarrassed or have thoughts like "That was dumb" or "I should have known better" or "This is fifteen dollars that I could have used for something useful. What a waste!" And, trying to push away all these feelings and thoughts, she puts the ticket in the glove compartment "for later." But, in fact, sometimes she "forgets" about it. Given that, at the university, an unpaid ticket doubles after two weeks, the price for the ticket becomes $30 instead of the initial $15. (Image 3.1)

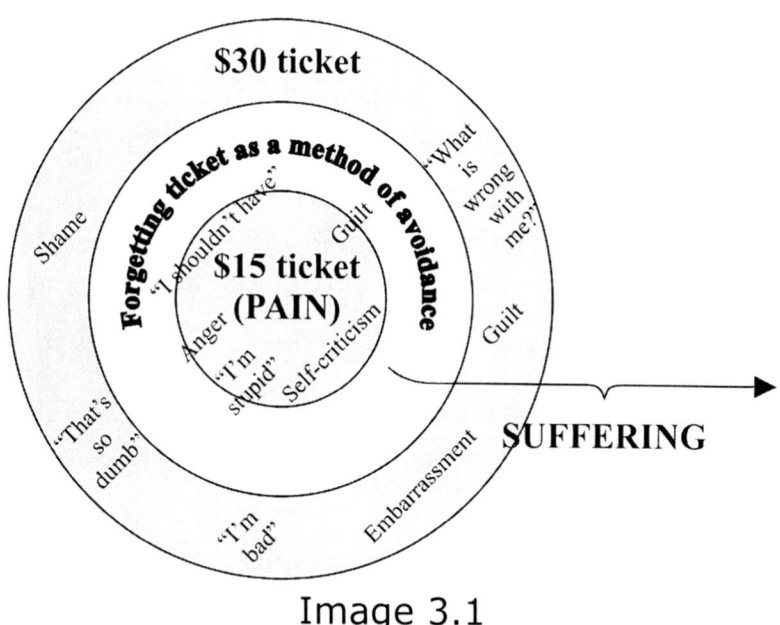

Image 3.1

Notice that, had she not tried to push away or deny the existence of the first pain and simply paid the ticket right away, she'd be $15 dollars richer right now. Of course, this example is a relatively minor inconvenience. We just use it to demonstrate the basic idea of how suffering gets added to pain. Sometimes in this book we will use smaller examples so that you can consider these ideas without too much judgment. We don't mean to equate this to your traumatic experience. These are just starting places.

Unfortunately, unneeded suffering can cost considerably more than $15. It can cost marriages, jobs, friendships, self-respect, dreams, and even lives. Although the issues of pain and suffering apply to all of us, regardless of our history, our clinical experience tells us that some people get caught in this cycle of suffering. Getting caught does not mean that you are broken or that there is something wrong with you. We are all fish in the same water, and what we are trying to look at here is a way of describing how you got stuck. 🔔[Notice any reactions to this sentence.]

Case Story: Angie's Pain and Suffering Circles

Let's look at the example of Angie, who experienced physical and sexual abuse from her stepfather while she was a young girl. Her stepfather was physically abusive to her mother and Angie witnessed a lot of violence in her childhood. Her mom was afraid to leave, and they remained trapped in this terrorizing situation. Any perceived breaking of the rules led to abuse. But of course, the truth was that nothing would have prevented the abuse. She was told she was stupid and bad just like her mother. Angie moved out of the house when she was eighteen, but the suffering associated with these events was not over even then.

As illustrated in the inner circle in the following illustration, all of the abuse can be viewed as one source of the pain in Angie's life. Something happened to her that was unfair, wrong, painful, and not at all her fault, which resulted in feelings of sadness, guilt, shame, and fear, and thoughts of "I'm bad" and "I'm broken," just like the average human being. Now, let's see what happened when Angie tried to forget or get away from the inner circle of pain.

As a young woman, Angie went away to college and did very well. She had learned to be perfect as a way to attempt to control her environment and avoid any potential criticism from those around her. Her efforts at perfection were not based on pursuing things she truly wanted in her life but rather on the avoidance of all the intense fears she had developed related to the abuse. She felt that if she could get some control in her life, she could avoid her feelings that she was bad or stupid.

She avoided close relationships, making sure that no one knew who she really was. She tried to be friendly, but social situations scared her. She learned that alcohol was one way to deal with those fears. During the week she studied and kept to herself. But on the weekends she began binge drinking at parties. This was the first ring of added suffering.

After repeated bouts of drinking and drug use, some of the initial pain in the form of self-judging thoughts and feelings of shame returned and these were intensified in response to the drinking and using. She developed guilt over drinking, and she stopped going to classes that met early in the morning. As a result, her grades began to deteriorate. The second ring of suffering was added.

When her best friend confronted her about the drinking, Angie yelled at her and picked a fight as a way of getting even further away from feelings of guilt and shame about her drinking. As a result, Angie spent even more time with the rowdy crowd at the college, and her grades declined even more as a result. In one of her drinking binges, she had casual sex with someone from this group so that she "didn't have to be alone." The third ring of suffering was added. 🧘[Notice any thoughts or emotions.]

As a result of the unprotected casual sex, Angie contracted a sexually transmitted disease (STD). When she started experiencing symptoms, she suspected she had contracted an STD and was embarrassed about the drinking and the casual sex. She felt guilty, ashamed, and regretted deeply having had casual sex with someone she hardly knew. Additionally, she began having the thought that perhaps her stepfather was right: He had always told her she was a slut. At this point she began to think about suicide, adding the fourth ring of suffering. (Image 3.2)

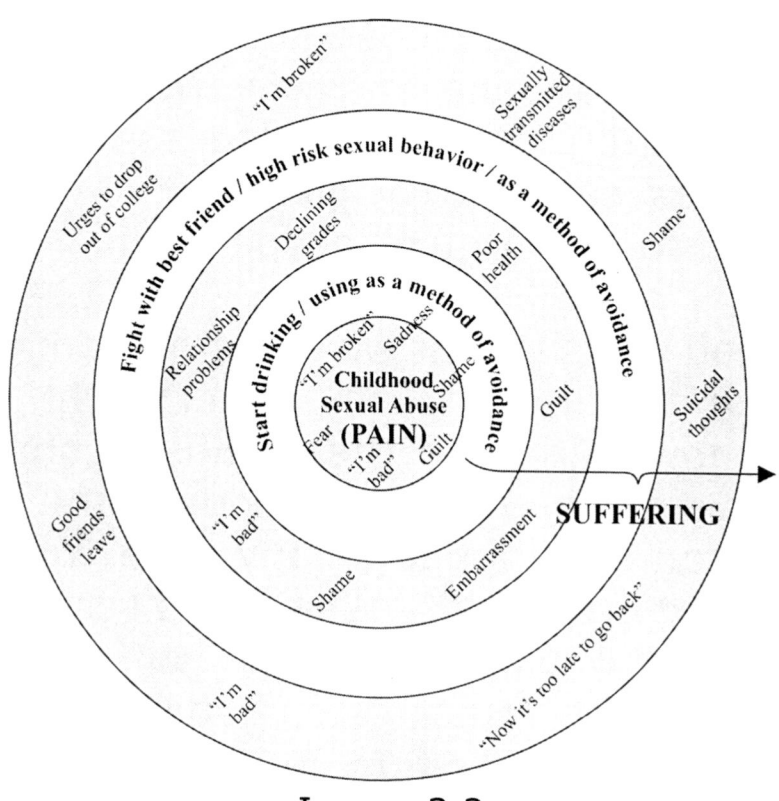

Image 3.2

Limiting the Rings of Suffering

We drew the inner and outer circles in the example above to help you get a visual of how suffering can build on pain.

The bad news is that, although we stopped after the fourth ring, rings can be added infinitely, as the arrow above suffering suggests. Angie, for example, could proceed by dropping out of college to avoid feeling the shame that comes up about her declining grades or moving on to harder drugs when alcohol isn't enough anymore to deaden the pain. In fact, we can all think of people whose lives followed such a trajectory and never recovered, with one ring of suffering being added to the next, sometimes leading to tragic or unfulfilled lives waded through in quiet desperation.

The good news is that we *can* stop adding the rings of suffering at any time. Right here, right now. Although the painful event may not have been avoidable, adding the outer circles can be stopped at any time. You may be asking yourself, "What if I've already added a couple of rings of suffering?" It doesn't matter. You can stop adding unneeded suffering no matter how much suffering has already been added to your original pain. For example, perhaps you are an abuse survivor or Vietnam veteran who's gotten divorced last year, and the divorce may be part of the rings of suffering already added or part of the original pain you are struggling with. It doesn't matter. You can still stop the unneeded suffering from being heaped onto the pain. We are not saying it's easy, because it isn't. But, in this book we will guide you through the process of addressing unneeded suffering, if you are willing. 🔔 [Notice your breathing at this moment.]

The first step is to identify the primary source of pain in your life and what you have done so far to try to get rid of this pain, to reduce, suppress, or eliminate it, and notice whether or not these very efforts have added to your suffering. Allow yourself to be open and honest while bringing a loving and kind sense of compassion toward yourself, no matter what has happened.

Thinly Veiled Suffering

Keep in mind that each of us can have a very different style of adding unneeded suffering to pain. Sometimes, the suffering being added may look positive. Consider the Vietnam veteran who came back from the war feeling numb, having no faith in human nature, and tried to get away from these feelings and the horrors of the war by becoming the perfect provider and protector, working overtime and weekends, fixing things around the house, preparing for potential problems, saving money, or always watching out for potential threats to the family by limiting where the children were allowed to go or who could come to the house. AND, in the process, he spent little to no time with his family, grew farther and farther away from his loved ones, did not see his kids grow up, and twenty years later was caught off guard when his wife asked for a divorce and the kids claimed not to know who he was. This is a sad but unfortunately not uncommon situation.

Exercise 3.2: Identifying Your Circles of Pain and Suffering

In the following graphic, we invite you to write down your pain and any suffering that may have been added. Please remember to approach this task with compassion for yourself. This is not a "gotcha" or blame exercise. This is what happened to you and what you did to survive. You did not know how to do something different. You may have thought there was a different way, but you weren't sure how to get there. You are taking the first step here in being willing to look at your life. In our experience, this is an exercise that may help you change how you live your life, if you let it.

There is an empty figure below for you to complete. This figure is composed of an inner pain circle surrounded by four rings of suffering. We encourage you to complete this exercise as thoroughly as possible. You may want to use a pencil in case you need to erase and re-write.

Step 1. On the inner circle below, where "Pain" is written, would you be willing to think of some of the most poignant, painful events in your life that are still emotionally present for you, perhaps the reason you picked up this book to read, or perhaps some other event(s) you are still struggling with? On the outer edges of the inner circle, write all the feelings, emotions, memories, bodily sensations, and thoughts that come up when you make contact with this original painful event. Some of the difficult emotions may include fear, anger, guilt, shame, sadness, loneliness, regret, and so on. Some of the difficult thoughts may include "I'm broken," "It's my fault," "I'm unlovable," and so forth. Some of the difficult bodily sensations may include pain, tension, body memories, and the like. Some of the memories may include flashbacks or intrusive fleeting images of things that happened to you or things you did.

Step 2. Now, on the second circle, write out all the initial ways you found to try to push away, not feel, suppress, avoid, minimize, or reduce the emotions, feelings, thoughts, and bodily reactions you listed in step 1. Try to think very hard about this, as some of these moves may be quite old for you and perhaps not even easy to remember. We gave one example above (drinking and using), but there are many, many ways to try to push away our feelings and thoughts that result in more suffering. See if you can notice what you have done in your life so far.

Step 3. On the third ring (gray), write all inner and outer consequences of what you wrote down on the previous step. First, think of all the feelings, emotions, memories, bodily sensations, and thoughts that come up when you think about things you wrote down in step 2. Now, also think of all the ways that what you wrote down in step 2 has been affecting your life. A couple of examples: one starts drinking and spends less time with nondrinking friends; one starts working a lot and spends less time with significant others, and so on.

Step 4. Now, on the fourth circle (white), write out all the ways you found yourself trying to push away any difficult feelings and thoughts you listed in step 3. For example, remember how Angie, whom we discussed earlier, felt embarrassed and ashamed about her drinking when confronted by her best friend, so she withdrew from her best friend and started hanging out with the wrong crowd. See if you can notice how you've tried to suppress, eliminate, reduce, or minimize any uncomfortable thoughts and feelings you listed in step 3.

Step 5. On the fifth ring (gray) write all inner and outer consequences of what you wrote down in step 4. First, think of all the feelings, emotions, memories, bodily sensations, and thoughts that come up when you think about things you wrote down in step 4. Now, also think of all the ways that this move (or moves) began affecting your life. What are the noticeable consequences of continuing to try to push away some of the feelings and thoughts associated with step 4?

Although we are stopping at this step, there might be even more layers on your circles of pain and suffering. Feel free to continue this exercise on your own, even if it requires a separate page.

Conversely, perhaps you could only identify a couple of circles above. That's understandable, particularly if you have found ways on your own of keeping the circles of suffering from being added. However, if you have a sneaking suspicion that there are more circles but you just can't notice them now, feel free to come back to this exercise later. (Image 3.3)

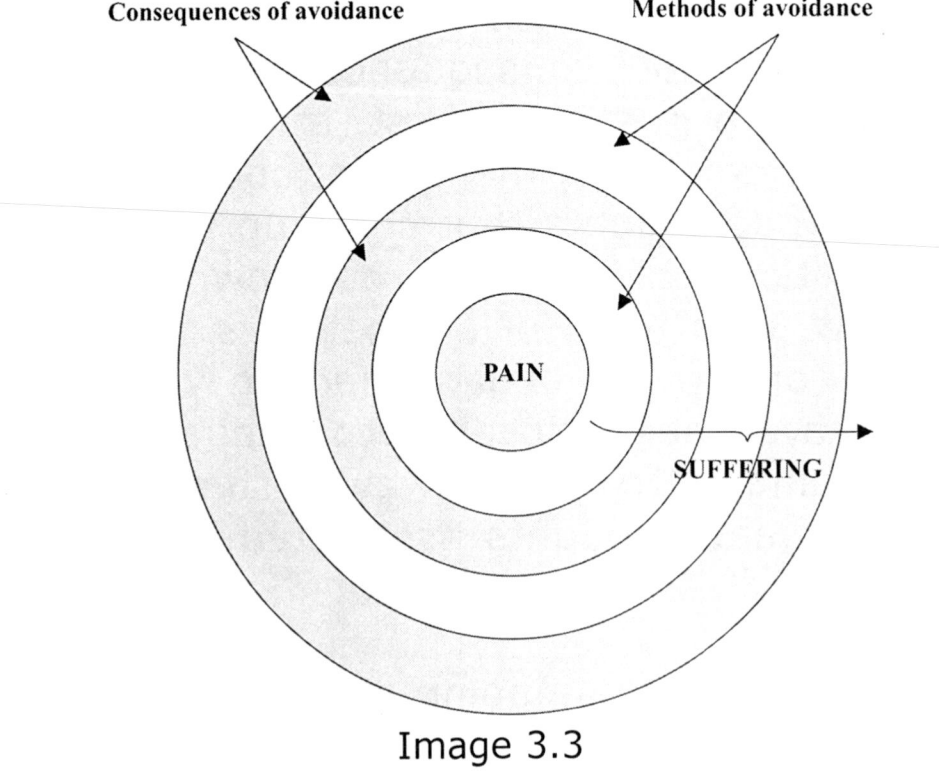

Image 3.3

Exercise 3.3: The "Where" Questions on Pain and Suffering

Looking at your pain and suffering circles above, please answer these two questions:

Question 1: Where Is Your Pain?

Is the original pain, whether throbbing and acute, dull and quiet, or dormant and unpredictably triggered, still with you at some level? Today, can you make contact with the pain you wrote down above, even if there have been several rings of suffering added since? How and when is your pain more likely to show up?

[space left intentionally blank in the original book]

Question 2: Where Are You? Inner or Outer Circles?

As you think about your current situation in life and the issue that is bringing you the most discomfort, perhaps the main reason you picked up this book, ask yourself the following question: Where are you right now in terms of the distress that is most interfering with your ability to function? Are you on your innermost circle or on one of the outer circles?

[space left intentionally blank in the original book]

The goal here is to become more aware of where you are in this moment. We want you to begin to really examine how your suffering has expanded into a variety of aspects of your life. Remember, the goal is not judgment. Rather, it is waking up and noticing where this path has led you. The rest of this book will be about showing you ways to sit with the inner circle of pain without turning it into suffering. However, starting right now, if you find yourself in the outer circles, stop and see if you can do something different that would keep you from adding unneeded suffering. Bringing a mindful stance to this process without judgment, justification, or defenses may be one way of responding differently to finding yourself in the outer circles at this point.

Eliminating the Suffering

There are three characteristics of pain and suffering worth highlighting prior to ending this chapter. First, as we have indicated above, pain is inevitable. Second, the path of recovery will weave in and out of added suffering. Third, you cannot get rid of your past history; you can only influence what happens from now on.

The Inner Circle of Pain Cannot Be Eliminated

Look back at your answer to question 1 in exercise 3.3. See if it isn't the case that no matter how many layers of suffering you have added, the original pain, in one way or another, has not completely disappeared. Some examples from our clinical experience:

The drinking wears off the next day or whenever the drinking stops, which could be years later, and the reasons one started drinking, such as sadness about a divorce, are still there, plus some.

Financial and academic accomplishments may never seem enough to get rid of thoughts like "I'm unworthy" or "I won't amount to anything." There are not enough successes in the world to quiet such thoughts forever—a fact to which many an accomplished person, including CEOs of multinational companies, can attest. There is always Bill Gates to compare oneself to, or Gandhi, or the street vendor on the corner who interacts lovingly with his daughter. For each of us, there will be different buttons pushed.

Reassurances from others that you are smart, lovable, or attractive may seem short-lived. You may find that you put yourself or others through endless tests: "Am I still lovable even if I tell you I hate you or I leave you waiting for three hours?" or "I know I was a straight-A student in high school, but the true test is whether or not I can make it in ... (fill in the blank—college, graduate school, business, medical school, etc.)." If your pain feels like a bottomless well, it probably is, because pain of this sort cannot be eliminated with reassurances, whether from others or oneself.

Even physically painful actions like cutting or burning oneself may remove the immediacy of some of the emotional pain, but it soon returns, with the addition of shame and guilt over the self-injurious behavior.

Sometimes pain seems to have disappeared, only to come back unexpectedly in full force. A father who lost a child, for example, may be able to go on with his life, deeply care for his other children, laugh aloud while seeing a comedy in the movie theater, or thoroughly enjoy a vacation in the Caribbean. AND, all of a sudden, he may be again overcome by sadness and grief years later, perhaps when one of his other children graduates from college or perhaps on his deceased son's birthday.

All these examples highlight the facts that the pain in the inner circle cannot be completely eliminated and that it's the nature of internal pain to come and go of its own accord. See if you can notice—as a fact, not something to believe or disbelieve—that pain cannot really be eliminated or pushed away permanently. 🔔[Notice any thoughts or judgments coming up for you.]

Unfortunately, there is no real escape by using ordinary, everyday means. Some people think that if they just do fun or positive things they can avoid reminders of old traumas. However, sometimes even a very pleasant event, like the graduation in the example above, may trigger remnants of an old pain. These positive experiences can remind us, for example, that we are alone and don't have someone to share a beautiful sunset with, or that this moment will soon pass, or even that we just went to the movies to try to avoid thinking of a relationship breakup. If our posture toward pain is that of defensiveness and attack, it leaves very little that can be done that is healthy and stops the rings of suffering from being added.

It Is Normal to Go In and Out of Suffering

Now look at your answer to question 2 in exercise 3.3. If you are like most of us, chances are you are noticing that you are on the outer circle or find yourself going back and forth between the inner and outer circles. That's to be expected.

If you find yourself judging yourself for being on an outer ring, see if you can notice that and let it go. Remember, this is not a game of "gotcha" or right and wrong. Instead of focusing on blame, the invitation is to have you stop adding rings of suffering as soon as possible in order to make your life work for you.

History Is Additive, Not Subtractive

The fundamental idea in this section is that you can never really get rid of your past, and trying to do so is part of the cause of suffering. We often act as if we can perform lobotomies on ourselves by essentially trying to find some way to get rid of part of our mind. However, that's not possible. When you try to get rid of the memories, the feelings, the sensations, or the connections with your trauma experiences, you are actually adding more layers to the parts of this memory in your brain. You cannot, in fact, take anything out. People try all types of strategies to get rid of parts of experience, including drinking, distracting, forgetting, and even the more extreme behavior of dissociating. The psychological gymnastics involved in dissociation may push memories, thoughts, and feelings aside for a while, but over time dissociation usually creates more suffering (Polusny and Follette 1995). To exemplify the fact that history is additive and not subtractive, we would like to try out an experiment that has been adapted from Hayes, Strosahl, and Wilson (1999, 126).

Exercise 3.4. What Are the Letters?

Let's imagine the following scenario. We come to you and say, "Guess what? We have a million dollars to give to you if you can perform one task. All you have to do to get the million is to remember the three letters we mention. We will repeat them only three times, and you will need to remember them—and then we'll give you a million dollars! Are you ready? Are you completely ready to hear these three letters that may make a difference in your finances forever? Here are the letters: a, b, c. The letters are a, b, and c."

What are the letters? _____

Can you say them aloud? Can you recall them? The letters are a, b, c.

Now, what are the letters? _____

Can you say them aloud? Now, if we come to you in an hour and ask you to repeat these letters, do you think you'll remember them? What about in a day? What about in a week?

What are the letters? _____

Now let's try a different experiment.

As you can well imagine, we do not actually have one million dollars to give you. It was a trick. So, we will now make a different

> request of you: Whatever you do, do not think of the letters we just told you.
>
> What are the letters? _____

What did your mind come up with? Check and see, even if you wrote out different letters than the ones we talked about before. How do you know that these aren't those letters? You do because, in your mind, you are saying, for example "d, e, and f are not a, b, and c," which means that in your mind the thought of "The letters are a, b, c" is still there. Try really, really, really hard not to think of the letters as a, b, c. Can you honestly do it? Probably not, right? Isn't this interesting? After something gets into our heads, it hardly ever gets out when we are trying to get it out. It's easy enough to inadvertently forget what we learn in class or something on our to-do list; however, the very attempt to try to forget something makes it more memorable (Wegner 1994). So, there is no way of displacing the thought "The letters are a, b, and c" with other thoughts such as "The letters are now d, e, and f" or "I should forget the letters a, b, and c." When you try, you simply end up with three thoughts in your head about the letters a, b, and c. We can only add more things to our brains; we're unable to deliberately take anything out. It just can't be done.

This exercise not only illustrates that history is additive and never subtractive, it also illustrates how easy it is to store very insignificant, inaccurate bits of information about anyone, even people we don't know or care about. Yet, these little bits can stay with us, sometimes for a long, long, time. Even right now, you can probably remember a joke that you hate or find offensive, and yet, there it is, somewhere in the back of your mind, even if you never repeat it. If you check in, based on your experience, you'll see that you cannot will yourself to forget something, even a simple string of letters like a, b, and c, let alone an important aspect of your history and who you are.

This is an important fact to make contact with, based on your experience and not just because we say so, because this means that the only way to find a life after trauma is *with* that trauma history. More will be said about that in the remainder of the book.

Now What?

You may have picked up this book hoping that perhaps within these pages you could find a way not to feel the sadness, guilt, shame, memories, anger, and self-critical thoughts and self-blame that typically come along with traumatic experiences. Perhaps these are some of the very feelings, thoughts, and experiences you listed in the outer edges of your inner circle. As you have learned, we cannot help you get rid of your pain. But by finding a way to deal with the pain, there might be an out towards a vital life. What if, as the quote by Robert Frost states at the beginning of this chapter, the only way out is through?

The next chapter will address the puzzle of how we end up in the outer circles and, more importantly, why it's so hard to stop adding circles of suffering. If you are like the rest of humanity, try as you might, you find yourself doing just that in your life, despite your best intentions.

Journaling

Thoughts

[space left intentionally blank in the original book]

Feelings or Emotions

[space left intentionally blank in the original book]

Self-Judgments

[space left intentionally blank in the original book]

Physical Sensations

[space left intentionally blank in the original book]

Action Urges (What Do You Feel Like Doing?)

[space left intentionally blank in the original book]

CHAPTER 4

Control Is the Problem

The significant problems we face cannot be solved at the same level of thinking we were at when we created them.

—Albert Einstein

We are going to talk about a new way of approaching your history that may seem counterintuitive or just plain strange. AND you have come this far, so we are asking you to continue to look at your trauma history in a new way. The title of this chapter, "Control Is the Problem," is taken from the work of Hayes, Strosahl, and Wilson (1999), and indicates that holding on to efforts to control your experiences is likely to increase your suffering. We guess that many things you have been doing up until now have been aimed at getting rid of, controlling, not having, or managing your traumatic thoughts, memories, and feelings. Reading this book may even be a part of that attempt. It would not be surprising if some of what you have done has worked to some degree. Check and see, though, if those strategies have had some costs associated with them or been some sort of half measure. So, for now we are going to ask you to read the next few pages with openness while always checking back with your experience. The goal of this chapter is to introduce a different level of thinking, as Einstein aptly put it, as the first step to a new way of living your life. But let's back up a bit.

Early Messages of Control

Does it ever seem to you that perhaps you've been fighting a game that just isn't fair? That you've tried very, very hard to feel better, but it's just not working? What if trying hard, doing all the right things, and trying to play by the rules is just not fixing what seems to be wrong with you? It may in fact be that this is not the way out of the tug-of-war with your history. Maybe everything you've tried is not going to work because the rules you learned very early on just don't work in the realm of thoughts and feelings. You might think, "No one taught me any rules about all this. What are you talking about?" Let's take another step back and look at what most of us learned about this game of life.

Very early on, most of us learn that good kids are those who do not cry or make a fuss, kids who try not to cause much trouble, who play by the rules and don't upset the grown-ups (Hayes, Strosahl, and Wilson 1999). Basically, if you're good, you don't rock the boat. Now, we're not trying to imply that this is some sort of grand conspiracy. We both have raised children and recognize how most of this starts. We tell our babies that they are good when they are quiet and cooperative. We smile and coo at our happy, easy babies. We ignore children when they're throwing a tantrum. Wow, think about the message here! Some of you may even remember the old saying that children should be seen and not heard. 🧘[Take a moment here to notice how you are feeling right now.] While you might not hear those exact words now, a lot of the same messages are there.

Sometimes these messages are conveyed directly, such as in praise for a child who does not complain. But more subtle messages are also being sent, and it's in these that the problems start. At times, parents imply to kids that adults do not feel or shouldn't feel fear, pain, or sadness by saying things like "See, Dad is not afraid," or "Big boys don't cry." In some families children are told "Stop crying or I'll give you something to cry about." And when there is abuse, the messages can be even deeper and darker. Children are told not to ever talk about what happened, at times even being threatened with death if they tell. Sometimes children are told to ignore their own natural instincts—being told "That doesn't hurt" even when it does. And so it begins: the pattern of denying your feelings, of denying yourself. Basically, by the time we get to adulthood, we have had a lifetime of learning to try to suppress feelings or thoughts that are unpleasant to ourselves or to others.

The intent of this learning can vary a lot. Sometimes it is really not badly intentioned but just a part of the status quo. Sometimes, it is to cover up a secret. Either way, we learn some pretty basic rules that are supposed to make life work. These messages can be conveyed indirectly, through modeling, such as a parent who never appears sad or afraid even in face of dire situations like divorce or death, or a parent who is ultraoptimistic and never allows a child to express fear, doubt, or sadness. Remember the hidden messages in expressions such as "Buck up" or "You can do anything you really put your mind into," or very quick solutions to expressed concerns, such as "Just do it" or "Don't worry, nothing will go wrong." Although often well-intentioned, these seemingly optimistic messages are simply teaching children (and adults) not to express emotions that make parents (or others) uncomfortable. Sometimes this message is passed on to children exactly because parents or others do not know how to resolve the problems either! 🔔 [Pay attention to your breathing at this moment.] Sometimes messages such as "Just think positive" can come across as "Don't tell me about things that make me uncomfortable," and in fact, sometimes we see that people whose illnesses are progressing despite treatment feel blamed by others for the worsening of the illness, as if they, by implication, haven't had enough positive thoughts to contain the illness.

The bottom line is that: we are constantly bombarded with messages such as these:

- Difficult emotions and thoughts should not exist.

- But if they do, they should be controlled.

- We can make our feelings positive.

- Having positive feelings can stop bad things from happening.

Can you really will yourself to feel different? You might try an experiment. For instance, you might try to make yourself have a crush on someone. Just pick someone and decide to make yourself feel those feelings that come with the first blush of infatuation. Make sure that you feel that warmth inside, the butterflies in your stomach, and the happy feelings you feel when the person walks into the room. The task is not to date the person or have any real interaction with him or her. The task is just to make yourself feel all those lovely, giddy, warm feelings you get when you meet someone who brings out those responses. If you're like everyone we have ever met, you can't just turn these feelings on or decide to have them. In our experience, feelings don't work that way. And yet we are told all the time to change our feelings. 🔔 [Notice what you are feeling right now as we say this.]

Exercise 4.1: Your Early Messages

This exercise is an effort to understand yourself and your specific history better. Take a few minutes right now and write down some of the messages that you received as a child that implied that negative emotions (or emotions that were judged to be negative), such as sadness, anger, fear, self-doubt, jealousy, envy, or guilt, should not be felt or should be suppressed. When you consider who taught you this idea of controlling feelings, think not just of your parents but also of siblings, relatives, teachers, schoolmates, books, magazines, newspapers, TV, and movies.

Messages that implied that negative emotions and thoughts are bad:

[space left intentionally blank in the original book]

Messages that implied that others either don't feel these emotions and thoughts or, if they do, that they can get rid of them:

[space left intentionally blank in the original book]

Where have you received these messages as an adult?

[space left intentionally blank in the original book]

If You're Not Willing to Have It, You've Got It

So, here we are...

First, we know from experience that pain is inevitable in life.

Yet, we are taught very early on that there is something "wrong"—read bad, abnormal, undesirable, even shameful—with experiencing pain in life.

In fact, as you probably found out with the exercise above, you've received plenty of messages in life to say that uncomfortable thoughts and feelings, as well as memories and bodily reactions, should be suppressed, reduced, or otherwise eliminated from your life.

So, guess what we do when we encounter pain in our lives?

Yes, that's it. We try to eliminate, reduce, or suppress emotions, thoughts, feelings, memories, and bodily sensations that are deemed negative as best we can.

But in the world of thoughts and feelings, the rule seems to be that if you are not willing to have it, you've got it! (Hayes, Strosahl, and Wilson 1999)

So what's the problem with all of this? The problem is that we are told to get rid of bad feelings, painful memories, and anything else that might cause someone to be upset. Frankly, this never works well. Even in the course of everyday life, people who are not survivors of trauma run into difficult or uncomfortable situations that lead to pain. They can't just get rid of bad feelings either. But for those people who have experienced more severe forms of pain and trauma, this effort becomes a very extreme form of a double bind. You have all this pain and suffering that is fairly big in your life, and you are told not to have it. Don't talk about it, show your pain, or even think about the event. Just *don't!* So, you do what you know how to do ... the things we have talked about. You run harder, faster, or better—in whatever style you have developed. We have looked at some of this—you know what these efforts are for you. (See what you identified in the circles of pain and suffering in chapter 3.) Maybe you avoid close relationships, or drink and use drugs, or starve yourself, or work all the time, or just find some way to shut down. And how has that worked?

Metaphor: Trying to Dig Your Way Out

There is a metaphor about wandering in a field that expresses these issues in a less verbal way so that you can get a different sense of this problem (Hayes, Strosahl, and Wilson 1999). Imagine that you are blindfolded, given a bag of tools, and told to go live your life in a field of trees, grass, creeks, and meadows. Oh, there are also some deep holes here and there. Some of the holes are small, but some are quite big. One day, you cross a creek and turn right after the tree with the really rough bark when, all of a sudden, *boom!* You fall into a big hole. It is dark, but even if it wasn't, remember, you're blindfolded and can't really see what's going on. You might sit there a while and think about this and even be mad at the whole situation. After a while you decide you need to get out of this hole. Well, first thing you do is reach into your tool bag to find that there is only one tool there—a shovel. You've learned that a shovel is good for digging, and here's life handing you a shovel, so you start digging. You are a hard worker, and you dig fast and nonstop, with a lot of enthusiasm. You try digging to the right but don't find the way out. You try digging to the left. You try digging under your feet. All this effort is to no avail. Then, exhausted, you stop and decide to think this through: "The problem is that I crossed the creek. I shouldn't have crossed the creek. And then, I turned right after the rough tree. I shouldn't have turned right. That was really dumb!" After much thinking about this, you realize that you're still in the hole. You then start thinking about how you were able to get out of a hole (albeit much smaller) last time by using your shovel, and you start getting angry about how the shovel does not appear to be working this time. Perhaps someone did something to your shovel. After all this thinking, you stop and decide to feel your way around, and at first there is enough space around you that you think that perhaps you're out of the hole. But then you realize that the hole has simply gotten bigger, with all sorts of caverns and side tunnels that are even interesting for a while. Interesting or not, you're still in the hole. Perhaps you pick up this book in the hope that we will hand you a gold-plated shovel, one that would allow you to dig really fast and deep. In fact, you might be so intent on digging that were we to throw you a ladder right now, chances are you would think it was for digging. "Wow! Here's a new, cool shovel with steps in it!" 🔔[Notice any thoughts, feelings, and judgments coming up for you right now.]

Okay, it might seem like we're being glib with you here, especially when we can't be right there with you as you are reading this. However, we are not trying to make light of this situation at all. We understand the discomfort not just from reading about it but from our own experience. We understand that this pain you are in may be so big, deep, and wide that there seems to be no way out at all, and you are doing the very best you can just to survive. AND what you have been doing is not working anymore. See if it isn't so that there are ways in which trying to get rid of the pain you were feeling worked like digging—and only got the hole bigger. See if you can notice the ways in which you can relate to this metaphor in your life. Remember, it's not your fault that you are in the hole: it is as if you were blindfolded and fell into the hole, and you used the only tool you had available (the only skills you were taught). So, this is not about blame or fault. What it is about is getting out of the hole.

So, here is our first suggestion to you: *put down the shovel.* Imagine us standing right here with you as you make this very big step and just stop digging.

Seeing with New Eyes

If you want to go back to your old tools later, you can do that. We can always go back to doing more of the same. But, for now, we invite you to begin to approach all of this with new eyes, even if it feels scary. Assume that whatever you've been doing to solve long-standing problems that don't seem to go away *is not* working. If it were, don't you think that it would have worked by now? For example, if your typical strategy is drinking to try to drown out the pain, ask yourself this: Has drinking really taken away the pain and memories in the long term? If drinking hasn't taken away the sadness and the memories of what has happened, why would one more beer or Scotch do it now? Has drinking not created other problems in your life that in fact have made the hole bigger?

If you cannot relate to the example of drinking, substitute whatever moves you have identified as your strategies to deal with your pain, be it working all the time, trying to be perfect, isolating, hurting yourself, keeping relationships superficial so that you won't get hurt, sleeping all day and not going out, and so on. We each have our own repertoire that is quite varied and sometimes very creative. And, as you move to put down the shovel, beware of trying to continue your digging with the ladder we are extending to you.

If you are a little confused, that's okay. 🔔 [Notice what shows up for you right now, as we say this.] If absolutely everything we are saying right now makes perfect sense to you and you know exactly what to do, then you're probably still digging in the old way. This work requires the "new level of thinking" that Einstein talked about. To make room for something truly different to arise within ourselves, we sometimes have to let go of the framework we have adopted. A friend of ours who grew up on a farm once told us that this new approach is like burning the fields so that next year something new can grow. There are lots of expressions that relate to this new way of looking at the world. You know them. If a tree falls in the forest and no one is there to hear it, is there a sound? What is the sound of one hand clapping? What we are proposing is that this is not an intellectual problem that you can work out with thinking. Rather, we are gently suggesting to you that this new way of seeing is more of an insight that you will sense rather than think. Whatever metaphor works for you, use it.

The bottom line is this: If what we are saying makes too much sense to you and doing something about it seems easy to do, entertain the possibility that you are about to engage in more of the same. For now, just put down the shovel and let go of reasoning your way out of this place.

There are many ways to look at the world, if we stay open.

Exercise 4.2: Seeing More Than One Alternative

Image 4.1

Because this point is so crucial, we want to use some other examples to illustrate it. Look at the picture below. (Image 4.1)

What do you see in this M.C. Escher print?

[space left intentionally blank in the original book]

Can you see the white riders? _____

Can you see the black riders? _____

Depending how you look at it, you will see either white riders mounted on white horses or black riders mounted on black horses. While you are focusing on the white images, it's hard to recognize the black images, and vice versa. Yet, neither the black riders and horses or the white riders and horses is the "truth." The illustration is of *both* black AND white images, but our minds often focus on one to the exclusion of the other.

This problem of perception is a human phenomenon, as it is difficult for us to entertain different possibilities at the same time or to entertain a different possibility after having made up our minds. Cognitive psychologists have discovered, for example, that we have a tendency to engage in *functional fixedness,* that is, a tendency to not be able to see other functions for the same object after we learned of one way to use that particular object (Solso 1991). So, it's wise to always entertain the possibility that, in our own situations and inner lives, there is something we are not seeing, despite how closely we are looking.

Life strategies may serve different functions, depending on the individual: What is digging for one person may be putting down the shovel for another. Only the person himself or herself can know what new behavior is truly different, and even then, sometimes only over time. We are really interested in whether this behavior functions to help you avoid unwanted thoughts and feelings or if it represents a way to help you to be more fully present in your life. For example, for a person who has problems related to alcohol or drugs, drinking and letting loose after reading this chapter might be more of the same. However, perhaps for someone else whose coping strategy is to be socially isolated and always in control, having one drink with coworkers at the end of the day may actually be putting down the shovel. It just depends. 🔔[Notice any thoughts coming up.] We invite you to adopt this questioning perspective about your own perception of what is going on in your life as you continue to read this book. It is out of this somewhat questioning perspective that drastic changes can sometimes take place.

We call this part of the treatment *creative hopelessness.* What we are trying to convey here is that your situation, as currently constructed, is indeed unworkable. However, out of this sense of confusion and lack of clarity, something unique, creative, and helpful can arise: a different level of thinking. We know what we are proposing here is fairly radical. And we want to acknowledge that some trauma survivors have been taught to doubt their own perception of everything and to go along with others' perceptions. If that is the case with you, then continuing to doubt yourself would be more of the same. So, we'd suggest you shake that loose also and go the other way, entertaining the possibility that perhaps perpetually doubting yourself is part of the problem. Remain aware that our minds are tricky, and it's almost like they are constantly at work in trying to keep us stuck. We'll talk more about the mind, for lack of a better term, later. But for now, entertain the possibility that not all that your mind says should be completely believed. If you are truly going to put down the shovel, ask yourself this: "Am I doing something really different?" If you start having the nagging suspicion that it's more of the same, try something else. 🔔[Notice your breathing right now.]

After hearing the person-in-the-hole metaphor, many of our clients have said, "That's exactly right. What I need is to put down the shovel." In one case, a few weeks went by and finally the client came back in saying, "How come I put down the shovel but I still feel depressed?" It turned out that this person's typical style of operating ("old move") was to jump enthusiastically into the new bandwagon, only to give up after things did not improve immediately. In fact, for her, enthusiastically believing the new therapist, whom she deemed "bigger, better" than the last one, was her own way of digging. Being enthusiastic about dropping the shovel wasn't really dropping the shovel for her; it was more of the same.

Being able to see how we are digging in life is half of the work. Because if it were easy to see, you probably would have already seen it. It takes bringing compassionate and honest illumination into the darkness of suffering to recognize our old moves.

Metaphor: The Rock Garden

In Kyoto, Japan, there is a rock garden with a very special feature: Although it's a small garden, there is no one spot in the garden from which one can see all fifteen rocks. As you move from one spot to another, you might be able to see a rock that was hidden previously, but then there is a different rock out of your field of vision. Whenever you find yourself stuck in a hole or on the outer circles of suffering (see chapter 3), ask yourself: "Is it possible that there is something (like a rock in this Kyoto garden) I cannot see right now? Where do I have to move, or whose perspective do I need to take, to be able to see what is missing from my current field of vision?" Even if you cannot possibly imagine that there is something missing from your perspective, we invite you to entertain the possibility that there might be, as this perspective alone may help you to hold yourself and your reactions lightly.

What if life is like that rock garden in Kyoto? What if sometimes it takes being in a different spot in life to see something that has been hidden from our awareness previously? Sometimes, the spot in life that allows us to see the previously unseen is pain. Sometimes, being in pain allows us to look at our lives and what we have been doing with different eyes. A client reported he had the experience of feeling a sense of disconnection toward a friend who had experienced the end of a relationship. This client would secretly judge his friend for "moping around" and would think "Get over it!" Years later, after his own marriage ended abruptly and painfully, our client saw his friend's earlier experience in a very different way. His own pain allowed him to look at his friend's experience with more compassion and understanding, in a way that he had never experienced before.

Consider the possibility that pain—not suffering, but simply the inner circle of pain, as discussed in the last chapter—far from being an enemy, can allow you to see previously unseen things and to motivate you to do something different in life. Pain can help us to see new things in ourselves and in the world. Strange as that may seem, pain can be an ally.

The Problem with Suppression

As we noted above, human beings receive plenty of training to suggest that controlling how we feel is imperative. Although this next exercise is similar to one we described in chapter 1, we think it is worth looking again at the issue of how control works or does not work inside our skin. It's crucial that you do exactly what we tell you to do.

Exercise 4.3: Don't Think of an Orange

• Don't think of an orange.

• Whatever you do, do *not* think of a juicy orange that smells sweet. Don't think of its round shape with dimpled skin that gives way when you peel it. Just don't think about that orange no matter what.

• Notice what showed up for you.

If you're like most people, you could not keep the image of an orange from coming into your mind. At least, this is what psychologist Daniel Wegner found when he conducted this study using the image of white bears (1994). He divided up a group of college students into two groups: one group was asked to think of a white bear and the other was asked to not think of a white bear. Interestingly, in this and other associated studies, it was found that those instructed not to think of a white bear actually thought more of a white bear than those who were asked to think of it. Trying to suppress certain thoughts led to a paradoxical, unexpected result of thinking even more about the item. Researchers have speculated that this paradoxical effect also applies to feelings, and studies currently underway are examining this phenomena in more detail. Sometimes, this effect happened right away; at other times, people noticed an increase in the thought or feeling later. Either way, suppression of a thought or feeling is generally not possible. In fact, we invite you to notice whether the image of an orange comes up for you later on, when you least expect it.

Metaphor: Perfect Polygraph Machine

Let's try another example. Imagine that we hook you up to a perfect polygraph machine (Hayes, Strosahl, and Wilson 1999). Every single change in body temperature, heart rate, breathing, sweating, we would know—every single one of them. This is a perfect polygraph machine, remember. Just to add a little incentive, we will hook this polygraph up to your bank account. Now, we ask you to nod your head or we will withdraw one thousand dollars from your account (or whatever amount you have left if less than this). Could you do it? Could you nod your head? Of course you could, and you would do it quite well so that we would be sure to see that you had nodded your head. Now, imagine a second scenario. Again, we connect the polygraph to your bank account, and then we say, "Don't feel anxious about losing your money or we will begin withdrawing money from your account. Every time you have an anxious thought, feeling, or breath, we will withdraw one thousand dollars from your account." Could you do it? Could you 100 percent not feel anxious if told to do so, even with our pulling big chunks of money out of your account? If you're being honest here, the answer is no. It's not that you personally cannot do it. Nobody can. You would be thinking about your bills, your overdraft protection, your child-support payment, rent or your house payment, being out on the street with nothing, and on it goes. So no matter how important it is for you not to have that thought, or any other thought, the fact is that we do not have the control inside the skin that we have outside the skin. In the outside world, you can do things like nodding your head without much problem. Inside the skin, things work differently. 🔔[How does your body feel right now?]

The Bottom Line on Control

There are several issues here, so let's review.

We have learned through a variety of experiences that controlling things is good. Using control, we can build houses, drive cars, fix broken objects, and engage in a variety of other useful tasks. However, in the world inside the skin, we have very little control of thoughts and feelings and other related phenomena.

Knowing that control has worked in the outside world, we try to use it on our thoughts and feelings. This seems like a good idea and lots of people may have told you to do it ("Stop crying!"), AND we have learned that the very attempt at controlling what goes on inside the skin turns pain into suffering.

In fact, most long-term outcomes of trauma, such as substance abuse, depression, suicidality, self-harming behaviors, and problems with relationships often arise as a result of efforts to try not to have feelings, memories, or thoughts associated with the trauma.

More on Experiential Avoidance

As we have discussed, we refer to this process of trying to escape feelings, thoughts, memories, and bodily sensations as experiential avoidance (Hayes et al. 1996). Research on trauma has considerable evidence to show that experiential avoidance—that is, attempts to get away from negative thoughts and feelings—is associated with more psychological problems (Polusny and Follette 1995). In fact, all forms of treatment for trauma that have some empirical support contain some aspect of an exposure component that includes facing the trauma in one way or another while also being given some tools to cope with the event (Follette and Ruzek 2006). Therefore, getting better from a traumatic experience involves letting go of attempts to control what goes on inside you: thoughts, feelings, memories, and bodily sensations. This is a good place in the process to look again at some of your behaviors that may be falling under the umbrella of avoidance. After reading more on this, you may have some new insight on your old moves.

Exercise 4.4: Old Moves in Sheep's Clothing

The feelings I most dread are _____

The thoughts I most dread are _____

The memories or images I most dread are _____

The bodily sensations I most dread are _____

When I experience, or fear experiencing, the above feelings, thoughts, memories, and bodily sensations, I tend to ... (old moves)

[space left intentionally blank in the original book]

Take a moment now and go back to your pain and suffering circle in chapter 3. Are the behaviors you identified in exercise 4.4 the same as the ones you identified earlier as adding suffering to your life? If they are the same, that's fine. If they are different, notice that your own understanding of yourself may be evolving as you read this book. This is not a problem and may in fact be a very good sign.

Trauma and Control

Our clients often recount that during their trauma, be it sexual abuse, war, or natural disaster, they had no control over the events happening to them. 🔔[Notice any bodily sensations coming up right now. Breathe.] Children being molested by an adult do not have control over the situation. Soldiers fighting a war do not get to pick whether or not they'll be at war with a particular nation or whether or not they'll be attacked or have to defend themselves and others at a particular time. The tsunami and hurricane survivors were not able to control the weather and its impact on loss of life and property.

We understand that the issue of control is very complicated. Sometimes other people may tell you that you did have control: "You should never have gone there by yourself" or "Well, you shouldn't have moved to Florida." But this kind of feedback is part of the problem. Most people want to have the illusion of control. It helps all of us to feel safe and to feel that we can protect ourselves and our loved ones. AND, as we consider this issue in this chapter, we see that it is pretty much impossible to get through life without falling into some holes—or experiencing painful events. Life is like that: a series of events, one following the other, with most of us engaging in what ifs when something painful happens, wondering if one action caused another.

The challenge is to notice when control will work and when it won't. Many trauma survivors feel totally helpless to address things that they actually can control but feel they can't. You can decide not to have contact with someone who is hurtful to you. You can clear dangerous substances out of your house. You can say no to someone when they pressure you to do something you don't want to do. What you can't control is how you feel about all of these situations. There are some strange paradoxes here. Our clients often report that when their lives feel out of control, there is even more pressure to try to control thoughts and feelings. Sometimes these control efforts can also involve trying to control the behavior of other people in ways that are not helpful. Some might say it's like moving deck chairs on the Titanic. That is, the ship is in big trouble and the person is rearranging things to make them look like everything is fine. AND we all do it to some degree. Basically, we are asking you to wake up and look at your life with new eyes.

When we suggest to trauma survivors to let go of control or that, from an ACT perspective, "control is the problem" (Hayes, Strosahl, and Wilson 1999), we have to make sure that we are all on the same page. Control of what? And, for what purpose? Both of these issues matter in gauging what is healthy and what isn't. Therefore, we would like to take some time to discuss the difference and the relative effectiveness of attempted control on the inside and on the outside of our skin, and we will invite you to notice what function your control behaviors serve in your life.

Control on the Inside Is Almost Always Unhealthy

To reiterate what we have been saying so far, attempts to control thoughts, feelings, memories, and bodily reactions (things that happen inside the skin), are almost always problematic. As noted earlier, that's the process by which we end up adding suffering to our original pain.

At this point, you may be thinking, "But there are some things that I do that help me not to focus on my trauma without adding suffering." And we would probably agree with you that some things may not be as damaging and may indeed be helpful to you. Nothing is black or white, really. As we discussed in chapter 2, there are skillful things you can do that may keep you from dwelling on difficult thoughts and emotions and that may help you to manage your everyday life. For example, sitting in a quiet place and having a cup of tea may be very effective in dealing with an urge to do something harmful to yourself.

However, as we move forward in this book, we would like to propose to you that the agenda of trying to control the world inside your skin—thoughts, feelings, and memories—is actually a big part of what is keeping you locked in a cycle of suffering.

Exercise 4.5: Rating Attempted Control on the Inside

On a scale of 0 to 10, with 0 being never and 10 being always, how often do you tend to try to suppress, get away from, forget, or eliminate the following inner experiences?

Feelings of inadequacy_____

Anger _____

Shame _____

Fear _____

Pride _____

Urges to harm yourself _____

Thoughts of "I'm bad" _____

Feelings of uncertainty _____

Memory of a trauma _____

Joy _____

Feelings of love _____

Other _____

Based on your answers above, how would you rate the extent to which excessive attempted control (suppressing, getting away from, eliminating, forgetting, minimizing) of uncomfortable or difficult thoughts, feelings, memories, and bodily reactions is a problem for you on a scale of 0 to 10, with 0 being not at all a problem and 10 being a very big problem? If it is a problem, how is excessive control of thoughts and feelings affecting your life?

[space left intentionally blank in the original book]

When you think about letting go of trying to control what is going on inside your skin, how much discomfort do you feel on a scale of 0 to 10, with 0 being none and 10 being the most you've ever felt? What emotions, thoughts, and action urges do you have?

[space left intentionally blank in the original book]

The last question in the preceding exercise—about the idea of letting go of control—probably has caused you some discomfort. That's natural, and we will help you through it. As mentioned in earlier chapters, we would encourage you not to stop reading this book now or in the future because you are feeling afraid. [What is your mind saying right now?] Experiencing fear is an inherent aspect of successfully working on trauma issues and should not be interpreted as cause for alarm or reason to stop the work. If fear or discomfort arises, see if you can let these feelings be like a wave that comes and goes, rising and then passing while you just ride the wave. This move has been described as being a bit like bodysurfing—just letting the emotions pass. Go back to exercise 2.7, on mindful breathing if necessary, and allow yourself to breathe in and out. And remember, whenever fear or discomfort descends as you're reading this book, take some time to go to the end of the chapter you are reading and jot down what you're feeling, thinking, and wanting to do. As we discussed in the introduction, doing this work is not just about putting yourself through the pain. Rather, it is in the service of living your valued life. This process is about your moving forward in ways that are important and meaningful to you.

Hopefully, exercise 4.5 has provided you with some ideas about which types of internal experiences you are most likely to try to control and given you some sense about how this has worked for you. Letting go of control and noticing the cost of attempted control on the inside will be a continuing theme throughout the book, as it is a central focus in ACT. For most of the book, when we say "control," we will be referring to attempted control of thoughts and feelings, something that, as a rule, does not work. However, before moving to another topic, we would also like to cover the issue of when attempted control outside the skin may also be unhealthy.

Control on the Outside Can Also Be Unhealthy

In the world of ACT, we suggest that, in general, attempted control is most useful outside the skin (Hayes, Strosahl, and Wilson 1999). That is true up to a point, of course. When it comes to trauma survivors, we know from the literature that control on the outside can become quite unhealthy as well (Herman 1992; Pistorello and Follette 1998). Sometimes individuals respond to the unpredictability of a traumatic experience by exerting too much control in their environment, trying to increase feelings of security. At other times, they may give up control in their lives altogether, erroneously believing, because of their trauma, that there is nothing they can do to control their life circumstances.

The issue of control, on the outside as well as on the inside, is a crucial one in trauma survivors' lives because the illusion of control can be temporarily soothing. Throughout this book, we will encourage you to apply control where and when it can work. Two comments on control of outside events: First, control on the outside can be healthy (for example, assertiveness) or unhealthy (for instance, an eating disorder). And second, too much control on the outside can be a form of digging for some people and, in fact, can lead to an inordinate number of problems interpersonally. Usually, too much control on the outside is associated with trying to run away from uncertainty, fear, or some other uncomfortable emotion. So, although we are encouraging you to take control of your life, only you will know what is healthy in that regard for you. There are many ways of taking control of one's life without being controlling.

Exercise 4.6: When Excessive Control on the Outside Is Unhealthy

Below are a few questions to help you assess whether you might be relying on excessive attempts at controlling things in your environment:

• Do you restrict your eating so much so that you have become underweight or anorexic, or do you alternate between restricting and then bingeing and purging.

• Do you find yourself attempting to control what others do via verbal threats, coercion, or physical means.

• Do you find yourself attempting to control what others do even when it has no direct impact on you, such as which jobs others will take, how they will vote, how they'll handle their money, which church they attend, or which degree they will pursue? A rule of thumb is to ask yourself two questions: "Does this choice affect me directly?" and "Even if it does affect me directly, do I have the right to ask this of this person?"🔔 [Any thoughts or judgments coming up?]

• Do you insist on always deciding where your family or friends will go to eat or to vacation, which movies they will watch, or how they will decorate the house. Do you become upset or worried that things will not turn out well if others are making these decisions instead of you, even if it's only occasionally

Based on your answers above, how would you rate the extent to which excessive attempted control on the outside is a problem for you on a scale of 0 to 10, with 0 being not at all a problem and 10 being a very big problem.

If it is a problem, how is excessive control affecting your life?

[space left intentionally blank in the original book]

If you rated excessive attempted control on the outside as a problem for you, how much discomfort do you feel when thinking about doing something different? What emotions, thoughts, and action urges do you experience? Rate it on a scale of 0 to 10, with 0 being none and 10 being the most you've ever felt.

[space left intentionally blank in the original book]

Exercise 4.7: When Lack of Control on the Outside Is Unhealthy

Below are a few questions to help you assess whether you might not be controlling things in your environment in situations where doing so could be helpful:

• Do you engage in impulsive actions just because you feel like it, without considering the consequences? Examples: binge eating;

gambling; drinking; having sex indiscriminately; driving too fast or recklessly; missing work, school, or other appointments; skipping on bills; failing regularly to correct your child when you know you should; or giving up quickly when things get difficult, such as in jobs, school, friendships, or hobbies you are pursuing?

• Do you find yourself almost always letting others make daily decisions, such as where to eat, what fun things to do, how to decorate things, and so on? If you do make decisions, do you worry excessively that others will disapprove of your choice, or do you quickly recant your suggestion if anyone opposes it? Do you find yourself saying things like "I really don't care" over and over again when these daily decisions are being discussed.

• Do you find yourself looking to others to make major life decisions for you, such as whom to date or marry, which job to take, how to vote, how to spend money, which church to attend, which sexual orientation to have, or which degree to pursue? This is beyond just discussing things with a friend. We are talking about really hoping that others will tell you what to do, directly or indirectly.

Only you can tell whether or not this applies to you. Others may not even be aware that you are making decisions based on their opinions. If you answer yes to this question, you might want to read chapters 7 and 8, on self and values clarification, carefully, as trying to get others to decide things for us is often associated with not knowing who we are or what we truly want. This is not unusual for some trauma survivors, so no need to judge yourself, AND you probably want to look at different choices.

• Do you allow yourself to be controlled by others via threats, or verbal, emotional, or physical means? An extreme example of too little control would be experiencing domestic violence, but there are various gradations of giving up control when subjected to pressure, coercion, or abuse.

Based on your answers above, how would you rate the extent to which lack of control on the outside is a problem for you on a scale of 0 to 10, with 0 being not at all a problem and 10 being a very big problem. If it is a problem, how is this lack of control affecting your life?

> [space left intentionally blank in the original book]
>
> If you rated lack of control on the outside as a problem for you, how much discomfort do you feel when thinking about doing something different? What emotions, thoughts, and action urges do you experience? Rate it on a scale of 0 to 10, with 0 being none and 10 being the most you've ever felt.
>
> [space left intentionally blank in the original book]

Please note that the distinction between control on the inside and control on the outside is some what arbitrary, given that unhealthy control on the outside (too little or too much) often boils down to attempting to control what is going on inside the person. For example, the veteran who imposes severe curfew guidelines on his teenage children may be trying to reduce his experience of fear for the safety of his children. If they are home by nine o'clock on Saturday night, he will experience a reduction in fear that they might get into a car accident. Similarly, the rape survivor who allows herself to be bossed around by her boyfriend may do so to avoid feeling the fears of rejection or abandonment that she might face if she disagreed with him. The bottom line is that all problematic control attempts have to do with individuals trying to get away from their own inner experiences.

So, if control on the inside is a problem, what do we do instead? You may be having the thought that this all sounds pretty crazy and that it will never help you. That's okay; you can have that thought and still go on to do the work. We know the efforts you're making are hard. We have spent countless hours with people who have gone through this process and found that it can make a real difference in their lives. It may feel dark and lonely in this hole, and you may wonder if there is any way out. If you're willing to keep turning the pages, there *is* a new way to live your life. And we are here to walk you through the process.

Journaling

Thoughts

[space left intentionally blank in the original book]

Feelings or Emotions

[space left intentionally blank in the original book]

Self-Judgments

[space left intentionally blank in the original book]

Physical Sensations

[space left intentionally blank in the original book]

Action Urges (What Do You Feel Like Doing?)

[space left intentionally blank in the original book]

CHAPTER 5

Letting Go of the Struggle: Are You Willing?

Let everything happen to you: beauty and terror. No feeling is final.

—Rainer Maria Rilke

Being Willing

We have talked about not getting caught up in the struggle of avoidance as it relates to pain and trauma and how this avoidance can turn pain into suffering. This can all make some intellectual sense to you and you may even agree that not avoiding is a good idea, in theory. We are at the point of asking you to make a leap that will take you beyond just thinking this through. Are you willing to make some big changes in your life? The type of changes we are talking about go beyond intellectual decisions to be different; we are talking about a whole new way of looking at life—something that might even be called a paradigm shift. A visual example of this shift might give you a sense of this new way of being in the world.

Metaphor: Chinese Handcuffs

Have you ever seen the toy that is sometimes called Chinese handcuffs (Hayes, Strosahl, and Wilson 1999; Hayes and Smith 2005)? (Image 5.1)

Image 5.1

These handcuffs are a tube that has some elasticity because it's made up of loosely interlaced straw strips. The unsuspecting child, or adult, is told to put a finger from each hand firmly into this tube first and then try to get the fingers out without destroying the tube. If you haven't seen one of these before or played with it, we highly recommend trying it. The usual first response is to try to pull the fingers out, which only makes the tube tighten around the fingertips as the straw laces draw closer together. Instead of loosening, the handcuffs' grip gets stronger. The more you pull, the worse it gets. We've seen people get so upset at being caught that they end up taking the handcuffs apart out of frustration. Paradoxically, the way out of the handcuffs is to push the fingers further into the tube to the point where the straw strips actually expand out in width as the finger trap becomes smaller in length. This is a situation where the intuitive reaction—to pull your fingers out—does not work. The effective, workable solution is illogical, counterintuitive. Sometimes the world of thoughts and feelings is like that.

Trying to suppress, get rid, or reduce our unwanted thoughts, feelings, and memories can be a trap too. On the surface it makes sense, and nobody can blame you for trying it out first. But, inevitably, something different and less logical may work better. Notice that to get out of the finger handcuffs, you have to stop struggling to get out and sit with the discomfort of feeling stuck. As Rilke states in the quote that opens this chapter, we are asking you to consider being open to all of your internal experiences. Paradoxically, becoming willing to move into this feeling of discomfort may free you from it. This can be a sticky idea for people, so this chapter is about trying to clarify how being willing can function in your life.

🔔[Take a moment here to notice any thoughts coming up.]

That ability to sit with discomfort is what we call *willingness* (Hayes and Smith 2005), which is not only easier said than done, but also easier said than understood! So, we will use many examples to explain what willingness is and isn't, including some real-life examples that you may relate to personally.

Willingness and Panic

One of our clients developed panic disorder after having been assaulted and robbed, and he started avoiding a series of situations. It first started with a panic attack that he felt came out of the blue when he was at a party a few months after the assault. Then, he became paralyzed by the fear that he might have another such panic attack and not be able to get out of the situation. That's when he started avoiding going out at night. The avoidance gradually expanded to other situations with crowds (shopping, movies), then situations where help might not be immediately available (driving or walking in unfamiliar places). He first came to treatment one year after the panic attacks started only because his partner was concerned and wanted him to return to his usual self. His partner reported that he would refuse to go shopping or on other errands and would only drive to close locations and only if someone came with him. When he came to therapy, he was starting to become anxious whenever his partner was out of sight, and his leaving to go to work had become a grueling ritual requiring many reassurances. This situation was putting a strain on the relationship, and they wanted help.

Panic attacks are not uncommon in people who have survived trauma, and we expect that some readers will relate to this client's predicament very well. 🔔[Are you having any bodily sensations, thoughts, or feelings as you read this?] Panics attacks are short and intense periods of anxiety that generally involve shortness of breath, heart palpitations, sweating, dizziness, feeling detached from your body, and feeling that you might die or go crazy. At times, the fear of having panic attacks can lead to agoraphobia, which is often characterized by a generalized fear of being in public places (APA 1994). Panic disorder with agoraphobia can be an extremely painful problem that has the potential to severely limit people in their everyday functioning. Lives can become smaller and smaller as these people try to eliminate the potential of experiencing panic or even any physiological reaction that seem to lead to panic. In fact, this disorder has been labeled "fear of fear." These people feel that if they can just avoid this or that situation, or bring enough safe people along, the fear will go away or become tolerable. The result of these strategies is more fear, and fear about more things and more situations. We often use the analogy of this being like feeding a baby lion in the hope that he will be less menacing (Hayes, Strosahl, and Wilson 1999). Every once in a while we just open the cage and quickly throw some meat in and slam the door. But, in fact, the meat only makes the cub bigger, and eventually we are facing a full-blown lion. Just like with the finger traps, the solution has become part of the problem. Trying to pull the fingers out gets one stuck more. Trying to pacify one's fear by avoiding more situations only makes the fear bigger.

So, what is the way out? If attempting to control your thoughts, feelings, and memories is a losing battle, what is the alternative? As we discussed in the last chapter, we'll start by putting down the shovel, letting go of the struggle, being willing.

What Is Willingness?

First, let's talk a bit about what we mean by willingness. For the purposes of this book and the work we have been doing, willingness is:

- Openness to experience

- Letting go of attempts to control

- Of or resulting from the process of choosing (American Heritage 1976)

- Acting or ready to act (American Heritage 1976)

- Being willing is an action, not a feeling (Hayes, Strosahl, and Wilson 1999)

Metaphors for Willingness

- It's like letting go of the shovel when digging fails to get you out of the hole (Hayes, Strosahl, and Wilson 1999).

- It's like pushing your fingers *into* a finger trap when your whole being feels that pulling them out is the way to go (Hayes, Strosahl, and Wilson 1999).

198

- It is like the lawn that allows the sunshine, the rain, and the snow to fall on it without trying to dodge any of it (Linehan 1993b).

- It is like the sand on the beach that allows the waves to come and go without trying to control their timing, length, or height.

Exercise 5.1: Willingness Is Like Jumping

We have adapted this exercise from the work of Steven Hayes and his colleagues (Hayes, Strosahl, and Wilson 1999). It will help you get a sense of how the sort of willingness we're talking about feels.

1. Get a hardcover book and a stable box or chair you can stand on with a few feet of available space around you.

2. Place the book on the floor to the left of the box or chair and stand to the left of the book.

3. Now, standing there, *try* to jump forward. Notice what happened. Remember

the task here is to *try*—don't jump, just try.

4. Notice how odd this trying is. How do you feel just trying?

5. Now, standing there, *jump* forward.

6. Next, stand on top of the book and ask yourself: "Am I 100 percent willing to jump from this book?" If you are, *jump.*

7. Now get on top of the box or chair and ask yourself: "Am I 100 percent willing to jump from this box (or chair)?" If you are (and your knees also concur), go for it.

What feelings and thoughts came up for you as you did this exercise when you only tried to jump forward?

What about when you asked yourself if you were 100 percent willing to jump off the floor? Off the book? Off the box or chair?

Now, what if we had asked you to jump off a five-foot ladder? Would you have been willing to do that? Maybe some of you said yes, but many would have said no. This exercise highlights two characteristics of willingness. First, *you can choose to be willing in some situations and not in others* (Hayes, Strosahl, and Wilson 1999). You can choose to jump off a box or chair but not off a five-foot ladder. Jumping off a five-foot ladder may not be safe, or even if it is, it may not be something that you truly value in your life. This is an important point: *We are not saying that you must bring willingness to simply sit with every uncomfortable feeling, emotion, or memory you experience.* Listening to feelings of discomfort in some situations is key to survival. Consider the case of the veteran who leaves a bar when he feels threatened by a group of intoxicated, angry men, or when an adult who was molested as a kid chooses not to hang out with her perpetrator, who continues to make sexual innuendoes. 🔔[Any thoughts coming up for you now?]

Second, *willingness is all or nothing* (Hayes, Strosahl, and Wilson 1999). You can choose which situations you will bring willingness to but not how much willingness. It is like jumping. You cannot touch the floor with the tip of your left foot and call that jumping. That's just touching the floor. You cannot step off the box or chair one foot at a time and call that jumping, because it isn't. Willingness is like that. You either do it or you don't. There is no "sort of" willing. Let's do an exercise that will help to make this point.

Exercise 5.2: Unwillingness in Willingness's Clothing

Sometimes it's hard to recognize willingness. One way is to be able to know when you are not being willing. The following items are meant to help you recognize when unwillingness is hiding in willingness's clothing. Not all examples will apply to you specifically; they are a way of helping illustrate how unwillingness may show up in life in several different situations. Remember that this is not a "gotcha" game, and you will need some compassion toward yourself to engage in this exercise. Read each of the statements below and circle the numbers and letters of those statements and examples, respectively, that apply to you.

1. I tend to wait to make overtures toward other people until I am certain that I will not be rejected or that I can easily dismiss the importance of the rejection if it happens. For example:

a. I may avoid potential connection with people altogether via excuses to myself or others, such as "I'm too picky."

b. I tend to select friends or partners who I think are beneath me or broken, or who I think are unlikely to reject me.

c. I tend to seek out people who I know would not be interested in me, such as someone of a different sexual orientation, or someone who is unavailable, such as a married person.

d. I tend to keep people from really knowing me by cooling things off when the relationship or friendship becomes more intimate.

e. When I feel afraid of getting hurt, I often find myself telling myself that I don't really want a relationship, friendship, or connection anyway.

2. I have often gone into situations that make me feel uncomfortable, such as parties, places with crowds, a class, driving, or job interviews but have not remained psychologically present. For example:

a. I may have distracted myself with mentally planning the rest of the day or week, monitoring changes in bodily sensations constantly, or focusing on some detail in the environment.

b. I have used drugs or alcohol to give myself courage to enter into these experiences.

c. I have dissociated during these experiences and missed most of the event or discussion.

3. I have forced myself to "white knuckle" discomfort by using willpower. For example:

a. When I am afraid of doing something, I call myself names until I can force myself to shut up and do it.

b. I almost never discuss my feelings about events, as I think it is a weak thing to do.

c. I often think that my ability to do something or not is a function of moral virtue.

4. I have allowed myself to sit with discomfort as a way of getting rid of discomfort. For example:

a. I may have gone into a situation that provokes anxiety, such as giving a speech or going to a movie theater or a party, hoping that this would result in my no longer having anxiety in that situation.

b. After experiencing a loss, I tried to accept it so that I could stop feeling so sad.

5. I have negotiated with myself with "If ... then" conditions under which I'd be willing to sit with discomfort. For example:

a. I may have gone into situations where I knew alcohol and drugs were available with the resolve not to drink or use as long as nobody offered me a drink, my favorite beverage or drug was not available, nobody said or did anything upsetting to me, or my anxiety level did not get too high.

b. I may have done something uncomfortable, such as giving a lecture or going to a PTA meeting, with the resolve that I would stay as long as my heart didn't race or my face didn't get red. If these things happened, I came up with excuses to leave or not engage in the action.

c. I may have sat with discomfort only until it got to a certain level, but then I felt justified in quitting, drinking, cutting, yelling, or engaging in whatever behavior I was trying to change.

d. I may have gone into family gatherings with the resolve not to engage in a physical or verbal fight with an estranged relative there unless he or she brings up a particular topic or I feel insulted by the person.

e. I find that I am willing to be respectful of my partner, and respect is a value I hold dear, as long as certain conditions are met, such as my feeling loved, her being respectful back, or my partner being a good provider.

6. I have attempted to sit with discomfort because I was afraid of losing others' respect or support if I didn't. For example:

a. I went into therapy to pacify my partner, but secretly I found myself setting up tests to prove it couldn't possibly help me or us.

b. I agreed to do something scary, like skiing down a steep hill or driving faster than I was comfortable, in order to impress those around me.

c. I suffer from panic disorder and agreed to go to the movies with a friend because my friend called me chicken. But I did not watch the movie and spent the whole time looking at my watch.

7. I think or speak of willingness as if it is a feeling, not an action. For example:

a. I find myself saying that I can't do something until I feel more willing.

b. I often think, and justify my actions with the thought, that other people with less severe traumas probably can feel more willing, but not me.

c. I often confuse willingness with the feeling of wanting. I may say that I don't want to go to a party when in fact I do want to AND I am not willing to at this point.

Take a few moments now to look over the items you have circled in the exercise above. The point of this exercise is to raise your awareness of what willingness is and what it isn't. As discussed in the last chapter, we need all the help we can get in catching our minds doing their usual tricks, which often perpetuate suffering. As we've said before, this is not a right versus wrong game. Nobody is keeping score. This is simply a way of bringing mindfulness to all your moves, including those that might be keeping you stuck—those old moves that are actually a form of digging but may look on the surface like letting go of the shovel. (See chapter 4 for the person-in-the-hole metaphor.) 🔔[Gently notice your thoughts and your breathing right now.]

From Willingness to Acceptance

Being willing to experience uncomfortable emotions allows us to move into acceptance. Attempts to control, suppress, or somehow change what we are experiencing within us perpetuates the struggle. As we pointed out earlier, words have acquired a great deal of power in our lives. When you label yourself as stupid, inept, or dysfunctional, those labels often become viewed as some sort of literal truth that can determine what you should and should not do. AND these words do not even need to have any real evidence to back them up. They're just labels that we learned to firmly attach to ourselves. And then suddenly we are following instructions that come with those words and labels. This may actually be a little difficult to explain verbally, so another metaphor will help us explain.

The Bus Metaphor

What if these feelings, emotions, thoughts, and sometimes bodily sensations that control what we do in our lives are like passengers on a bus we are driving (Hayes, Strosahl, and Wilson 1999)? This notion of driving a bus serves well as a metaphor for taking purposeful control of your life's path. As the bus driver, you often have to make decisions about things like speeding up, slowing down, and, most importantly, making turns at different intersections. You have some ideas about your route (what you would like to do with your life), AND there are some passengers on your bus who look pretty scary. Some of these characters who have somehow managed to get on your bus are acting menacingly. They sneer and frown at you, bulging out their eyes and making rude noises. Sometimes they can be quiet then suddenly run up to the front of the bus and yell "Turn left here, or else!" while shaking their fists at you. You get scared—and who wouldn't? It seems best to do what these creeps tell you to do; otherwise, they might really go crazy and take over altogether. What if other people saw these passengers on your bus and thought you picked them up on purpose? What if everyone knew you spent time with passengers like this? So you turn when these passengers tell you to. You keep off the main highway so people don't see you. You do what you can to keep them quiet. The times you've tried to argue with them, they got louder, closer to you, and even ganged up on you. So, over time, you have learned that when you get to a particular intersection, you turn left, even though you really would like to turn right. You've become so accustomed to this pattern that when an intersection is coming up, all the nasty passengers have to do is merely look in your direction and you turn left without their having to lift a finger.

What you may not be aware of is that the passengers—these thoughts, feeling, memories, and sensations—can't actually do anything to you. You are the driver and they can always only be passengers, yelling and shaking their fists. They cannot actually touch you or effect any change in you that you don't allow. They can *say* things, like "You can't do it," "You're stupid," or "Bad things will happen if you turn right." They can yell, scream, make threats, and generally be very persuasive about what they might do to you, but the fact of the matter is they can't get to you. They might even be able to speed up your heart or your breathing with all this commotion, but it's really all bark and no bite.

It may have occurred to you that it would be a lot easier driving the bus without these clowns. You could take the bus exactly where you wanted to go if only the passengers weren't there. So, you stop the bus and try, to no avail, to push some of them off. But, as it turns out, they cannot leave the bus. They live there. They also cannot leave the back of the bus and get into the driver's seat. The only way they can actually control where the bus goes is through you, by directing you, threatening you, screaming and waving at you. 🔔[Who or what are the passengers on your bus right now? What are the thoughts, feelings, judgments, and reactions you are having?]

Now, one thing that you might do is stop the bus and start arguing with the passengers, but notice what happens. Your bus (your life) stops so that you can argue with or try to get rid of the passengers. You're not going anywhere while you're engaged with these folks. Arguing or efforts at expulsion turn out to be futile, because they can't leave the bus, no matter how hard you try. The bus is just as much their home as it is yours. Some of the passengers may not even be big and scary but rather small and meek and say things like "You're being selfish for trying to go right when everyone prefers you to go left." Others may be tall, good-looking, and confident and say things like "You're better than other people, so why should you compromise?" or "You're absolutely brilliant." [Notice if you have ever had passengers like that on your bus. Are they lurking around now?]

Getting Hooked By Passengers on the Bus

At different times in our lives, some of these passengers may be more vocal and persuasive than others. This will vary according to the person and the situation. When you are more vulnerable, these passengers can seem more powerful. As we discussed in chapter 2, when you don't get enough sleep, don't eat well, become isolated, or use substances and engage in related behaviors you have a higher probability of getting hooked by passengers on your bus. Have you ever noticed, for example, how easy it is when you're tired, sleepy, or hungry to listen to those passengers who say things like "How irritating so-and-so is" or "Life is horrible"?

Sometimes our culture, including the world of psychotherapy, tells us that the solution is to focus on "positive" rather than "negative" passengers. You may have heard of therapy techniques that will invite you to replace negative thoughts with positive ones, for example. In ACT, and mindfulness in general, this is not considered helpful because the actual *content* of your passengers is not as important as the *process* of not getting hooked by the passengers on the bus. As discussed in chapter 2, mindfulness involves being able to see thoughts as thoughts, feelings as feelings, memories as memories, and so on.

By the way, we put the terms "negative" and "positive" in quotes precisely because emotions such as fear and sadness or thoughts of "I'm bad" are not negative—or positive. They simply are feelings and thoughts that we may evaluate as negative or positive. In fact, in ACT we use a language convention that, albeit a bit wordy, helps to remind us of this fact. We would like to use it here with you, to help you remember this point from now on. Instead of referring to thoughts, feelings, memories, and bodily sensations as negative or positive, we will use the terms "negatively evaluated" or "positively evaluated" instead (Hayes, Strosahl, and Wilson 1999). They are more accurate and may help you not get hooked by the content of your passengers.

Although the content of your thoughts and feelings is not important, it is important to know which type of content (either negatively evaluated or positively evaluated) tends to hook you. In general, we tend to more readily recognize and more often discuss in therapy the ill effects of getting hooked by negatively evaluated content, such as a thought like "I'm a failure" or a feeling of anger. This can indeed be problematic and add even more suffering to some mental disorders. When you feed the lion, it can get very strong and persuasive. So some people can feed their anger by spending time with other angry people, thinking about all the unfair things that others have done to them, and getting people to corroborate their angry story. Guess what happens then? The anger gets bigger and stronger. The same is true for depression. You can put on sad songs, stay isolated, look at photos of old loves, and just generally curl up into a ball of sadness. Of course, these labels for groups of feelings ("depression" or "anger") are arbitrary and overly simplistic, and in our opinion, these feelings are present in all of us at different times in our lives. However, it might be useful for you to know if you have a propensity toward a particular emotional way of responding to issues, because the process of buying into what these passengers say and do is the problem, and not the passengers themselves! To be clear, there is nothing wrong with being sad or angry. These are natural feelings—inevitable passengers—that may be there for a very valid reason. AND they don't have to drive the bus.

As we mentioned above, sometimes people think the cure to all this is to just be sure to buy into thoughts that carry a positive content ("I'm very smart"). However, if you find yourself following the passenger that says "You're the greatest" now, chances are you'll heed the passenger that says "You'll never amount to anything" later. The trick here is not to find passengers with "good" content but to be able to recognize all of this content as simply part of the passengers on your bus.

Exercise 5.3: Identifying the Passengers on Your Bus

Passenger	Type of passenger	How likely to get hooked (0–10)?
"This is not fair"	Thought	Typically, a 10.
Shame	Emotion	Typically, a 9.
Memory of trauma	Memory	Used to be a 10. Now, it's a 5 or 6.

Table 5.1

It is very important to know which are the scary, difficult, obnoxious, or seductive passengers on your bus. Later we will also help you clarify which direction you want your bus to go. But for now, let's see if you can identify some of the passengers on your bus.

1. In the left-hand column, write down passengers on your bus who easily hook you.

2. In the middle column, write what type of passenger each is: emotion, thought, memory, image, saying, or bodily reaction.

3. In the right-hand column, rate how likely you are to get hooked by this passenger. That is, when this passenger comes up, how likely are you to believe it, argue with it, try to prove it or disprove it, or in some way react based on its content? Use a scale of 0 to 10, where 0 is not at all and 10 is completely buying into it. (Table 5.1)

Acceptance is about driving the bus yourself, turning right or left as you personally choose according to your values, *with* all your scary passengers along for the ride.

What we want to help you experience at some level is this new idea that these thoughts and feelings are not actually real in the way that they seem. You are in this present moment, and you have survived some very painful experiences. The thoughts and memories are simply phantom passengers. They exist only in your mind and only have the power and importance you give to them. For example:

- Images of the war are not the war itself—they are simply images that your mind is producing. Sometimes these images may be accurate and sometimes not, as in the case of nightmares that include elements that did not happen.

- Thoughts in the vein of "I'll never amount to anything" are probably something you heard from a parental figure. But, the origin of the thought does not mean that the content is correct. This thought, like every other, is only a *thought.*

- You may experience a racing heart, rapid breathing, and upset stomach when you go through a part of town that was destroyed by a tornado while you were trapped in the basement. But remember, these are just bodily sensations that are associated with anxiety. They can be unpleasant, but you can survive with these feelings.

You don't have to like or want or be happy about any of these passengers. We do not mean to minimize the experiences you had. All your passengers are on your bus for a reason. It could be a memory of an experience. Someone may have said something to you. It could be a valid reaction to an experience—sadness or anger. They belong on your bus, AND they do not need to drive it. You are here now, you have survived, and we want you to begin to be the driver of your life.

Case Story: Mike, the Vietnam Veteran

Sometimes, these passengers run in gangs. A client of ours, a Vietnam veteran named Mike, once described the following scenario. He had reluctantly agreed to go to a Fourth of July celebration only to become triggered by the sound of fireworks. As he sat there in the dark with his wife and kids around him, he started having flashbacks of the war (we'll call these flashbacks Passenger A). Then he had thoughts of "I could have saved my buddy" (Passenger B), which led to "I'm such a coward" (Passenger C), sensations of feeling choked up and wanting to cry (Passenger D), feelings of shame about crying in front of his kids (Passenger E), and feeling angry at himself (Passenger F) for being so "weak" (Passenger G). He jumped up abruptly and stormed off, later blaming his exit on his eight- and ten-year-old kids for "making too much noise and being so obnoxious." In session, he cried profusely when he described how his youngest kid followed him home, missing the fireworks himself and apologizing all the while for ruining his dad's enjoyment of the fireworks. The client went home, locked himself in his bedroom, and cried, covering up his mouth so that his kid couldn't hear it.

Mike's story is an example of being ganged up on by passengers. Sometimes we may be prepared to recognize one type of passenger, a thought, let's say. But when multiple passengers of different types show up (such as feelings in addition to thoughts), it gets easier to get hooked.

Mike also found himself buying into the content of his passengers. He experienced several internal events: memories, feelings, thoughts, and evaluations. These were aversive and unwanted, no doubt about it. However, none of these internal events really required any action. Had Mike sat there and viewed the fireworks, letting the passengers chatter or scream or threaten, they wouldn't have been able to get to him. He may have found himself feeling uncomfortable, and these passengers may even have inspired some tears. But they couldn't truly hurt him or his kids. His behavior when he got hooked by the content ("I can't cry in front of my kids"), however, hurt them all.

What would an acceptance approach have looked like for Mike? As the saying goes, many roads lead to Rome. The crucial thing is what we end up doing in our environments, and how that fits with what we want our lives to be about. In this case, what most perturbed Mike was having blamed his kids for his leaving the fireworks, something he attempted to repair with his kids, now adults, during our therapy work together. The type of moves that might have helped him avoid taking it out on his kids would basically start with his being able to be mindful of what was happening inside him (see chapter 2). For example, some mindfulness exercises that might have helped him get un-hooked from his passengers could include:

- Coming back to his breath

- Trying to picture the reactions he was having as leaves on a stream, clouds in the sky, or passengers on his bus

- Focusing on the process and not the content (for instance, noting to himself, "That's a thought," "That's a feeling," "That's an evaluation," or "That's a memory")

When he started having the war flashbacks, he could have gently reminded himself to breathe in and out and notice that they were just flashbacks, that he was safe and sound today, and that there was nothing that he needed to do right this minute.

After noticing his reaction, he could have alerted his wife that he was struggling. He could have let her know that he would try to make it but might need to leave early. It would have been even better if he had alerted his wife and kids in advance that viewing the fireworks might be difficult for him and discussed with them ways to help him through it.

Another acceptance move for Mike, depending on what his values were and how far along he was in his recovery, might have been not to agree to go to the Fourth of July celebration. Having been mindful of his current limitations in coping with becoming triggered in a public environment, he might have elected to say no to his wife and kids.

Acceptance Is Not Approval or Forgiveness

🔔[Notice any reactions you may have had to reading this heading.] Sometimes the term "acceptance" gives rise to some uncomfortable passengers in trauma survivors' minds: "But what happened was wrong—how can I possibly accept it?" or "I'm not ever going to forgive the government for putting me through this!"

But rest assured: What we're talking about here is not about approval or forgiveness or putting up with wrongs done to you, or any of the other passengers that might hang out in this gang. Acceptance does not mean condoning or agreeing with what happened. Acceptance of your history does not mean that what happened should have happened. Acceptance of your history means letting go of the struggle with memories, feelings, thoughts, or bodily sensations associated with your history.

Acceptance of your history does not mean having to forgive people, as in absolving someone of responsibility. It is important to us that we make this point clearly: *Acceptance of your history does not mean what happened to you was okay.* As therapists, we often feel a great deal of sadness over the kind of pain and suffering that our clients have endured, particularly when it was at the hands of people who should have protected them. We would not presume to tell you that you must forgive those individuals in the traditional sense of the meaning of forgiveness. We believe that in your heart you will find what is most useful for you in regard to this specific matter. What we are talking about is finding a way to let go of the past in the service of having your life *now*. Acceptance is about not turning over the rest of your life to these traumatic experiences. In chapter 9, we will discuss forgiveness, particularly toward yourself, in a different way—as a way of letting you move in your valued directions.

Some of the ways acceptance has been discussed or portrayed more recently in the self-help community and the popular culture can be very helpful. We'll focus on two such examples: the serentiy prayer and the film *A Beautiful Mind.*

The Serenity Prayer

The serenity prayer, most often seen in the context of 12-step programs, provides some wise direction. We paraphrase it below:

"Accept things that you cannot change"

Thoughts, feelings, memories, bodily reactions, and other people would fall in this category.

"Change the things you can"

This includes *our own behavior* or current injustices you see in the world.

"Have the wisdom to know the difference"

The ability to make this distinction can come through clarification of your values and through mindfulness—letting your experience (and not your mind) teach you.

A Beautiful Mind

An excellent example of the type of acceptance we are discussing here appears in *A Beautiful Mind,* a 2001 movie about John Nash, a Nobel Prize winner in economics. The movie portrays his struggles with psychotic symptoms throughout his life. One of the powerful aspects of this movie is that the viewers see things from John Nash's perspective and therefore get to experience what it's like to be overwhelmed by images, thoughts, and feelings that are totally in his mind. As the movie progresses, the viewers, like the main character, experience a change in perspective as the hallucinations are revealed to be passengers on his bus (our wording). That is, the main character starts treating these very convincing, often flattering persons as characters conjured up by his mind and not what they claim they are: an FBI agent recruiting him for a special assignment or a best friend who rescues him from his loneliness. In a very moving scene toward the end of the film, John tells the images, "I will not be able to speak to you anymore" and walks away. It is understood that although he will no longer be engaging in conversations with them, these characters created by his mind will continue to follow him.

If you haven't seen this movie before, or even if you have but don't remember much about it, it would be a good accompaniment to this book to see it again from the acceptance perspective we are presenting here. While the actual content of the passengers in this movie may be quite different from yours, we have seen no better portrayal of the idea of distancing from the passengers, who can seem so real and terrifying. Please know that we are in no way suggesting that your struggles are hallucinations or that there is something crazy about this process. Buying the content of the passengers on our bus is a perfectly normal process. As the title of the Magritte painting in chapter 2 reminds us, this is the human condition.

The discussion about various acceptance moves and examples is meant to provide you with some ideas for doing something different when

226

the usual suspects show up at the front of your bus. What if instead of an old move you could do something really different? To bring this concept closer to home, the next exercise will ask you to consider which acceptance moves you could engage in when tempted to resort to old moves in the context of difficult passengers. Remember that willingness is an all-or-nothing move, AND we can choose to jump off a book but not off a chair. Therefore, pick acceptance moves that you are 100 percent willing to commit to doing. What matters is doing something, however small, that is functionally different from your old strategies to give you a taste of what it would be like to try to accept, instead of control or suppress, the passengers on your bus.

Exercise 5.4: Accepting Your Passengers

Think of some of the passengers that show up for you, the context in which they appear (where, when, or around whom), and what you typically do when you get hooked by those private experiences. Then, think about some things that might help you try to accept the passengers without adding suffering to your life. We filled in the first row with an example to help you to complete the rest. (Table 5.2)

Passenger (Thought, feeling, memory, bodily reaction, etc.)	Context (When does the passenger show up?)	Typical move (If I get hooked by the passenger, I do this.)	Acceptance move (This is what I can do to accept the passenger.)
Flashback to when I was abused	During sex	Have sex, dissociated, feeling like a little girl	Notice that flashback is just a memory. Stop and look husband in the eye.

Table 5.2

Acceptance Inside the Skin

So far, we have discussed how easy it is to get trapped into adding suffering to our wounds by trying to escape, reduce, or eliminate the inner circle of pain. Attempting to control what goes on inside the skin is the problem, and willingness and acceptance provide an alternative. As the driver, we can continue to head in a valued direction while also bringing along unwanted passengers on our bus. We don't have to like these passengers or want them there. All we need to do is let them be. This may seem very straightforward in theory, but in practice there are many pitfalls. To help you walk the path of acceptance, we will spend the next chapter discussing barriers to it. If you've tried to accept these uncomfortable thoughts, feelings, and sensations but feel that you just can't, why might that be the case? Most often, this inability is because you've fallen prey to one of the enemies of acceptance—the topic of the next chapter

Journaling

Thoughts

[space left intentionally blank in the original book]

Feelings or Emotions

[space left intentionally blank in the original book]

Self-Judgments

[space left intentionally blank in the original book]

Physical Sensations

[space left intentionally blank in the original book]

Action Urges (What Do You Feel Like Doing?)

[space left intentionally blank in the original book]

CHAPTER 6

Barriers to Acceptance

If we all worked on the assumption that what is accepted as true is really true, there would be little hope of advance.

—Orville Wright

If you feel that you have been trying to accept difficult thoughts and feelings but it seems that somehow things go awry, you are not alone. In many ways what we're talking about here may seem like an old message. For a long time, people may have been telling you to let it go, forget the past, move on. That's not what we are saying. We know that if you could do that, you would have by now. This chapter is about looking at what it is about being human that can get in the way of acceptance and developing new ways to look at letting go of the struggle. The topics here are ones that we ourselves come back to over and over—because we know it is easy to get caught up in denying and rejecting difficult emotions. This chapter may serve as a touchstone to come back to if you find yourself struggling.

In this part of the book, we need to go into a bit of theory to make our point. We know that if we went into great detail on these issues you would find yourself struggling with a new problem—boredom. Just try to go with us for a bit as we build a foundation that will give you some context for the next phase of the work. First we're going to talk about one of the biggest problems (and assets of course) of being human—language. 🔔[Notice any thoughts, feelings, and judgments coming up for you right now.] We've mentioned it before, but now it's time that you understand the full weight of the problems that language can bring.

Like most things that we have been discussing, there are two sides to this issue. Language has been a huge asset to humans, and many would argue that this is part of what makes us unique in the animal world. At the same time, it is part of what brings suffering into our experience (Hayes, Strosahl, and Wilson 1999). Read this chapter from beginning to end, even if it's tempting to skip ahead. There is a process to getting where we are going that requires us to build a foundation from the bottom up. Part of the goal here is to help you to *experience* what we are going to present, not just understand the intellectual aspects of it.

First Barrier: Language and the Two Sides of the Coin

The benefits of language are undeniable. Language has allowed us to provide clothing and food for ourselves, construct buildings, carve roads into steep terrain, and go to the moon. The fact that we can write this book and know that you can actually follow it and find something useful occurs thanks to language. Language allows us to engage in planning activities and to live successfully in a difficult and changing environment. Language is a powerful tool. AND, sometimes, it can cause problems. The next exercise will help begin to demonstrate some of the issues we'll be dealing with.

Exercise 6.1: The Power of Language

Think about a very embarrassing moment. Write briefly about the situation below: What happened, where were you, who else was there, when did it happen, and how was it embarrassing?

[space left intentionally blank in the original book]

What feelings, thoughts, bodily sensations, or urges did you have while writing about this embarrassing situation, or even while just thinking about it?

[space left intentionally blank in the original book]

Imagine that you've won a million dollars free and clear. What will you do with that money?

[space left intentionally blank in the original book]

What feelings, thoughts, or bodily sensations did you have while writing about winning a lot of money, or even while just thinking about it?

[space left intentionally blank in the original book]

Write down the three most important aspects of your life, such as family, job, friends, health, pets, or whatever else matters to you.

[space left intentionally blank in the original book]

Now, imagine that all of a sudden you no longer had these three aspects in your life. What if they totally disappeared or were gone from your life? What would that feel like for you?

[space left intentionally blank in the original book]

Now imagine cutting a lemon in two and taking a large, juicy bite into one of the lemon halves. Take a moment to really imagine that. What sensations did you experience in your mouth?

[space left intentionally blank in the original book]

We know that for at least some, if not all, of the situations above you experienced reactions just by thinking about these events. Yet, none of these situations are *here right now.* Some were in the past and some could be in the future. The only reason that you had an experience of these events psychologically, physically, and emotionally is because we described them with words. Think about that. Language brought the past and the future here for you.

So, in fact, language allows us to travel in time. That's the good and the bad news.

The fact that language can transport us like that has many adaptive functions. For example, being able to remember the past and access it readily via language makes learning of all sorts possible. Language is the tool we use to transmit ideas and to build a culture of information. This ranges from information that is relatively basic to knowledge that is remarkable. At a basic level, if you have already been to a friend's house and someone asks you for directions, you might be able to describe how to get there. Imagine how ineffi-cient it would be if we could not tell someone directions, but instead had to take the person there ourselves! At a more remarkable level, someone can describe a theory of the universe, as Stephen Hawking does in *A Brief History of Time* (1988). Both the pedestrian and the ex-traordinary can be transmitted through lan-guage.

When we use the term "language," we mean more than just spoken and written words. We mean all symbolic forms of behavior, including gestures, signs, images, pictures, and symbols. Of course, thinking involves language, and that's where some of the trouble can start.

Notice if it isn't the case that sometimes the type of communication we most struggle with occurs within ourselves, as with internalized messages and self-judgments. 🔔[Notice any thoughts or bodily sensations coming up right now.] We all have that committee in our head, commenting on almost everything we do.

ACT and Language

Acceptance and commitment therapy is based on a theory that attributes a great deal of our experience of human suffering to language (Hayes, Barnes-Holmes, and Roche 2001; Hayes, Strosahl, and Wilson 1999). As we have stated many times, we are not denying that painful things happen to people. Pain is just part of living this life. However, suffering happens because that sense of pain can be brought from the past into the present and even the future as a function of language. Language can also have a dark side that is not typically recognized. For the purposes of this book, we want to discuss two aspects of language that can contribute to psychological suffering: "time travel" and unexpected connections.

Time Travel
As mentioned above, language can transport us to the past and the future. Most of our

immediate experiences are not full of pain. The pain comes when we think back to painful past experiences or project onto feared future events, neither of which is currently here. For example, at this very moment (right now), while you are reading this book, your life is probably not in danger, you are reasonably comfortable, you're not being subjected to embarrassment and humiliation, being thrown out of your house for not paying the bills, having a fight with your spouse, or experiencing unbearable pain. Yet, with a snap of your fingers, language can take you to all these past and future experiences, simply by their mere mention in this paragraph. The exercise below is meant to help you recognize how much traveling your mind has been doing.

Exercise 6.2: Tracking Your Traveling Minds

List below all the worries and fears you have experienced recently, then note whether the potential problem, issue, or concern is happening right now (meaning this very moment, here, not ten minutes ago or ten minutes from now), in the past, or in the future. Write down your worry or fear, then add "past," "present," or "future" to indicate when it is

238

happening. We filled in the first one as an example. (Table 6.1)

Worry or fear	Past, present, or future
What if I can't get better?	*Future*

Table 6.1

Most people find in completing the above exercise that very few thoughts, feelings, or concerns that are generating distress for them actually pertain to this very moment. The distress is usually about past or future events. When we were first exposed to this idea, we fought it, thinking, "Yes, but what if the rent is due in three days and I don't have money?" Well, even this situation is not *right at this moment*—it's three days from now. In fact, wondering what will be in the next paragraph in this book is not in the present moment; it's a minute from now. And, often, what we do to ourselves in the present moment, such as not sleeping, picking a fight with a loved one, drinking, worrying, or other types of avoidance in response to concerns about the past or future are not particularly effective in terms of life goals. 🔔[Any thoughts coming up in response to this last sentence?] And these problematic strategies can't even control the event. They are just ways of trying to get rid of or avoid our internal experience about the event. Now, mobilizing ourselves and doing something about a dreaded future event at this moment would be helpful, but notice that doing something about it is different from worrying about it or avoiding it.

One example of how our minds can take us to a future or a past that is not here is that of a robbery survivor we treated. He was coping reasonably well with the aftermath of his assault until he heard years later that his perpetrator had killed his next victim. Learning that "he could have died" (again, language taking us away from the present) brought about a different set of feelings and thoughts for this client. He was overcome with terror and rage and became afraid to leave the house. So, while his experience had not actually changed, this new information impacted his thoughts and feelings in a significant way. It was at this point that he decided to enter therapy to deal with the experience that had happened twenty years ago.

One of the outcomes associated with trauma is an increased risk of suicide (Polusny and Follette 1995). Suicide is perhaps the greatest example of language's ability to transport us to places we have never been in ways that can have final and unchangeable consequences (Hayes, Strosahl, and Wilson 1999; Hayes and Smith 2005). When people attempt suicide, they are often predicting a future: "I will no longer be in pain," "People will be better off," or "I'll go to heaven," to name a few. 🔔[Notice what your mind is saying, if anything, about this.] In fact, none of us *know* whether any of these futures will actually occur. We are predicting a future as if we have experienced something like it before. The ability to even think about the future happens because of language. Other types of life on this planet, including our beloved pets, cannot engage in this type of activity. Animals do not attempt suicide, not even the frequently cited lemmings, which often end up drowning when they accidentally fall into the water after running amok under crowded conditions. However, when they do fall into the water, they actually try to swim out, whereas human beings after failing one suicide attempt may proceed with another (Hayes, Strosahl, and Wilson 1999; Hayes and Smith 2005). Research shows that 20 percent of humans have considered suicide (Chiles and

Strosahl 2004), and the rate is even higher among trauma survivors. This is an extreme example of the potential danger of language.

Unexpected Connections

In addition to readily transporting us to the past or the future, we know from laboratory studies that language can also make two or more completely unrelated events have a similar impact on us (Hayes, Barnes-Holmes, and Roche 2001). Without going into too much technical explanation, we would like to elaborate on this a bit and provide a couple of examples. We know in trauma that when an aversive experience, such as getting burned, is paired in space and time with another initially neutral experience, such as the clothes the person was wearing when she got burned, the initially neutral event becomes aversive too. For example, one of our clients had accidentally grabbed a pot of boiling water from the stove when she was six years old, resulting in some second-degree burns and a subsequent hospitalization. After this episode, she would cry whenever she saw the clothes that she had been wearing at the time of the accident. This type of association, for lack of a better term, between events that are similar or close in time is well recognized in the trauma field: war veterans may get panicky with loud noises, a rape survivor may feel anger when exposed to the same scent worn by a perpetrator, or an earthquake survivor may experience fear when dogs start barking—something that can happen between aftershocks.

However, what we have learned more recently is that, through language, the connection among events can be much more pervasive and unpredictable. Things acquire the same "function" or impact on the person even when they are not similar or occur at a different time (Hayes, Barnes-Holmes, and Roche 2001). The problem is that, due to language, even things that are not logically connected can become psychologically related to trauma, and, in the presence of mindlessness, it becomes easy to fall prey to them. For example, we had a client who had remained hidden in a very small hole for days on end during the Vietnam War in absolute fear for his life. After he returned home and began talking to us about how trapped he was feeling in his marriage, he started having panic attacks similar to those he'd been having in elevators and other confined spaces since being home. What do a marriage and an elevator have in common? Not much, except that, through language, the idea of being "trapped" transferred this feeling to his marriage. This impact of language means that you are constantly taking your history to places that it doesn't belong. Therefore, you cannot eliminate difficult reactions simply by avoiding things that might remind you of your trauma, because the number of such things may be infinite. Therefore, we need to learn to transcend the power of language, such as through mindfulness, so that we can minimize the potential of these processes to add unneeded suffering.

Transcending Language, and Why It's Useful

So, right now you may be having the thought "This is very interesting and all, but how exactly can this be helpful to me?" Finding a way to transcend the content of thoughts and other internal events may be the most useful strategy for being able to start living life after surviving a traumatic experience. Because of the power of language, we know that initially you may start avoiding one or two things that remind you of your trauma, but, over time, a wider circle of events will start having the same impact on you. Chances are, you've already noticed this impact of an ever-widening circle of things that cannot happen, places that you can't go, people you feel you shouldn't see, or things you cannot talk about. Eventually, you may simply be wracked with tension and no longer able to trace it all the way back to the original trauma. That's the impact of language: Events, including mental events such as thoughts and feelings, start having the same impact on you as the trauma itself.

As you know by now, we don't think that you have to change the memory of your traumatic event or your internal content in relation to it. In our experience, it just does not work to try to get rid of or replace the content of a thought, memory, or feeling. Instead, we are suggesting a way of helping you ease the hold these experiences have over how you live your life.

If experiencing X (a flashback, a thought of "I'm bad," or an increase in heart rate) does not automatically lead to Y (avoiding sex, drinking, or leaving the mall), then X is no longer something that must be avoided and suppressed at all costs.

Your life can become about something other than trying to get away from a big part of yourself: your memories, your feelings, your thoughts, your own bodily sensations—basically, the passengers on your bus. In ACT, instead of changing *what* you experience (thoughts, feelings, memories), we focus on changing *how* you experience them. If you can experience all aspects of yourself with awareness and without all the pitfalls associated with language, you can begin to move forward in ways that are consistent with values and goals in your life.

One way you can work on transcending language is using mindfulness or being grounded in the present moment. When you find yourself getting caught up in the past or future, you can use one of the mindfulness exercises from chapter 2 to help bring you back to the present. Also, you can think back to one of the metaphors we've presented to help you see your thoughts, feelings, and bodily sensations for what they are. Some of the metaphors we discuss in this book that might be helpful with this are passengers on a bus, leaves on a stream, or chess pieces on a chessboard. We've already talked about some of these, and others will be discussed later.

Defusion: Unhooking from Words

In ACT, the main strategy for undermining the power of language is *defusion,* which means getting some distance or unhooking from the literal meaning of the words (Hayes, Strosahl, and Wilson 1999; Hayes and Smith 2005). In some ways, we get far too caught up in the content of words—what ACT researchers call *fusion.* Defusion, conversely, has to do with finding ways to separate the words from what they are referring to. Try to read these words without understanding them. Try very hard not to understand the words you are reading at this moment. You couldn't do it, could you? However, if we wrote "Tente bastante não entender estas palavras que está lendo neste momento" only some of you may have been able to do what we asked in Portuguese: "Try really hard not to understand the words you are reading at this moment." The issue is this: When we get caught by the content of some of these troubling thoughts, even though they are just words or images, it's hard to detach some from them, and we end up getting hooked and doing things that are not workable in our lives.

Another way to think of how fusion can work is to go back to the Magritte painting in chapter 2. See how the image of the painting is viewed from such a perspective that it merges with the scene being painted, to such an extent that one can only tell the difference because of the small white border of the painting and the base of the easel? Becoming fused with words or getting hooked by words (we use these terms interchangeably) is like being in the painting but thinking that you are in the actual landscape. It's like getting so caught up in your own thoughts, stories, memories, and self-judgments about your past that you forget that that's all they are: thoughts, stories, memories, and self-judgments. Then you begin to act as though these things are real in the present moment—when they are not. It's very easy to get hooked. The difference between being able to see thoughts as thoughts versus what they say ("You're stupid") is a matter of a fleeting second.

A crucial skill to learn is to be able to notice this process of getting fused and back up from thoughts and feelings enough so that you have some flexibility in how you respond to them. For example, if you have the thought "I just can't take this" and experience it as the truth, you may act accordingly and perhaps even proceed with a plan to self-harm. However, if you can experience the same thought with some distance, with the awareness that it is just a thought, other, more flexible ways of responding are possible. Fusion is like walking around with a purple bubble in your head and assuming that everything you see through the bubble is the truth, with all its distortions and the ever-present purple color (Hayes and Smith 2005). Defusion is like removing the bubble and holding it out in front of you, with some distance, and noticing how the bubble may distort things and make them appear purple.

The next section will focus on defusion strategies. These will help you get a different perspective that lets you disconnect a bit from the attachment to content so that you can differentiate the painting from the scene in a way that will help you live a more effective life. 🔔[Any thoughts coming up in response to this last sentence?] Some of these exercises may seem silly at first, but, as we did with the mindfulness exercises, we ask you to go ahead and have that thought—and hang in there anyway. Research shows that some of these exercises (such as the next one) can actually work to help people disconnect from the tyranny of words (Masuda et al. 2004).

Exercise 6.3: Milk, Milk, Milk

This is a classic exercise first suggested by Tichener (1916) and currently regularly used in ACT treatments (Hayes, Strosahl, and Wilson 1999; Hayes and Smith 2005).

1. Sit comfortably in a chair in a private place.

2. Imagine a glass of milk. Imagine its color and taste and the glass and notice if there are any sensations in your mouth even as you think about milk.

3. Start saying the word "milk" out loud over and over again.

4. Say it faster and faster, louder and louder.

5. Continue for one minute.

After you stop saying the word "milk" very fast and loud, ask yourself what happened to "milk" while you were saying it. Did you find that the taste, color, and vividness just went away? That's the experience most people have when doing this exercise. Now, imagine the following situation: One of our clients had been forced to drink a glass of milk each evening as her perpetrator (her father) came into her room at night. For her, doing an exercise such as this one allowed her to get some distance from the word "milk" and some of her automatic reactions to it, such as feeling anxious, gagging, and wanting to hide.

We know that, unlike our client, most people will not struggle specifically with the word "milk." But what about other words, such as "stupid," "bad," "fat," "selfish," "sissy," "ugly," "unlovable," "coward," or "lazy"? Do any of those words touch some old pain for you? 🔔 [Notice any bodily sensations coming up.]

Some of us have spent a lifetime running away from words. One of our clients who was a very financially successful physician, a meticulous mother to her two children, a popular chef (something she did as a hobby on weekends), and an award-winning tennis player later told us that she realized she had spent a big chunk of her life trying to eliminate the possibility that the word "lazy" would ever apply to her because her mother detested lazy people and would frequently comment on this attribute in people.

Some words have a powerful impact on us, and we spend a great deal of our time trying to push them away. As we described in the introduction to the book, we can never really separate two sides of the same coin. What we mean here is that for our client above, for example, even when she was working all that time and getting consistent praise for her work ethic, it was always in the service of avoiding being lazy. So "lazy" was always present. She hadn't defeated it—she lived with it every day.

This example of the power of words is why we need to find a different path. Part of this work is about becoming free from this tyranny of words. The next two examples will make the issue clearer.

Many of our clients have had derogatory sexual words used to describe them by their perpetrators. 🔔[Gently notice your breathing.] We work with them to help them see this as a strategy that was used to shame and control them, but that's still a rather intellectual understanding of the problem. One client described how her abusive uncle frequently called her a slut. Although he was no longer alive, she could still hear him calling her this ugly word in her head. She also realized that this label had had a lot of influence on her life. She would alternate between periods where she was running away from the word and periods where she rather compulsively engaged in sexualized behavior. During her adolescence, for example, she deliberately dressed provocatively, wore a lot of makeup, and had many sexual partners. This was not in the service of sexuality but seemed to serve the function of avoidance of her real feelings and also of giving her a sense of control. She'd had no control over the abuse that happened at the hands of her uncle, and it seemed to her that in her adult sexual encounters she had control. The client noted that "If he thinks I'm a slut, I'll show him." Later in her life, however, she moved to the opposite pole of sexuality and became avoidant of anything involving physical contact. She deliberately attempted to look unattractive, avoided any type of physical contact, and shied away from sexual relations with her husband. Both her compulsive sexuality and her later avoidance of physical expressions are forms of being controlled by the content of that old word. Even though she could articulate these ideas intellectually in treatment, she did not know how to find a way to move in the direction she valued, which was to have a loving emotional and physical relationship with her husband.

A combat veteran reported that when he was growing up, his father had repeatedly called him a coward. His father had been a career military officer, and he treated his children like they were in boot camp. When he was a young boy, this client was more interested in books and science than he was in sports and other rough-and-tumble activities. Even when provoked, he avoided fights, something his father found intolerable. Although he had a strong aptitude as a mathematician and truly would have preferred to attend college and become a teacher, at the end of high school, this client decided to prove to himself and his father that he was not a coward by joining the military. When he was sent overseas to Vietnam and was thrown into jungle combat situations, he was terrified of the intensity of the situations he encountered. And in his head, he heard his father calling him a coward. Alcohol and drugs helped some, but he also found himself taking very dangerous risks in order to make sure that none of his peers would ever think him a coward. And at night, he would throw up as he thought of the horror of the events of that day. The process of his reaction was similar to the woman above, even though the content was very different. Even now, years later, he struggles with these battles that are long over.

As you read these examples, you may have recognized your hooks right away. On the other hand, you may not be sure if there are words that serve this function in your life. Here is one exercise that might help you recognize them.

Exercise 6.4: Recognizing Words That Hook You

I secretly fear that I am _____, but most people around me would not know that about me.

One of the qualities that I try the hardest to keep people from seeing in me is _____

I feel extremely pleased when people say that I am _____

I get the angriest when people imply or say that I am _____

For my mom/dad/parent figure, the worst quality for someone to have was/is _____

For my mom/dad/parent figure, the best quality for someone to have was/is _____

The situations that I get most upset in have to do with

[space left intentionally blank in the original book]

🔔 [Notice any emotions or memories coming up in response to the last exercise.]

Exercise 6.5: Word, Word, Word

Similar to the earlier "milk, milk, milk" exercise, we ask you to again say one word over and over again, faster and faster. However, this time we want you to pick a word that has historically been difficult for you. Don't start with a word that brings up the most intense feelings first; select something that has impacted how you live and what choices you make. Just pick one word, not a sentence or a phrase. The shorter the word, the better. This is about breaking that word down to what it really is—just a collected bunch of sounds.

1. Select a word for yourself.

2. The word I'd like to let go of or defuse from is _____

3. The things I do to try to prove that this word does not apply to me (or *does* apply to me) are [space left intentionally blank in the original book]

4. Sit comfortably in a chair in a private place. *It is important that it be private.*

5. Say the word you picked aloud, slowly and carefully. What does this word evoke for you? Any images, memories, feelings, associations? [space left intentionally blank in the original book]

6. Start saying the word over and over again, loudly.

7. Say it faster and faster, louder and louder.

8. Continue for forty-five seconds.

9. After you stop, notice any reactions to the word that were different from when you were saying it fast and loud. We recommend trying this out whenever you feel hooked by a word.

Description vs. Evaluation

Description and evaluations are two different things, but we often use evaluations as if they are descriptions (Hayes, Strosahl, and Wilson 1999; Hayes and Smith 2005). An example might help clarify this point.

If we tell you, "The Statue of Liberty is in New York," would you agree? Most folks would know this and would readily agree, right?

If we say, "The Statue of Liberty was given to the Americans by the French," would you agree? Unless you are a history buff and want to add some caveats, you probably could nod your head yes.

If we say, "The Statue of Liberty is 151 feet from base to torch" and if you go look it up yourself, you'd agree.

Now, if we say, "The Statue of Liberty is a beautiful American landmark," would everyone reading this agree? The answer is no. Some of you may agree; others may say that it's interesting but not beautiful, or argue with us about what "beautiful" means.

If we say, "The Statue of Liberty is the best symbol of freedom in the world," would everyone agree? Probably not, particularly if we were able to question people from a variety of countries.

The last two questions about the Statue of Liberty are *evaluations.* They move beyond merely describing the Statue of Liberty to judging it in one dimension or another. Evaluations belong to the person thinking or saying them. They are not, in fact, part of the object itself. Being the best at anything is not *in* the Statue of Liberty; it's an evaluation of the statue offered by someone.

There are a number of things we can all mostly agree on as *descriptions.* These are just the facts: the what, where, when, and who. They tend not to be emotion laden or specific to one point of view. Given that the statement is correct, we would all agree. Some examples of descriptions are:

- This chair is made of leather and steel.

- I work from nine to five, four days a week.

- My sister often cries at the movies.

As we noted above, evaluations are different from descriptions. These concepts depend on who you are and how you see the world. Some people might agree with you, but even in the case of a very common point of view you could probably find someone who would see polka dots where you see green. Some might say evaluations are a horse of a different color. Some examples of evaluations include:

- This is a great chair.

- I'm a hard worker.

- My sister is such a drama queen.

The thing about evaluations is that they are not constant. Look at the difference between the examples of descriptions and those of evaluations provided above.

Evaluations change depending on several factors. First, they may change depending on the intended purpose: "A great chair for what? If it is to read, yes; if it is to change a light bulb, no."

Evaluations can change in comparison with other things or people: "Most people work five days a week. Why do you think you are a hard worker when you work four?"

The mood of the evaluator can also factor in: "I didn't think that movie was sad. Why did she?"

Descriptions don't change. Regardless of your mood or whether you had just been to a furniture show featuring the most comfortable chairs in the world, if I say, "This chair is made of leather and steel" (and let's say it is!), you would agree.

The problem is that evaluations tend to get us fused or tied to our thoughts, feelings, memories, and bodily sensations in a way that descriptions don't. Evaluation has its place and time: In school and work, for example, evaluation can provide useful feedback to people on how well they are doing. Sometimes evaluations can be a way of saying something in an efficient manner without too many words. For example, if it's your job to get imperfect fruit off of a quickly moving conveyor belt and you hear someone say, "That's a bad apple," you'd know to get the apple off the belt fast without having to hear the whole explanation of what made the apple bad.

However, in other contexts, particularly when it comes to our relationship to difficult thoughts and other experiences, evaluations are frequently not that useful. They tend to get us pulled in emotionally, usually because of a history where particular evaluations, either negative or positive, got associated with strong consequences. Furthermore, evaluations, unlike descriptions, tend not to be too informative. For example if you brought home a new boyfriend to meet your parents and they said,

"He's a bad apple," it might be hard to know what they meant or if this really told you anything about who he really is.

The other problem with evaluation is that it doesn't suggest ways of addressing the issue. For example, let's imagine that you heard that you were dumb or stupid growing up and you find yourself having a great deal of difficulty in college courses. One possibility is to tell yourself or a friend, "I'm stupid," and stay there. 🔔[Any thoughts or feelings coming up?] That's a rather stable characteristic and does not give you much room to move. However, a description would be more like "I got a D on this exam, but I only studied for two hours and have never taken calculus before." This takes the emotion out of it and also offers more information. From that description you can recognize that you might need outside help and that you may need to devote more time to calculus class. It is a difficult part of our work as therapists to hear how frequently children are given labels like this that they then carry with them for a lifetime. When we have groups for trauma survivors, the stories often have a remarkable similarity.

It's worth pointing out here that no one is immune to the impact of evaluations. They are an omnipresent feature in our culture. People are always looking for the best, the brightest, the prettiest, or the strongest. The list goes on and on, and you can't totally escape evaluation. But you *can* become better at noticing when it happens and not buying into it. If you have a history of being called stupid while growing up, there will probably still be a passenger on your bus who every so often, or perhaps all the time, yells "Stupid!" from the back of the bus. When that happens, description could be one among several other potential strategies that might help you defuse from the word. The first step would involve being able to notice that this is an evaluation and not a description. The second step would involve conjuring up the description that might go with that evaluation. If we follow the example from above, the counterpart description for "Stupid" might be, as we said, "I got a D on this exam, but I only studied for two hours and have never taken calculus before." If one becomes fused with the word "stupid," the person may start avoiding going to classes or doing homework, or may even impulsively drop out of the class or college altogether. The description, however, may provide the person just enough distance from the power of loaded words from the past, such as "stupid," to allow for other, more flexible responses, such as studying harder or asking the professor for advice. Alternatively, a description in this case may involve not just rephrasing content, as we have described above, but also labeling or describing the process: "This is a thought, a verbal echo of an old experience." The description is not meant to change that passenger or to replace it. It's only a strategy to use so that one "Stupid!" passenger does not end up dictating the direction of your bus.

Exercise 6.6: Evaluation Is in the Eye of the Beholder

Look around you right now. Select an object. Any object.

1. The object I picked was _____

2. Find some positive evaluations for the object. Come up with as many as you can.

[space left intentionally blank in the original book]

3. Find some negative evaluations for this object. Come up with as many as you can.

[space left intentionally blank in the original book]

4. What was your experience while evaluating this object? What showed up?

[space left intentionally blank in the original book]

5. Look around the room again and see if there is anything that you couldn't evaluate negatively if you were asked to.

6. Now, think of the person you most like or love in your life.

7. Find some positive evaluations for him or her. Come up with as many as you can.

[space left intentionally blank in the original book]

8. Find some negative evaluations for him or her.

9. Come up with as many as you can.

[space left intentionally blank in the original book]

10. What was your experience evaluating someone close to you so purposefully? What thoughts and feelings did you have? [space left intentionally blank in the original book]

The central idea is that, if we wanted to, we could go around evaluating people, places, and things constantly. And these evaluations can be ever-changing: We can go from evaluating someone as wonderful to evaluating them as the most hateful person we've ever met. Yet, the person may not have changed at all. AND these evaluations can impact how we relate to a person or situation. If you work for me and I decide you are a bad person, I may avoid contact with you and try to make sure that others communicate your job tasks to you. I may avoid you in the lunchroom and give you unpleasant tasks to do. What do you think would happen in this situation? We're sure you get the picture, and this happens all the time. Watch your mind on a busy day and see what happens. Our minds are constantly evaluating, comparing, critiquing, and categorizing.

Another way to think of evaluations is as judgments (Linehan 1993b). We find that trauma survivors, particularly those who experienced their traumas early in life, struggle a lot with self-judgment. It's not surprising that many of the people we work with grew up in fairly unhappy and judgmental families. Part of the abuse was often verbal, and these words became very painful. In fact, many clients have commented on the irony of the old children's saying that goes "Sticks and stones can break my bones, but words can never hurt me." So many of us learn these judgments from an early age, and when one is judgmental of one's self, the tendency to judge tends to snowball. It becomes easy to see the world through the lens of judgment, where everyone and everything gets an evaluation. This can be a very unhappy place to live, and when you first really become aware of this in your life, the realization can be a painful one. Yet, noticing and letting go of judgments of self and others can be quite freeing.

Exercise 6.7: Catching Judgment

1. Think of a situation that is currently upsetting you. Pick something that is moderately upsetting (5 to 7 on a scale of 0 to 10, with 0 being not at all upsetting and 10 being the most upsetting thing you've experienced), and write about it below. Try to write all the thoughts about yourself and others that have

gone through your mind pertaining to this matter. Write everything, without censoring any thoughts or feelings.

[space left intentionally blank in the original book]

2. Get a highlighter or a pen or pencil of a different color. Go back to step 1 and under-line or highlight all judgments of yourself and others. Notice what the ratio was for you of descriptions versus evaluations or judgments. This may give you a sense of how much this may be a problem for you. 🔔 [Any self-judg-ments coming up about how much you evalu-ate or judge?]

3. Try not to "judge your judging" (Linehan 1993b, 208). This is an exercise to catch your judgments, not to pass judgment on them. As we pointed out earlier, judging is embed-ded in the culture, just as you are. The trick here is to become mindful of all this judging and to consider alternatives.

How You Talk Does Matter

Sometimes adopting some new language con-ventions can help make the difference between getting completely pulled into an experience and viewing it in a more defused or distanced way. Although some of these conventions will be a bit awkward at first, we highly recommend that you try to see if you can include some of this way of speaking into your language. We're not trying to push jargon or psychobabble. As we've already noted, it is very easy to start living your life in accordance with your language. Catching yourself with some of these new ways of speaking can serve as a reminder that there is another way to look at the situation. How we talk may just give us enough distance from the power of words to be able to detect the white border on the canvas, thus being able to distinguish the painting from the scene. ACT therapists are known to talk this way in their personal and professional lives, and you can almost spot one in a hall or waiting room if you listen to how they talk! Sometimes it's sort of funny—AND it works for us. Also, remember that when we say "talk," it can also mean the things you say to yourself. In fact, this is probably the most important talking that goes on—the talk that's all inside your mind.

Use "And" Instead of "But"

In this book, we've often used the technique of replacing "but" with "and," as we discussed in the introduction. The word "but" originates from the words "be" and "out," as is noted by Hayes, Strosahl, and Wilson (1999). The typical usage of "but" is to contradict what goes before it. For example, "I would go the store, but I'm afraid." This statement implies two things: first, the person is not going to the store; second, fear caused the person not to go (the conclusion being that if the person wasn't afraid, he or she could go to the store). By using "and" instead of "but," particularly with an emphasis, the fact that emotions and thoughts are not causes of our behavior, but rather co-occurring events, becomes clear. The typical view is that we should not or cannot have certain internal experiences, such as painful thoughts and feelings. And if we do have these experiences, they can control our behavior.

Don't worry, this way of talking is not another thing that you are doing wrong. You learned this the old-fashioned way, in the culture. If you think about how often we describe experiencing some unwanted internal event in opposition to doing what needs to be done, it's pretty amazing: "I was supposed to go to work, but I was sad and stayed home" or "I wanted to go out on a date, but I was afraid I would get upset." The fact of the matter is that these experiences are not mutually exclusive. We can be sad AND go to work. We can be anxious

AND go out on a date. The problem with "but" is that it implies either the first part or the second part is okay, but that both things can't exist together. Using AND can help you see that both experiences can occur simultaneously: You don't need to get rid of sadness to be able to go to work. This is such a powerful concept that we've emphasized it throughout the book with our capitalized ANDs.

Verbally Defuse

We often say things like "I'm sad" or "I'm stupid," as if our whole being is the experience that follows from those words: sad or stupid. However, the fact is that these are thoughts, self-judgments, and evaluations that you are having. They are not *you*. 🔔 [Any reactions to this sentence?]

"Sad" and "stupid"—along with any other evaluation you make about yourself—are only your passengers. They are with you for a reason, but they are not you. So, another language convention we use is to say things such as "I am feeling sadness" or "I'm having the thought that I'm stupid." We believe that these small changes, when made regularly, help you to see these subtle but important distinctions. In fact, you might find it interesting to teach those close to you to adopt these same language conventions, thus helping you develop a community that maintains perspective on these issues.

Similarly, as discussed in the last chapter and reinforced by our discussion of description versus evaluation in this one, we find it helpful to refrain from calling thoughts, feelings, and so on, either positive or negative. Instead, we draw attention to the fact that these are evaluations we have about these private experiences. Therefore, instead of saying happiness is a positive emotion, we say happiness is a positively evaluated emotion. As with some other language conventions, we think this strategy can help us become defused or unhooked from our own thoughts and emotions.

Use "Being Willing" Instead of "Want"

Often, we describe our approach toward things or activities as a matter of want: "I want to go to work, but I'm sad." If we are not truly feeling like we "want" to, it's almost hard to say it, isn't it? "I want to fly in an airplane to the conference, but I'm afraid." Notice your experience and see if you don't relate to this in some way. We lower our eyes, sigh a bit, and then say it, because there is something about that statement that is not quite true. So, we recommend that in such situations you say instead, "I'm willing to go to work AND have this feeling of sadness" or "I am afraid AND I am willing to take the airplane to the conference." Much of this willingness is in the service of our valued goals, which we will talk about more later. This language approach allows us to get a little perspective on the distinction between thoughts and feelings (wants) and our stance toward life and what needs to be done (willingness).

Speak of Your Mind as if It's a Separate Entity

Sometimes, if we speak in a way that highlights the process of thinking as opposed to its content, it is easier to get a different perspective. An example may help you see how this might be helpful to you. Some trauma survivors, when experiencing a great deal of stress, may become a bit hypersensitive about their ability to trust others around them, particularly if the trauma involved some sort of betrayal. One of our clients who had been quite stable abruptly became increasingly concerned about several coworkers' stance toward him after he was bypassed for a promotion. He started feeling fear and having difficulty being himself even among colleagues whom he used to like. In session, he reported having an ongoing string of thoughts like "This person doesn't really want to speak to me, he's just killing time" or "I know that they'll be talking about me when I leave the room." To the extent that he became fused with these thoughts and feelings, he started withdrawing from colleagues, acting distant, and this, in turn, was creating more tension. He tried a couple of strategies, such as reminding himself that some of these colleagues were friends or looking for evidence that might disprove that they were really talking about him. However, these strategies paradoxically generated even more doubtful thoughts. In fact, he could not convince himself to trust them again right away, and he still didn't know if some of them may have had a role in his being bypassed for the promotion.

In session, we worked on his mindfulness skills, not only of the present, but of past experiences that might help him understand this reaction. He noted a history of becoming suspicious when under stress, harking back to various prior experiences of betrayal in his own family, with individuals indeed speaking ill of him behind his back. One of the main strategies that ended up working for this client was to constantly thank his mind when the string of suspicious thoughts and uncomfortable emotions would show up at work. He'd say to himself, "Thank you, Mind, for that thought or feeling" or "Thank you, Mind, for doing your job" or "There goes my mind again ... (in the tone you'd use with a beloved child, such as 'that's my girl')." Although he wasn't certain that the content of these thoughts wasn't correct, this string of thoughts and feelings felt suspiciously familiar, like old passengers possibly, and getting hooked by them, even if there was a grain of truth somewhere in their content, was just not working for him. In fact, this fusion was about to create one of those situations of "If you are not willing to have it, you've got it." This is an example of how speaking of your mind as a separate entity may help you focus on the process instead of the content of the thoughts, particularly when you feel bombarded by thoughts and feelings.

By the way, a couple of shorthand terms we use in this book for this type of fused ongoing stream of thoughts or self-conversation are "mindy talk" and "negative chatter" (Hayes, Strosahl, and Wilson 1999; Hayes and Smith 2005). We all have it. Avoid judging yourself for it—just label it.

Exercise 6.8: Practicing New Language Conventions

In this exercise, we'd like you to write down some situations that are often problematic for you. Then use the remaining space to come up with some responses that you can make to yourself or others using the language conventions we've been discussing. Consider first the three examples we've provided to get the hang of the exercise. Then see if you can identify your own problematic situations and practice these language conventions. (Table 6.2)

Problem situation	What I would typically say	New language convention
When I get angry, I tend to say things that I regret later.	I said things I regretted, but I was angry.	I am angry AND will not say things I'll regret.
During my last evaluation at work, my supervisor gave me several compliments and I wanted to say that I didn't deserve them, that others did the work too.	Well, you're giving me too much credit here. What about so-and-so, they also...	I am having the thought that I want to say, "I don't deserve this," AND I will say thank you instead.

Problem situation	What I would typically say	New language convention
When I get stressed, I tend to go over in my mind all the things that have gone wrong recently.	When I get stressed, I tend to go over in my mind all the things that have gone wrong recently.	There goes my mind again. It makes sense, given that I'm stressed out.
Situation to use "and" instead of "but":		
Situation to thank your mind:		
Situation to say "willing" instead of "want":		
Situation to say "I'm having the thoughts...":		

Table 6.2

More Strategies for Changing Your Relation to Language

We have outlined several ways of trying to transcend language or loosen its grip over our behavior. Although we have given you some of our own examples and will provide others, we encourage you to come up with your own metaphors and ways to defuse from language in ways that work for you. We know that not every metaphor and exercise will appeal to everyone. Our hope is that by covering the same idea with so many different strategies, at least some will resonate with you and be of help.

Here is a table of various different strategies for letting go of some of the literality of language. These strategies were adapted from Hayes and Smith (2005), with their permission. (Table 6.3)

Additional Defusion Strategies

A Beautiful Mind	If you are a movie buff and enjoyed this movie about John Nash, see if you can picture your negative chatter as different people that follow you everywhere, whom you acknowledge, allow to be there, AND need not talk to, be friends with, or fight against.
Pop-Up Mind	Imagine that your thoughts, feelings, emotions, and bodily sensations are like Internet pop-up ads that just keep popping up when you least want them to, and which you can simply let pop.
Cell Phone	Imagine that your negative chatter is like a cell phone that you cannot turn off and you always carry around. Let it squawk as much as it likes.
Passengers on the Bus	Imagine that your difficult thoughts and experiences are passengers on your bus, folks that may be scary, but who need not leave for the bus to move.
Gollum Mind	Again for the movie buffs: If you are a Lord of the Rings fan, imagine that your mind is like Smeagle or Gollum, and tries to trick you sometimes just as Gollum did with Frodo by implying he could not trust his best friend, or who craves something that is not good for you ("Precious, precious...").

Thoughts Are Not Causes	If you find yourself identifying particular thoughts, feelings, and so on as barriers to moving forward in your life, ask yourself: "Could I have this uncomfortable thought, feeling, or memory and still do X (whatever it is you want your life to stand for: go to work, be kind to your partner, etc.) if someone was threatening a loved one?"
Think One Think One Another	Try to say or think that you can't do something while doing it. "I really can't go to the gym to-day" while lacing up your shoes, opening the car door ("I really can't"), getting in ("Maybe tomor-row"), and getting to the gym ("I'm way too busy to go to the gym") and then exercising.
Waves in the Ocean	This one's good if you find yourself impulsively acting on some urge (substances, food, shopping, sex, gambling). When you are experiencing the urge, picture it as a wave coming into the shore that later will retreat ... and come back again ... and retreat again ... Be the sand that receives it without having to do anything but just notice it coming and going.
Purse/ Wal-let Items	Identify difficult thoughts and experiences as different items in your purse or wallet, such as different credit cards, keys, lipstick, money holder, and so on. This act will remind you that you can carry your history around without letting it control what you do.
Painting vs. Scene	When you feel stressed, out of control, and overwhelmed, think about the Magritte painting in chapter 2 and ask yourself: "Am I on the can-vas being painted or in the actual scene?"

279

Finding the Middle Path	Sometimes trauma survivors, particularly those who experienced early trauma, may get stuck in viewing the world in black-and-white terms—great versus horrible; excited to be alive versus not worth living. Imagine a fork in the road that looks like it has only two offshoots until you see that there's a hill between them with a small walking trail over it. When you hear your mind speaking in black-and-white terms, stop and ask yourself: "Where is the middle path here, however difficult to see?"
Leaves on a Stream	Imagine that your thoughts, feelings, emotions, and bodily sensations are leaves on a stream that just keeps running and carrying the leaves along.
Fun House Mirror	When your negative chatter really gets going, ask yourself: "What if this chatter is like the images one sees in the mirrors at a fun house?" In the fun house, there might also be some regular mirrors, but one never knows which ones are the accurate images. The particular image in front of you may be accurate or not. Would you want to bet your life on those reflections?

Table 6.3

This barrier to acceptance we have been discussing so far in this chapter, language and its dark side, is perhaps the most pervasive barrier to acceptance. Being able to develop a different relationship with language is difficult. Language is something that always seems to be creating reality. Adopting this new understanding of language is tricky, and frankly, even after years of practice, we still fall into language's trap all the time. AND if you continue to work on these new habits of mind, you will come to see some real changes over time. Sometimes you won't be able to see the whole journey; but step-by-step, it's amazing how you get there.

At some level, fusion, or excessive literality, is the foundation of all other barriers to acceptance, including those we will discuss below. However, many roads lead to Rome, and we hope that some of the content we cover in the next section might be helpful to you in finding ways to become less entangled in difficult internal experiences.

Second Barrier: Lack of Compassion for the Self

One of the first things we pointed out in this book is that it's impossible to do this type of work without compassion toward oneself. This is a good reminder to do a compassion check when a string of judgments kicks in. If you don't sense compassion for yourself and what or who you're judging (especially yourself), see if you can bring it along on the journey with you. Doing work related to your trauma is difficult and can take a lot of energy. If you could have solved these problems easily, we're sure you would have done it already. And to make matters even trickier, problems with feelings often include a layer of guilt or shame. Unlike most other medical problems, when it comes to mental health, people are often worried that they will be judged for their struggle. In fact, they often judge themselves first! So, if you realize that there are problems as you work through this book, that's a good thing. That's why you picked up the book. Compassion comes with being open to whatever is there to see. If there are some things that are working well, that's great to know. If there are some things that are not working well, then it gives us a place to start.

We have come to believe that a lack of compassion for one's self (and all the problems that result from that lack) comes from believing our own evaluations (or those of others). Following is a list of some of these problems, things that may snag you as you work through the book and may hold you back. See if any of these tendencies have appeared while you've been moving through the process of learning ACT.

• *Internalizing blame.* Have you found yourself going into a litany of snowballing self-judgments like "I'm a mess" or "I should have been doing this sooner. I've wasted my youth"?

• *Engaging in reason giving.* If you believe the thought that you are a mess literally, then you have to try to justify, argue against, and defend against the content of this thought. You can, for example, get stuck in trying to explain why you're not to blame.

• *Externalizing blame.* Perhaps as a form of reason giving, if you become fused with self-judgmental thoughts, you might spend time thinking about who and what is to blame for your being a mess.

• *Losing hope and giving up.* If you become really fused with the thought that you are hopeless and believe the self-judgments that you're a mess or are worthless, you might be tempted to give up hope, thinking, "This is as good as life can be for me, so I should just forget about change." 🔔 [Any thoughts coming up in response to this last sentence?]

With compassion as its foundation, defusion can give you more options. We want to give you options for action that might not have been there before. The problem with assigning blame to self or others, engaging in reason giving, and giving up hope is that there isn't much room for progress. Language is the raw material that allows us to create a story about our life.

If you are human, you probably have a history that includes many what-ifs, should haves, and could haves. You probably wish you had done things differently here and there, and maybe even today. And this becomes yet another way to judge yourself as being at fault or somehow a bad person. We want to suggest that you begin to have some of the compassion and caring for yourself that you would for another vulnerable human being.

Compassion is not something that can be adopted just by intellectual means. It happens as a leap of faith. You welcome compassion toward yourself just because—there needs to be no reason or justification for it. In fact, the moment one starts to give reasons for being compassionate (some may even say loving) to oneself, it becomes something else. Imagine that you are bringing compassion in because you have "good reasons," or thoughts, for having compassion toward yourself: "I had a hard childhood" or "There was nothing I could have done about it" or "I'm a good person." Now, if these reasons or thoughts are the only things keeping compassion in place, what happens when these reasons or thoughts change, as they certainly will given the constantly changing nature of thoughts and emotions? What if tomorrow you have different thoughts that might serve as reasons *not* to be compassionate toward yourself, such as "I'm a bad person" or "I don't deserve compassion" or "I could have tried harder"? The point here is that a compassionate stance is a leap of faith. If it is based on reasons, it becomes about a story to defend instead of an opening to experience.

Some trauma survivors tell us that they don't deserve compassion. If you are having that thought, first of all, thank your mind for it and try to see it for what it is: a thought. How did this thought get to be a passenger on your bus? Think about it a little bit, not as a way of finding reasons for not believing it, but just so you see that this passenger comes to be on your bus because someone gave you the idea that it belongs there. The thought may be on your bus, but it doesn't have to drive it. It can sit there and say, "You don't deserve compassion," as much as it wants, while you, the driver, continue to drive the bus in the direction of self-compassion.

One of the things that always strikes us when trauma survivors say that they don't deserve compassion (or happiness, or whatever) is the question "If you don't deserve it, then who does?" Inevitably people come up with "young children," to which we point out that they were young kids once, young children who were vulnerable and dependent on their caretakers, young kids who feared disapproval and disappointments and who craved love and nurturance. Can you bring compassion toward that child you once were (even if you can't do this for yourself as an adult)? 🧘 [Notice any bodily sensations or judgments.]

Exercise 6.9: How Much Compassion Do You Feel for Yourself?

1. Please rate how much compassion you feel for the following people on a scale of 0 to 10, with 0 being no compassion at all and 10 being the most compassion you can possibly feel for anyone. How much compassion do you feel toward:

A homeless person who is out in the cold? _____

A soldier who died in Iraq? _____

The family of the soldier who died? _____

Children 0 to 5 years old around you? _____

Children 6 to 17 years old around you? _____

Survivors of Hurricane Katrina? _____

Starving children in Africa? _____

People who lost a loved one in the Asian tsunami? _____

The person who has hurt you the most in your life? _____

Yourself? _____

2. Now notice how much compassion you have toward yourself relative to others.

3. Could you, as a leap of faith, bring as much compassion toward yourself as you have toward the person or group you rated the highest? _____

4. If the answer is no, notice what your barriers are to self-compassion. My barriers are [space left intentionally blank in the original book]

5. What would it take for you to overcome these barriers? How many of them have to

do with becoming fused with your own evaluations? Could you find a way of defusing from these evaluations?

[space left intentionally blank in the original book]

Third Barrier: Focusing on Right and Wrong Instead of Workability

We are not saying that everyone should just sit around feeling their feelings all the time. We actually don't believe that. When we talk about making room for our thoughts and feelings, we say so in the context of making life work for you. We are talking about having these feelings so that you get to move forward in your life. The key issue is workability. Are you currently living in a way that takes you in a direction you value in life?

Sometimes we get so stuck in what is right or wrong that we lose sight of what actually works for us. One of the authors went home to Brazil for a visit, and her brother-in-law came to pick her up at the airport. Brazil, like some other countries, is notorious for aggressive driving, and her brother-in-law was at that time probably more aggressive than most. During the drive home on two-lane roads, a semi truck was passing a car and therefore was coming right at them in their lane. After a few seconds (that felt like minutes) of her brother-in-law maintaining the speed of 120 kilometers per hour without slowing down and the truck not being able to pull back into his lane, she couldn't resist anymore and said, "Aren't you going to pull to the side?" To this frantic question (it wasn't said calmly), he retorted, "This is *my* lane; he is in the wrong lane. He shouldn't have passed." Yes, her brother-in-law was right. The truck was in the wrong lane, AND they would have all died if he hadn't finally pulled to the side.

Life can be like that sometimes. We may be absolutely right in our positions, AND if we want to make things work for us, we have to let go of being right or wrong and move into an altogether different dimension. One of the authors had a dying plant at home, and she decided it was not getting enough water. She spent several weeks trying to adjust more or less water, only to find out later (after the plant died) that the problem was not enough light. Sometimes we get stuck in one dimension when the problem is in another altogether.

Being right versus workability is like that. How often have we done something like "this is my lane; he's in the wrong lane" with dire consequences? Some of the expressions we popularly use for this are "winning the battle but losing the war" and "cutting off one's nose to spite one's face." However, not all situations that we feel strongly about are like that. In fact, some great injustices in the world have been corrected because people got motivated by being relentless, goal-directed, and sometimes even spurred by anger. Apartheid and the civil rights movement come to mind. The wisdom, as the serenity prayer says, is to be able to tell the difference between what to accept and what to change. The next exercise is designed to be helpful to you in that regard.

The issue of right versus wrong is a tricky one to discuss with trauma survivors. Depending on the type of traumatic experience you've had, you may know that things that were done to you or that happened were wrong. We don't have any problem with that—in fact, we agree. Part of our work involves preventing additional trauma, including abuse of children. We understand that all of us have a moral compass that provides a sense of direction in our lives. We know that evaluating right versus wrong is a useful tool in life. However, we want you to consider areas where it may perpetuate suffering for you. That's the function of exercise 6.10: to help you identify areas where your investment in being right may be costing you too much, where letting it go would not interfere with your own self-respect. Being mindful of the impact on your self-respect is important. Many of our clients have been told to let go of issues because these issues made the people around them uncomfortable, such as when someone is suing a perpetrator and the rest of the family gets upset. Such instances may even involve considerable losses to the person, such as losing contact with other family members or spending money on a lawyer. Yet, simply giving up on this issue because of these costs without looking at self-respect would miss the point that persisting in such a lawsuit might be a value-driven choice, a violation of which could result in a significant loss of self-respect. No two situations are the same, so you will need to look at each situation carefully, with an eye toward doing what works for you, within your current circumstances, keeping your specific values in mind.

Exercise 6.10: Differentiating Workability from Being Right

Situation	Cost of attachment (0 to 10); explain	Cost of letting go (0 to 10); explain
Someone in my battalion in Vietnam got awarded a Purple Heart, and I am certain he did not earn it. People know about this, but superiors don't want to do anything about it. One said, "What's done is done." I feel resentful because it's damaging to those who did earn it.	*Rating: 7 (high cost).* *I feel that it has affected my ability to get assignments that I want, as I'm viewed as a troublemaker for bringing it up. I spent hours over weekends researching the issue, and my wife became upset with me.*	*Rating: 0-1.* *Probably not much, because I've said my piece and those who should do something about it know about it. Letting this go would not hurt anyone.*

Table 6.4

1. Take some time to think about some of the situations in your life that you currently feel most invested in about being right. In the left-hand column, write a summary of each.

2. In the middle column, rate each item in terms of how much it's getting in the way of achieving your goals. Use a scale of 0 to 10, with 0 being not at all and 10 being completely keeping you from reaching your goals. In this column, also explain how the situation interferes with achieving your goals.

3. In the right-hand column, rate how much it would cost you, in terms of self-respect, if you were to let go of needing to be right in that situation. Use a scale of 0 to 10, with 0 being no impact on your self-respect and 10 being completely eliminating your self-respect. Explain your rating. (Table 6.4)

Fourth Barrier: Being Stuck on Blame Instead of Response-Ability

It's very important that you recognize a basic truth about this issue: Responsibility and blame are two different things. Sometimes trauma survivors may get stuck on blame of self or others while feeling helpless to change their lives today. If you find yourself feeling stuck and unable to move into acceptance, check and see if this may possibly be the culprit.

The root of the word responsibility is actually "response-ability" or the ability to respond (Hayes, Strosahl, and Wilson 1999). This ability is something that can empower people to take control over their lives.

Blame is not particularly useful as a strategy. Usually, people suggest that the function of blame is to motivate people to correct what they did or to not do it again. Well, the same can be accomplished with response-ability, in that it can assist you in identifying what you are capable of doing to change your life. For example, by making contact with the anger toward those who hurt you as a child, you can make a decision to support the work of local agencies that contribute to the well-being of children. Simply being angry at society and blaming the culture for a lack of values is not very likely to be helpful, unless it leads to action or some sort.

Blame is usually about making the other person wrong. Is this really useful to or working for you? While blame can be very effective and appropriate in a court of law, it most often brings unnecessary suffering to the realm of interpersonal relationships. In fact, there is a saying that holding onto resentment is like drinking poison and hoping the other person will die.

Blame versus taking response-ability can be a difficult issue for trauma survivors who did not choose their traumatic history and yet are left with the aftermath. There is a distinction between responsibility for the trauma and response-ability in the present moment. By *response-ability,* we mean what you can do right now. What are you willing and able to do in your life in order to have the life that you value?

Exercise 6.11: What Is Your Response-Ability Right Now?

Impact of trauma	Ability to respond (0 to 10); explain	Barriers
Difficulty maintaining employment.	*Rating: 6. I can get jobs easily, but I often find it difficult to manage work and the kids by myself. I also get fed up with my bosses and end up quitting because they usually remind me of my abusive father.*	*I think, "Why should I get a job and work hard when the system just takes advantage of me? Whenever I get a stable job, my boss starts making too many demands on me."*

Table 6.5

1. Think about your trauma and which areas of your life have been most affected by it. List those impacts in the left-hand column. We've provided an example in the first row.

2. In the middle column, rate your ability to respond to that impact. Use a scale of 0 to 10, with 0 being that you're completely unable to deal with it and 10 being that you are

> absolutely able to respond. Explain your response.
>
> 3. In the right-hand column, describe your barriers to being able to respond to that impact. (Table 6.5)
>
> 4. Review your answers and notice what types of issues come up for you.

🔔 [Any thoughts coming up in response to this exercise?]

These are difficult questions to answer, and they should be considered alongside answers to values clarification exercises that we will be doing later. In the example provided above, the person realized over time that having or not having a job was his response-ability, even though his father had hit him and then abandoned the family. This man explained that deep inside he had struggled with whether or not he was to blame for hanging in there for so long and not standing up to his father. He had put all this adult responsibility on the child he was then. Staying stuck in this cycle of blame was interfering with his ability to be effective now. The discussion on focusing on response-ability instead of blame allowed him to feel more empowered to take control of his life. It became an issue of letting go of being right so that he could build a stable life for his family, something he valued.

Who would you be now if you could let go of the struggle with judgment, blame, being right (or wrong), and all the other passengers on your bus? What if you begin to have compassion and acceptance for yourself? For many trauma survivors, the first step in this direction is to begin to identify a sense of self—the you who has always been present. That is the topic of the next chapter.

Journaling

Thoughts

[space left intentionally blank in the original book]

Feelings or Emotions

[space left intentionally blank in the original book]

Self-Judgments

[space left intentionally blank in the original book]

Physical Sensations

[space left intentionally blank in the original book]

Action Urges (What Do You Feel Like Doing?)

[space left intentionally blank in the original book]

CHAPTER 7

Finding Your True Self

It takes courage to grow up and turn out to be who you really are.

—e.e. cummings

Trauma and the Self

One of the difficulties of surviving intense traumatic experiences can be a sense of losing yourself in the process of dealing with the aftermath. As the statement above illustrates, sometimes it takes a lot of courage to figure out who we actually have turned out to be. To an extent, that's the focus of this chapter. Traumatic experiences can sometimes distort the natural light of who you are, and you may begin to think of your self as the memories you have or what the passengers on the bus say about you. In the last chapter, we spent quite a bit of time dealing with the issue of learning to be aware that you are not your thoughts or feelings. The problem of buying into what our minds tell us is part of the general human condition, as the Magritte painting in chapter 2 illustrates. But this problem goes beyond thoughts and feelings—you are also not your memories, or roles, or any of the factors related to these phenomena.

This of course leads to the question "Who am I then?" We are going to try to answer this question from a psychological perspective, but you may find some more existential answers to the question as you do this work. Needless to say, the problem of finding one's true self has perplexed humankind for a long time. Yet, as author Jon Kabat-Zinn puts it, no matter where you go, there you are (1994)!

Not having a sense of your self can be especially true for people who experienced significant trauma as children in their family of origin. Some of the tasks any child needs to learn are to differentiate one's self from others, to notice and label feelings, and to gain a sense of one's identity in the world. Unfortunately, in severely disrupted families, this learning is often stymied. Sometimes parents' needs and wishes are so powerful that the child is not taught to differentiate his or her own identity from that of the parent. Children are sent mixed messages about developing their own identity that can severely interfere with this essential developmental process. We have worked with many adults who report that, as children, their basic physical and emotional needs frequently went unmet.

Children learn about themselves through parental descriptors of their behavior, and if this process is a healthy one, it can set a positive tone that lasts a lifetime. For example, when a child falls and breaks a favorite toy, she is likely to cry. The first task of the parent is to attend to this event. Noticing the child is upset is a beginning to validating this as a reasonable response. The father then may say, "Oh, you fell and hurt your knee, and your truck is broken." 🔔[Notice what thoughts, feelings, and judgments are coming up right now.] The child, wailing, may then be held and comforted, and the father can label this as sadness and upset. The father then may begin to sort things out, gently washing the child's skinned knee and putting on a bandage. He sits with the child and comforts her, and she begins to calm down as she is lovingly cared for. The father may then take a look at the toy and see what can be done to repair it. Contrast this experience with a similar situation where the child who is sad and upset is told by her father that nothing is wrong. The child may be told not to cry because it upsets Mommy or that she'd better cheer up because no one likes a crybaby. Several different things can be learned in situations like this. In the first example, the child can learn that she is someone worth noticing and that she has feelings that can be labeled. In contrast, if her needs are marginalized as in the second example, she may learn to ignore or mislabel feelings. She can learn that feelings should be ignored, or she may get a confusing message about who is having the feelings—the child or Mommy. She can also learn to care for herself, bandaging a hurt knee and soothing her own emotional upset.

For some who experienced sexual abuse, the abuse was labeled as positive and loving or as something the child wanted or caused. Many women have reported to us that when they told someone about the abuse, the response was that it was all in their imagination, or the message was completely ignored. When you read this, you can probably see how damaging these experiences can be on many levels, including that at a very basic level a child may not learn to trust his or her own experience, may not even know who he or she really is. Is the child a liar? Too sensitive? Selfish? That's what the child is being told. It's not surprising that this combination of not having had parents who helped to build a grounded identity coupled with repeated abuse and possibly periods of not feeling connected to one's body or the world can lead to an unclear sense of self.

If you look back over the last two paragraphs, you will notice that we used the word "learn" quite a bit. This is a hint about what's positive in this situation. Like most of what happens to you in life, there is learning involved in gaining a sense of self, and it is not too late to address any issue and learn what's required, if you're willing. So whether you missed out on the chance to develop a strong sense of self as a child or you somehow just lost touch with that part of you along the way, you can develop that sense of identity as you begin to work with the skills in this book. We believe you have always been there—you just need a little help getting back in touch with your true self.

Exercise 7.1: Reflections on Where You Are Now

Take a few moments to reflect on how these issues about who you are have turned up in your life. If you are not your thoughts and feelings, as we discussed in the last chapter, who are you? When you were growing up, did anyone ever see *you?* Write a bit about your thoughts as you think this issue through.

[space left intentionally blank in the original book]

🔔 [Notice what you are feeling right now.]

What you might notice as you reflect on these issues is a sense of sadness or loneliness. If feelings like that come up, can you just sit with them for a bit? You don't have to be a trauma survivor to have the sense that no one has seen the real you, the you that is behind the mask many of us end up wearing. The you that has been there all along, that is more than just your thoughts, feelings, history, and roles. Using an ACT perspective, there are three senses of self that we can talk about: self as conceptualized identity, self as awareness, and self as context.

Self as Conceptualized Identity

If they think about self at all most people think about what, in ACT, we call the conceptualized self. The *conceptualized self* is made up of a large set of verbal descriptions that we use to describe ourselves in relationship to our world. Everyone has a life story, and frequently we have many labels to describe ourselves. Most of these labels have some evaluation or judgment associated with them. However, as we discussed in the preceding chapter, language allows us to construct or reconstruct things, including our sense of identity. Much of what we think of as our identity is constructed. There is no absolute truth about this identity, but rather we have all agreed to describe ourselves and others in terms of some common values (what's "good" and "bad") and definitions ("a friend is someone who..."). This sense of self is the one labeled "friend," or "partner," or "teacher." We often use roles as a big part of this definition. We also use personality attributes to describe this self, things like kind, weak, smart, dumb, fearful, depressed, and selfless. In addition, our culture often focuses on physical descriptors such as tall, fat, man, Asian American, young, old, pretty, and plain. 🔔 [Notice any bodily reactions you might be feeling right now.]

Exercise 7.2: Knowing Your Conceptualized Self

Please complete the sentences below based on both what you think about yourself and what you think others say about you.

I have the following physical attributes (for example, height, ethnicity, gender):

[space left intentionally blank in the original book]

I come from the following geographic area (for example, city, state, country, neighborhood; places that you think define you in some ways): _____

I have the following desired and undesired qualities:

[space left intentionally blank in the original book]

I have the following roles in my life (for example, father, coworker, student, reader):

[space left intentionally blank in the original book]

I am someone who is (use labels to describe your history or patterns of behaviors, such as "veteran," "high achiever," "firstborn child," "alcoholic," or "rape survivor"):

[space left intentionally blank in the original book]

Your answers in exercise 7.2 will give you a sense of your conceptualized self. It may be that a big part of the way you think of this self is as someone who has survived a trauma. And you may link a number of other aspects of yourself to that experience or story. Our goal here is to help you to step way from that conceptualized self. It's okay to have it, as long as you recognize this self for what it is—just a set of labels that don't have to necessarily be accurate or to define who and what you are. There is some danger with this sense of self because it often has the most evaluations associated with it, and buying into those evaluations can lead to trouble. For instance, if you were told enough times as a child that you were bad, you may have come to believe that label and even act it out in your life. You may spend a huge amount of energy thinking about being bad or trying not to be bad. Even when you think about your trauma history, you may think it happened because you are bad. What we come back to over and over again in ACT is that "bad" is just a word, just like the hundreds of others that we somehow learned to apply to our selves. We think they define us, but they don't.

Part of the problem with using labels in identification is that those very labels pull us into attachment with both parts of the characteristic. For example, if one is very concerned with being attractive, being unattractive is essentially connected to that idea. Basically we know that the two poles of any attribute are inherently connected for us by language, and you cannot really have one side of an issue without the other. We will discuss this idea in more detail below, but first let's try a little experiment. When you read each of the words listed below, what pops up in your mind?

Good

Thin

Smart

Beginning

If you're like most people, you probably came up with bad, fat, dumb, and ending. A way of looking at this idea is that it is like two sides of a coin. You cannot have one side without the other—heads and tails are always linked. So, if you are overly committed to all the ways that you are good, you will be reminded at the same time of the ways in which you consider yourself to be bad. If you dedicate your life to being good, your mind will periodically come up with the thought that you're bad. In fact, some research shows that when people tried to use the image of a red Volkswagen to suppress thoughts of a white bear, the red Volkswagen took on some of the same features of the white bear—basically, the two became associated (Wegner 1994). Essentially this intense attachment to labels as a way to identify yourself functions as yet another form of avoidance, resulting in even more of what is being avoided. As you struggle to be nothing but "nice," you've initiated a struggle with "mean," and your mind won't let you forget it. This type of connection is not only present with labels but also with a variety of other phenomena, including perspectives on a situation.

The attachment to one point of view is also a problem in that it tends to blind us to other aspects of a situation (Hayes, Strosahl, and Wilson 1999). For many survivors of trauma, there is an over-identification with the negatively evaluated aspects of the self. This identification with the negative may block the person from seeing alternatives and being able to respond with psychological flexibility in a given situation. Let's say the person buys into the conceptualized self feature "I'm a failure" and becomes fused with it. This might preclude the person from seeing other aspects of the situation, such as ways to perform more effectively at work. Please note, however, that attachment to positively evaluated aspects of the conceptualized self, such as "I'm successful," is also problematic. This might be made clearer with the following exercise.

Exercise 7.3: Mental Polarity

1. Think of three characteristics about yourself.

2. Write each characteristic down and list its opposite.

3. Each time you list one characteristic, on the next line, take that up one level of intensity. For example, if you characterize yourself as intelligent, take that up to the level of brilliant on the next line. Attractive would go up to beautiful.

4. Remember, as you list each characteristic, also attach its opposite in the second column. (Table 7.1)

Characteristic	Its opposite
Example of characteristic:	Dim
Example of characteristic notched up:	
1a.	
1b.	
2a.	
2b.	
3a.	
3b.	

Table 7.1

🔔 [Notice what showed up as you did this exercise.]

As you label things, you are always tied to their opposites. Having one side of the pole always brings in the other. So if you identified yourself as pretty, that is connected to being unattractive and, in a sense, you become tied to avoiding the opposite. The more we come to believe that these words define who we are, the more we are tied to a more superficial sense of ourselves. These labels can then become very important to us and have a sig-

312

nificant impact on how we interact in the world.

The basic message is this: If your self is identified by these characteristics, you are always stuck at the level of content, and content is always connected to evaluation and liking or disliking. Further, becoming fused with these labels, even positive ones, can render you vulnerable to responding poorly to life's curveballs. Let's say that you are someone who is very attached to "I'm beautiful" as a conceptualized self, and then you suffer a disfiguring car accident. Who are you then?

Our goal here is to help you to identify with a different level of self that is more transcendent than language or labels.

Self as Awareness

In ACT we also talk about another sense of self: self as awareness. This self is seen as a process of being aware of our ongoing experience (Hayes, Strosahl, and Wilson 1999; Hayes and Smith 2005). This process may be thought of as an internal set of steps that transforms our experience. Essentially, this is our ongoing sense of what we are experiencing in the moment: "Now, I'm having this thought" or "Now, I'm doing that" This part of our experience can include things such as noticing what we are feeling or thinking in the current moment. For example, you might be noticing that you are cold or tired or that you are feeling sad. Being able to notice our experiences and label them is at the core of self as awareness. Like everything we have been discussing in this book, this sense of self is a learned experience that can change. In fact, learning to be aware or present in your life is a key element in learning to deal with your trauma. As a person who has survived a traumatic experience, you may feel numb or disconnected from both your inside and outside experiences (Bryant 2006), and this may have hindered your ability to develop this sense of self as awareness. This may be particularly true if your trauma happened as a child. Many researchers have suggested that children are especially able to separate from their feelings or bodies, in a sense disconnecting from the world around them. As discussed in chapter 1, this capacity to pull away from your experience is sometimes called dissociation. 🔔[If your attention wanders, gently bring it back to reading this page.]

There is nothing magical about the phenomenon of dissociation; it is simply a way of disconnecting from painful experiences. People talk about this coping strategy in lots of different ways.

They may have a sense of lost time, floating above a room, or being disconnected from their bodies. Not surprisingly, people who experience repeated and severe traumas may find themselves doing this more and more frequently as they try to cope. Dissociation as a way of dealing with traumatic experiences is essentially a way to disconnect from your current contact with thoughts, emotions, and physical feelings. This is one of those strategies that can work in the short run but in the long run ends up shortchanging important aspects of your life, as well as increasing your risk for revictimization (Cloitre and Rosenberg 2006). It doesn't seem to be the case that people can selectively remove contact with only the negatively evaluated thoughts and feelings through dissociation. Rather, people end up feeling numb and disconnected from all parts of their experience. So people don't experience pain—but they also don't experience joy. There is a vague sense of disconnect from the world, as if you are looking at it through a foggy pair of glasses. This idea of contact with the present moment is what we discussed in detail in chapter 2 when we explored mindfulness. And to reiterate the point, being mindful—present or aware—is a skill that takes daily practice.

An important part of being mindful or aware is the ability to have a sense of your physical body. A lack of physical awareness can be particularly salient to trauma survivors. You may have been injured or experienced a great deal of pain as a part of the trauma. Physical or sexual abuse as a child is frequently associated with extremely painful bodily sensations (Polusny and Follette 1995). But these sensations can also be the result of accidents, combat, and a variety of other traumatic experiences. As a coping mechanism, you may have learned to disconnect from all physical sensations.

Exercise 7.4: Awareness of Your Body

This exercise is from Hayes and Smith's book *Get Out of Your Mind and Into Your Life* (2005) and is used with permission.

We would like you to take the next few minutes to track your bodily sensations as they come and go. On the next page you will find a figure of the human body. To the left of this diagram is a list of words that describe various sensations that commonly arise in the human body. To do this exercise, take a few moments to center yourself.

Then start to notice the different sensations that come up in your body. Perhaps your back aches from lifting too much at work. Or perhaps your stomach is knotted up with nervousness. Just notice how your body feels.

As the feelings arise, use your left hand to point to the word on the left-hand side of the page that most accurately describes your feeling. With your right hand, point to the place in your body where the sensation resides. For example, if your shoulders are tight, you would point to the word "tight" with your left index finger and to the shoulder in the diagram with your right index finger. Take five minutes to notice bodily sensations as they come in and go out of your body now.

This exercise will be awkward at first (especially since initially you will need to search for the words). As you repeat it, however, it will become more fluid and you will be able to focus on observing, while allowing your fingers to do the "describing."

Self as Context

The third sense of self is the self as context (Hayes, Strosahl, and Wilson 1999; Hayes and

Smith 2005). This is not a concept that is frequently considered in everyday life, and frankly, it's a bit tricky to describe with words. We talk about this self in a variety of ways, most commonly as the self as context, but also as the observer self. This is the core sense of "you" as a place from which observations are made—the you that has always been present and is not defined by your history, labels, thoughts, feelings, or really anything that is typically of our physical or verbal world. As young children, we learn not just that we see things, but that we see them from a consistent locus or perspective: I, here, now. Once you learn you see from "here," for example, everywhere you go, that "here" follows. Once you see that now is "now," everything you experience you experience now (not then, not in the past, not in the future). And finally, once you learn a consistent sense of "I"—the person behind your eyes, who is aware—you are "I" forever.

Self as context is not content, it is the place from which observations are made. At first, this may sound similar to self as awareness. However, the observer self is more encompassing than that. If you think of the three senses of self we are discussing here—conceptualized self, self as awareness, and self as context—think of each as layers in an expanding circle of awareness, with self as context being the last, all-encompassing one. Although this sense of self can only be truly understood through experience and not words, one way to draw the distinction between self as context and self as awareness is this: (Image 7.1)

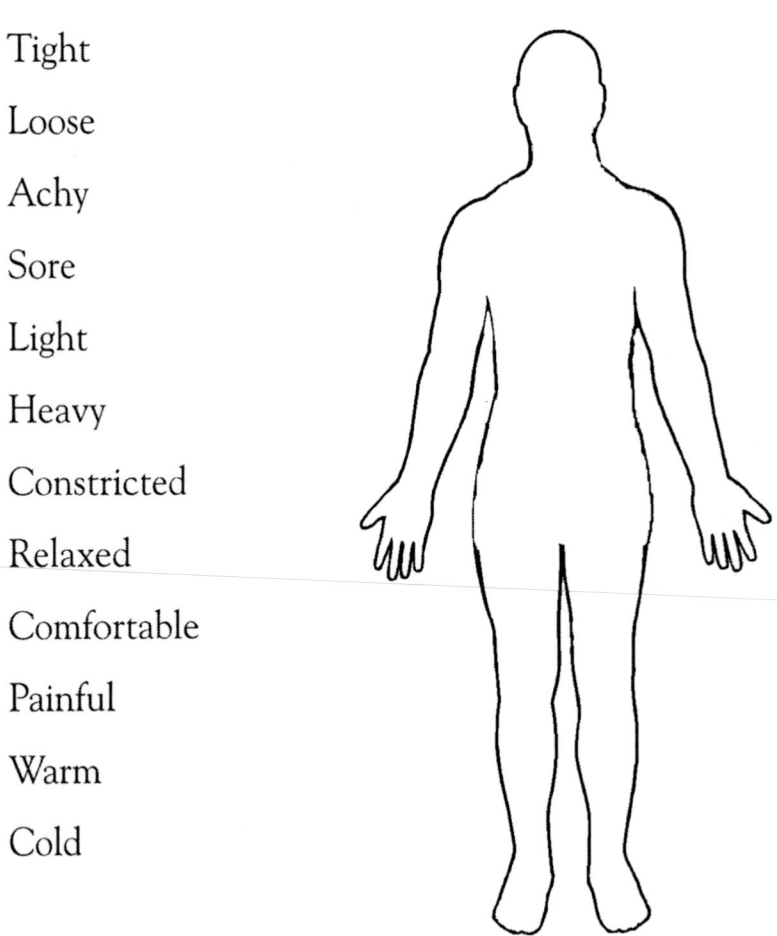

Tight

Loose

Achy

Sore

Light

Heavy

Constricted

Relaxed

Comfortable

Painful

Warm

Cold

Image 7.1

When you are saying to yourself, "Now, I'm feeling this," or "Now, I'm doing that" (self as awareness), can you make contact with the fact that there is a you there who is noticing that you are noticing (self as context)? We don't have the ability to measure or put clearly identifiable labels on this sense of self. And you may not have a full awareness or contact with this part of you, although it has always been there and, to an extent, you have always known it. It is a matter of reminding yourself of that fact. It's sort of like when you know there is something you've forgotten, even if you don't what it is. It's in the back of your mind, even though you cannot wrap words around it. This sense of self, albeit a bit nebulous to you at this point, will in fact be extremely helpful to you in finding life after trauma, as it will provide you a predictable and constant place from which to experience life, however turbulent that life may be. As we stated above, however, this sense of self is better contacted through experience than intellectual understanding. At this point we want you to try an exercise that we use to help people experience self as context (Hayes, Strosahl, and Wilson 1999; Hayes and Smith 2005).

Exercise 7.5: Experiencing the Observing Self

1. First, read the instructions below. Don't do the meditation right away. Read through it first.

The goal of this meditative exercise is to be able to notice who is underneath all your external layers. You can't do this exercise incorrectly. Your experience of this type of exercise will change over time. Just start where you are now, with whatever understanding you've gleaned so far. Read through this exercise and just go through it in your mind. You don't have to remember every single part—just go with a general sense of noticing yourself and your process. You do not have to do this exercise in an exact way to get a sense of your observer self.

Find a comfortable place to sit where you will not be disturbed. You can do this exercise with your eyes open or closed. Some of our clients have told us that they feel too vulnerable if they close their eyes. That's fine—either way will work. If you prefer to keep your eyes open, find a place on the floor on which to fix your gaze so that you don't get too distracted by your surroundings. First, just notice yourself sitting in the room you are in. Notice or picture the shape of the room and where you are sitting in it. Be aware of the chair you're sitting in.

Now go inside of yourself and just notice yourself sitting in the chair. Notice your legs against the chair, your back touching the chair, and your feet on the floor. Take a moment to notice how it feels to just sit in this chair. Notice that at times your body feels comfortable; at other times uncomfortable. Your body experiences many different sensations: cold, warmth, relaxation, tension, fatigue, and more. So, your bodily sensations are many and constantly changing. See if you can notice as a fact that there is a *you* noticing all these bodily sensations. Your body is yours, but you are not just your body.

Now, shift your attention to your mind. It may well be chattering away, saying all kinds of things. It might comment that this is stupid or that you can't do this or that you'd better get up and do the housework. You know how your mind is—talk, talk, talk. That's okay. You don't have to stop it or change it. Just notice it. Sometimes it helps to just gently label these thoughts as "Thinking." Notice that there are many thoughts going through your mind; they are constantly changing. Yet, there is a you noticing all these thoughts.

Now, see if you can notice that you have many emotions, and they are constantly changing: sadness, happiness, boredom, interest, joy, guilt, shame, envy, relief. You have many emotions, but you are more than just your emotions. There is a part of you that remains the same even though your emotions are constantly changing.

Now, shift your attention to the fact that you have many roles in your life. You may play the role of father or mother, sister or brother, grandmother or grandfather, son or daughter, student or teacher, friend, partner, coworker, secretary, or doctor, and right now you are playing the role of the reader. You have many roles, and they are constantly changing. Yet, notice that there is a you that can notice all these roles and stays the same.

As you do this exercise, notice the part of you that is noticing the chair, your skin, the thoughts, the emotions, and the roles—the you that is just observing.

Now, we want you to remember something that happened last winter. Just pick a neutral event. Bring the situation to mind and remember where you were. Mentally look around and really notice the setting you were in. Were there any other people there? Just notice them. Remember the sounds, the scents, and the colors. Remember how you felt and what you heard. As you remember all of this, see if you can notice the person behind your eyes who was there having that experience. There was a you present that experienced those moments in time last winter, just as there is a you here now, doing this exercise. See if you can notice that there is a you that is constant, that was there last winter and is here now. A you that was and is in contact with your bodily sensations, thoughts, feelings, memories, and roles, but that is not *just* your bodily sensations, thoughts, feelings, memories, and roles. See if you can sense this as an experience, not a thought or belief.

Now come back to this room and again notice yourself sitting in this chair, in this room, at this time. Come back to this time and place.

A word of caution: As we discussed earlier, some trauma survivors develop a way of dissociating from their bodies and minds as a way of coping with the trauma while it is happening (Bryant 2006). This is *not* what we are asking you to do with this exercise. 🔔 [Pay attention to your breathing at this moment. Where is your mind taking you?] Although we use the term "observing," the quality of the experience is more like the "connecting" self, that part that is aware of all these experiences and yet is not just these experiences. We are asking you to stay connected and present with these various aspects of yourself. If you find yourself simply dissociating, gently bring your mind back to the task at hand. Mindfulness is the opposite of dissociation: it is about being present to the moment, whatever it has to offer, like the sand that receives the waves at the beach or the lawn that receives rain, snow, or sunshine. The beach and the lawn are in contact with their experience AND they don't need to do anything about it. The quality is of being awake and having clarity. If it feels foggy and detached, gently bring your mind back to this present moment.

2. Now, before actually doing the exercise, you may want to review the instructions above. After rereading the instructions, go ahead and proceed with closing your eyes or directing your gaze to the floor and doing the exercise. It's okay if you do not do it exactly in the order or manner we suggested above the first time you do this exercise. Ideally, you will engage in it several times. For now, do the best you can and let go of any judgments toward yourself.

3. After actually engaging in the exercise, take some time to write your thoughts about the experience of trying to connect with your self as context. Just let this experience percolate a little bit as you continue on with your day. [space left intentionally blank in the original book]

Try this exercise a few times just as described above. If intrusive thoughts or images pop up, just notice those and try again to come in contact with that part of your self that is constant and noticing that you are noticing everything. As mentioned earlier, there is no wrong way to do this—it is just a matter of sitting with it for a while and getting a sense of your self as context or observer self. After you've done the meditation a few times, we want you to try this again with some parts added to it this time.

Exercise 7.6: Observer Perspective with Teenage Memory

Start in the same way as in exercise 7.5, using the same directions. This time, after you have considered a more recent experience, go back to an experience that happened when you were a teenager. For now, just stay with a neutral or mildly positive experience. You might think of a time when you were in school. Think of the environment you were in, noticing all the sights and sounds and scents around you. Take some time to really see what things looked like. Who was there? How were they dressed? Was there music or talking? Really let yourself be in that experience. Notice yourself, too. What did you look like? What were you wearing? Was your hair long or short? Notice your thoughts and feelings at that time. Can you remember what it was like to be that age? 🔔[Pay attention to your breathing at this moment.] And now, once again see if you can notice the person behind your eyes at that time (both the teenager and the you right now), the person looking out who is seeing and observing all of these events. Notice that there was a you there that has been there all along: a you that has been there when you were young, as you got older, and now; a you that has lived this life and experienced all of these feelings. Just take some time to try to catch that sense of you. You may notice that it's elusive, but over time you will have more glimmers of this you. And again, bring yourself back to this time, noticing this room, this place, where you are sitting right now.

Wherever you are with finding your observer self is just fine. For some people it's easy to sense, and others have a very difficult time coming into contact with this self. But over time, as you practice, you will notice that there is always a you who has not changed, even as your body and roles and thoughts and feelings have changed. Everything around you can be different and there is still a you that remains a continuous self. As you go through your daily life, see if you can take little opportunities to practice this—to notice the you that is noticing the world around you. This ability to have some distance helps us to be aware of ourselves in a new way.

Learning to do this can be a bit tough. Sometimes going back and practicing some of the basic mindfulness skills in chapter 2 can be a help in this endeavor. The ability to just be and notice your thoughts as thoughts, feelings as feelings, and objects in your environment is good practice. In fact, some people devote a lifetime to this practice. But don't worry—you can get there from here without moving to a monastery! You don't need to master this ability to contact your self as context before you go on. But don't just leave it behind either. Come back to this practice and notice how it changes over time. In fact, some of our clients tape-record this exercise so that they can do the exercise repeatedly, and we would encourage you to do the same.

Exercise 7.7: Noticing the You Across Time

	Photo 1	Photo 2	Photo 3
Brief description: age, event, and what was going on in your life.			
What bodily sensations might you have been experiencing?			
What thoughts might you have been having?			
What emotions or feelings might you have been having?			
What memories might have been coming up at that time?			
What roles might you have been playing at that time?			

Table 7.2

1. Get three photos of yourself that you are willing to cut up. Ideally, we recommend selecting photos from different stages in your life: one from when you were between five and ten, one from between thirteen and eighteen, and one from recent years. If you

don't have photos from these periods, feel free to get any three photos, as long as they are at least a year apart.

A word of caution: This exercise may stir up difficult feelings for some of you. If you feel this is too much, feel free to proceed to the next exercise and skip this one. However, if you are able and willing to engage in this exercise, it may be helpful to you.

2. Glue your three photos into the following three oval spaces.

3. Below each photo, write about the experience that you remember or that you assume you might have had around that time: bodily sensations, thoughts, feelings, memories, and roles. (Table 7.2)

4. Can you make contact with the fact that, although these photos are from different times in your life, with different bodily sensations, thoughts, feelings, memories, and roles, there was a part of you that remained constant?

Exercise 7.8: Reactions to the Concept of the Transcendent Self

What if you are not just your bodily sensations, your thoughts, your feelings, your memories, and your roles? Notice what you are feeling right now.

We have talked about a variety of perspectives on who you are, but we have come back again to this idea that you are more than your thoughts and feelings and all the rest of the labels the world attaches to you. This is a radical way of looking at things. Take a few minutes to write about your reactions to reading this. What would happen if you gave up all these ideas of who you are and found a way to start from a different place?

[space left intentionally blank in the original book]

You may have come into contact with some fear about letting go of some of these labels. Some of them seem good to you. And there's the rub. It's like you have these good labels and bad ones and they are in there struggling to win the war inside you. But this might be better explained using a metaphor.

The Chessboard Metaphor

Imagine a chessboard spreading out to infinity in all directions (Hayes, Strosahl, and Wilson 1999; Hayes and Smith 2005). All the different pieces are placed on this board. Some are black and some are white, just as in a chess game. Also, just as in the game of chess, these pieces begin to form themselves into teams. These pieces represent your thoughts, feelings, sensations, evaluations, and memories. Some of the thoughts are things we label as positive, such as memories of happy times we've had with friends, feelings of joy, thoughts about success at work or school, or sensations associated with being relaxed. On the other team are the things that are seen as negative, such as feeling depressed, memories about traumatic events or abuse, thoughts of being lonely, and even physical sensations of pain. In our experience, everyone's teams have some similar aspects—the usual suspects. While everyone does not have the same trauma experience or history, it is amazing how similar we are in feelings of inadequacy, sadness, and a sense of being alone.

The different pieces begin to work as teams, doing battle with each other. The battle can consume our lives with the efforts to get rid of all the negatively evaluated pieces. We try hard to not be depressed, not to think about our painful history, not to notice feeling angry at our situation. We work diligently to get rid of all the painful, negative stuff that we don't want to be there.

We try to stay on the good team, riding the back of the white knight and doing battle with all the black pieces (the negative stuff). In a sense, it feels like we need to be on the back of the white king or queen, trying to stay upbeat and positive and thinking only thoughts we perceive as good.

If you have seen *Harry Potter and the Sorcerer's Stone* (2001), we encourage you to picture this metaphor as the scene where Harry and his friends are faced with the challenge of winning a chess game. During this scene, you will remember that even to the audience, when the characters were riding their own chess pieces, which were being attacked by the pieces on the other team, if felt very scary. We knew that unless they made the right move, the piece, and the rider along with it, would be killed.

In the movie, that was the way it actually was. However, in our own minds, it doesn't have to be that way. 🔔[Notice any reactions coming up.] The white pieces (say, confidence, happiness, and thoughts of "I'm great") do not need to win or beat the black pieces (say, sadness, feelings of inadequacy, or perhaps even a thought of "I hate her!"). Yet, it often feels like they do—that if we don't stomp out the black pieces, we will somehow be destroyed.

We stay in this battle as if our lives depended on it. Because it feels like our lives *do* depend on it. It feels as though someone criticizing us may bust us apart. It seems like, if we or others judge us as ugly, incompetent, or lazy, we will shrivel up and die. Therefore, we feel we have to work hard at keeping these pieces at bay. It can feel like all the good stuff will be overcome by the negatives, and we will be lost, that there will be no battle left to fight. And it's not surprising that we feel this way. We have been taught all of our lives that this is the way to be. It is not just in your head—our culture teaches us this. We're supposed to clean house, get rid of all the dirty, negative, bad stuff and just shine with clean, positive thoughts and feelings.

However, what if we looked at this chess game from a different perspective? What if inside our own skin, the chess game is not like the one in the Harry Potter movie? What if, although it feels like your life is on the line, in fact it isn't? What if, unlike the much admired teenage wizard, you *don't* have to ride on the back of the white queen?

Consider that you don't need to defend or defend against pieces like "I'm a failure" or "I am the best student in the class" or "I'm right and he's wrong." What would it mean to your life if you weren't the pieces, not the thoughts of "I am good" or "I am bad"? What if, instead of being on the back of each piece, you are the *board* on which this game is being played?

If you are not defined by these pieces that we label good or bad, black or white, and you are the board, then you are the "context" that holds and encompasses all of these thoughts, feelings, sensations, evaluations, and memories. You can be in intimate contact with all of these pieces—in fact, that is an important part of the process. You don't need to distance or dissociate or pull away from any of this. In fact, pulling away would just be another way of playing out the battle. So, part of letting go of the battle is beginning to see yourself at board level.

If it feels scary to give up the battle, like you need to defend yourself against a particular thought, experience, memory, bodily sensation, or view of yourself, then consider the possibility that you are stuck at the "piece" level, and unlike Potter and his friends, you don't need to be. The pieces cannot harm the board (you). 🔔[Notice any thoughts coming up.] However, the way things work inside the skin is that if you get fused with the content of some of these thoughts and feelings, it is almost like a virtual reality game gets launched without your approval or full awareness, and all of a sudden it feels like slaying sadness or finding a way of getting rid of the thought "I'm a failure" is a matter of life and death. The way to turn off the virtual reality game is to get yourself back at the board level. Although your mind may say it's so, see if you can become aware, not as a thought but as a fact, that you are *not* riding on the back of the white queen ("I'm competent at my work"), nor does that piece need to be saved from the black queen ("You're a failure"). They are both on your board, and you are aware of both. One is not better than the other—they are both just pieces on your board. Neither needs to be killed, destroyed, or otherwise suppressed.

So, as the chessboard, what can you do? You can hold all of these pieces and decide to move in a direction that is consistent with your valued life.

You don't have to get rid of your history or your pain or your sadness to move forward. In fact, you probably already have some experience of that if you think about it. Most people can identify times when they moved forward with their life even when it was hard and they didn't feel like doing it. This is something like that but on a more radical level.

You can decide to live your life at the level of the board and move forward in a conscious way with your life. You can also go back and forth between board and piece level. Don't worry. No one we know can be at the board level all the time. In fact, we sometimes joke with each other about being at piece level. Like everything else in life, it is a process of moving back and forth, with the goal of spending more time at board level.

Exercise 7.9: Reactions to Being at Board Level

Notice what shows up for you right now. Just sit with this idea of being at board level for a bit. Notice it as not just a thought but as an experience of who you could be. After you sit with it for a few minutes, write about your response to what it would be like to walk away from the battle and be at the level of the board.

[space left intentionally blank in the original book]

One of the things that you may have been wondering as you read through all of this is how it relates to your trauma experience. In fact, these concepts are important to everyone who is struggling with some aspect of life, not just trauma survivors. AND we know that you or someone close to you has experienced something very painful that has led you to read this book. An exercise that might be helpful to you at this point is to understand when and how you are most likely to get caught at the piece level. Which are the pieces you find yourself trying to defend (white pieces) or push off the board (black pieces)?

Writing about your history may help you with this process.

Exercise 7.10: Writing About Your Trauma History

At this point we want you to take some time to write about your traumatic experience. This is not just about the what, who, when, and how. This is also about your responses to what happened. This is to be emotional writing. You are to write about your deepest thoughts and feelings about your experience. Your goal is to be willing to write whatever comes up for you in relation to the event. Just write about anything that comes up related to the trauma, making sure to include your emotions as part of this writing.

Do your best to take care of yourself as you do this work. We cannot be there with you, and we are very aware that this can be hard to go through on your own. But our experience tells us that you *can* do this. A great deal has been written on the benefits of writing about and coming into contact with your trauma experience. That being said, be mindful of how this experience is going for you. If you ever feel unsafe or that you need outside support completing this process, please honor that feeling. We know you have gone through the worst—you have survived your experience. AND we want you to get the support of a friend or even a therapist if you find the process too difficult on your own. This is about finding a middle path. It is not that you are broken or unable to do this. Haven't you been doing it for a substantial portion of your life—living with these thoughts, feelings, and memories that are so painful? So you have already done some of the hardest part of this work. Some people will find that they are able to progress through this exercise on their own, and others will feel like it would help to have someone to act as a sort of coach as they walk through it. Neither way is better. It is just a choice. We are asking you to be aware of your own needs, approaching this work mindfully and with compassion for yourself.

There are some special instructions here to note closely. James Pennebaker has written an important book called *Writing to Heal* (2004), and we are using instructions very similar to his with his permission. Pennebaker has a long history of research in this area, and the data indicate that writing can have a very beneficial impact. There are several guidelines that he has developed:

• Write for twenty minutes each day. You can write for more than twenty minutes, but in general you should not go over forty minutes the first time you write about your trauma history

• Write every day for four days in a row. The amount of time you write and the number of days are both important and seem to be a part of the healing process.

• Write continuously. Don't worry about being grammatically correct or even having it make sense. The goal is to write. If you run out of things to say, just repeat things.

• Write only for yourself. This is not for anyone else, so do not write a letter or give it to anyone. It is only for you. Start with a traumatic experience that is at a medium or low level of intensity. We don't start with the highest intensity experience in this work. Write about something that you are willing to experience now.

• The length of your description will vary, so you need to write it on your own paper, not in this book. Also, this written description may be something you want to be able to destroy when you are done.

• Begin your writing days now, and after each writing episode use the following guide to rate your writing (Pennebaker 2004).

Each day after writing, on a separate piece of paper, answer the following three questions by rating your experience using a scale of 0 to 10, where 0 is not at all and 10 is a great deal:

1. To what degree did you express your deepest thoughts and feelings?

2. To what degree are you having intense feelings?

3. To what degree was today's writing valuable and meaningful for you?

Whatever you felt, it is okay. This is part of your process. If this writing exercise has been helpful to you, pick another experience and write about it in the same way for four days.

Then stop. Assess the process. Writing can be used to deal with any number of current and past stressors. If this process is useful for you, continue to use it when you think it might help. If it is not something that seems useful, let it go. Writing in this way is a tool, and like any tool its utility depends on the person using it and the situation. The goal of this writing is to have some contact with your experience in a safe setting. This writing can give you a chance to look at what happened to you and to see that it was an event that is separate from you at the level of self. This is just one part of the work. If it is useful to you, you might want to look at Pennebaker's book *Writing to Heal* (2004) for more suggestions.

Now, we want you to take some time to consider what you wrote about in light of what we have been discussing in this chapter. Can you take a different perspective on this part of your life? Can you experience this story as the observer, as self as context, having the sense of it as something that happened to you but not as something that defines you or *is* you?

This is part of your history, and at the board level you can be in contact with this experience and move forward in a valued direction in your life. Remember, there is a you there that is not defined by your thoughts, feelings, or even your history. You don't have to get rid of or change your history to move forward with your life. The event you wrote about may well be an important part of your life, but it is not you. No matter how big it was, you are more than any part of your history or experience.

The work of this chapter is central to the process of acceptance and change. These exercises were designed with several goals in mind: First, we want you to come in contact with the experience of being more than your thoughts, feelings, and memories. A part of this process is also experiencing yourself nonjudgmentally. This entails seeing yourself as you are, not as all the evaluations and labels that you and others have applied to you. Finally, we hope to put you in contact with your history and help you realize that your history is something you have survived. You don't have to get rid of it or change it to live your valued life. Can you bring it along as a passenger on your bus or as a piece on your chessboard without letting it dictate the direction of your bus or your chessboard?

Comparisons, evaluations, and judgments, when taken literally, tend to get us further away from connecting with our selves. Cognitive fusion tempts us into creating a world full of dangers and menacing chess pieces that cannot really harm us, except in our own language-generated virtual-reality minds. This work is about honoring who you are, who you have been, and who you are becoming.

Journaling

Thoughts

[space left intentionally blank in the original book]

Feelings or Emotions

[space left intentionally blank in the original book]

Self-Judgments

[space left intentionally blank in the original book]

Physical Sensations

[space left intentionally blank in the original book]

Action Urges (What Do You Feel Like Doing?)

[space left intentionally blank in the original book]

CHAPTER 8

Creating a Valued Life

With Adria Pearson

Live as if you were to die tomorrow.
Learn as if you were to live forever.

—Gandhi

Living Large

Imagine that one day you wake up and realized that you have been living in a comfortable area of about four by eight feet in dimension. You've made it nice and cozy, with a comfortable couch, plush carpet, decorations, music, and so on. You feel fairly comfortable there, but every so often you look up, and with your binoculars you see that a mile away there is a beach. You notice that, although you like your comfortable space, your life is rather limited. You realize that you would really love to feel the waves of the ocean on your legs and the sand beneath your feet, so you start out toward the beach. As you do so, you notice that surrounding your living area there are small pieces of shattered glass scattered around in patches, and you experience a minor cut on one of your feet. Alarmed, you retreat into your old space. You look longingly toward the beach, but thinking back on getting cut, you tell yourself that you don't really care for all that sand anyway and that the water might be cold. You make yourself comfortable in your living area and decide that the solution is to keep busy and not to look out of your small space. That way, you won't notice that you're not at the beach. Perhaps if you work hard enough, eventually you won't even miss the beach anymore.

Working through this book is like raising your eyes, taking a look at your life, and asking yourself if that's enough. 🔔[Any thoughts coming up for you right now?] This chapter is about choosing to move in a direction that you value AND being willing to come into contact with some shards here and there. You may think, "I can manage shards of glass, but it's more like land mines outside my space." We know the risks seem large, and we are talking about getting back your life. In our experience, people often already have an idea about which direction they would like to move toward, but they have become fused with a lot of negative chatter, like "I don't really know that I'll like the beach. What if I get there and don't like it?" or "I can't stand the pain of stepping onto small pieces of glass" or "I like my cozy little space; it's very comfortable" or even "I might die if I go out there. I've already been hurt too badly."

Within this chapter, we will ask you to lift up your head and examine your life. By doing so, you can look in all directions and choose which one you would like to head toward. Values clarification is the process of choosing a life direction (Hayes and Smith 2005; Wilson and Murrell 2004).

When we discussed in chapter 3 that in order to stop adding rings of suffering to your life you might have to sit with pain, we weren't simply talking about feeling your feelings for its own sake. The reason to be present with your feelings is that by doing so, you have a better chance at creating a more meaningful life. We ask you to gauge your willingness to experience the cuts on your feet not because we think there is something inherently good, worthy, or moral about experiencing pain. What if willingness to go forward and take some risks is necessary in order for you to experience the water, the waves, the sand, and the sun at the beach?

Before we progress any further, we would like you to try to do something bold right now.

Exercise 8.1: A Year to Live

Imagine that you walked into your doctor's office and were told that you have one year to live (Hayes, Strosahl, and Wilson 1999). See if you can bring that experience right here, right now, not just as a thought but as an actual possibility. Close your eyes and picture the experience in your mind's eye, noticing what feelings, thoughts, and sensations show up as you imagine this scene. Ask yourself: "What if I only had one year to live? What, if anything, would I do differently?" Please take some time now and write below what comes to your mind, without any censoring or judging.

[space left intentionally blank in the original book]

It is from this perspective, remaining aware of the present moment and the potential that it may be nearly your last moment, that we invite you to continue reading this chapter. Values clarification is not about the future; it is about this very moment. It is about living your life now. As you read through this chapter, your mind may start saying things like "I will do that later, when I have more time, when I feel more confident, when..." Gently thank your mind and bring your attention back to making your life work for you now. The year to live exercise above is a way of helping us get unstuck from thoughts and feelings about the past and the future that distance us from the present moment and what we really value. In fact, we never know how much time we do have left, and there is much to be gained in living as if we were to die tomorrow, as Gandhi aptly put it in the quote at the beginning of this chapter.

What Are Values?

Before starting the process of values clarification, we need to define values. Values are chosen life directions (Hayes and Smith 2005; Wilson and Murrell 2004). They are not right or wrong. They don't need to be explained, defended, or argued about. They are not goals. They are not feelings. They are not what others want from you; they are what you want for yourself and from others. They are not another reason for beating yourself up. Knowing your values should empower you, not make you feel bad about yourself in a paralyzing way. Values are continuous; they are more about process than outcome. Values can give dignity and meaning to your life, even when the desired outcome is not reached. We will explain these characteristics of values in more detail below.

Values Cannot Be Right or Wrong

🔔 [Any thoughts or judgments coming up?]

We view values as choices, so they are not about being right or wrong. This is a different sense of values than as traditionally defined in religion, although those traditions might well inform your personal values. The ACT perspective is that the values that are right for you are the ones that work for you in creating a meaningful, vital life. While it might seem a trivial example, choosing your values is almost like choosing a favorite color. People around you may prefer white, blue, or green, while you may choose yellow. Which one is right? None of them. This is a subjective choice. It does not have to be defended. I choose yellow because ... What can you possibly say that would absolutely convince someone else and change their views?

When we say that there are no right values, you might think, "What about people who do bad things to others?" In our experience, we have never met anyone who claims that they truly value hurting others as much as possible or doing other destructive things. They may have hurt others, but we have not heard people declare that this is what they would like their lives to be about, had they a year left to live. Even among individuals who have committed horrible crimes, we don't usually see that. Now, there could be people out there with such values; all we are saying is that we haven't met them yet. Even if you personally have hurt others, the very fact that you are reading this book probably indicates that this is not what you want your life to be about. You're looking for a different way. Our experience is that there tends to be some similarity in terms of values across individuals, with most people choosing values that are life affirming. We really encourage you to look at your life long and hard and choose which values are important to you for your own sake, not because someone else told you that you should have that value.

Values Are Not Goals

A value is different from a goal (Hayes, Strosahl, and Wilson 1999). Going back to our bus metaphor, a goal might be to get to San Francisco from Reno. A value might be to head west. This distinction may seem odd, so we'll give you some context for this idea.

Goals can be achieved, finished, completed. If our goal was to get to San Francisco and we look up and find ourselves by the Golden Gate Bridge, we could say that we accomplished our goal. If I have as a goal getting a degree in psychology and I get that piece of paper that says I have a college degree, my goal is accomplished.

Values are never finally, completely accomplished. If I value heading west and I get to San Francisco, I can catch a boat or plane and continue heading west. If I value learning and improving myself, that value does not go away after graduation. There will always be more learning to do: I can read the paper each morning, watch the news, attend workshops, listen attentively to colleagues with more experience, or buy a book like *Finding Life Beyond Trauma* to continue my education.

Values can start right here and right now. If I want to head west, I can do so right this second. Goals frequently involve planning and waiting. For example, I cannot be in San Francisco right now. Values are a direction, not a destination, and therefore are always available to you. At any point in you life, you can stop and answer the question "Am I headed in my valued direction?" even if you are not yet at your final destination. You can start living your values the moment you start planning the trip to San Francisco. That's already about heading west.

Let's consider the situation of a survivor of sexual assault who has not dated since the incident for fear of being pressured for sexual intimacy. While this strategy has "worked" so far, this woman is feeling increasingly lonely and isolated. She might become aware that she values what could potentially come from an emotionally intimate relationship: human connection and companionship. 🔔[Notice any action urges right now? What do you feel like doing at this moment?] In living the value of connection and relationship, she might come up with several goals. She might make a goal to go on a date with someone. Even within this goal, there might be several steps. Here are some examples:

- Joining clubs or organizations where I can meet different people

- Socializing with others on group dates

- Identifying qualities I like and dislike in a potential romantic partner

- Identifying a person I am interested in

- Meeting for coffee (a date alone!)

As you can see, several steps (or goals) might take place before the larger goal is met. Each goal can be done, finished. She could check off "Meeting for coffee." However, all these goals are driven by the same value: human connection and companionship, which is a continuous direction. AND we want to be clear that you get to choose your values. There are many ways to be connected and close to someone without being in a romantic relationship. This is just one direction that some people choose.

Values Are About Process, Not Outcome

Values are a direction, not an outcome (Hayes, Strosahl, and Wilson 1999). If the goal was to get to the bottom of the mountain, why would any of us go skiing or snowboarding? Although one is headed toward the bottom of the mountain, the goal in skiing is about the experience of skiing: feeling the wind in your face, sensing your body making turns, and being in touch with nature. Often in life, process and outcome get confused for us. If you value learning, then all other things being the same, how long it's taking to get your degree is not the crucial factor unless spending several years in school conflicts with another value. Don't worry, we know how quickly such confusion can happen—sometimes both of us just wanted to get out of school!

Here's another example of how outcome and process are not the same: Let's imagine that you tell yourself that you want to have a child and, thanks to a magic wand, it's twenty years later and you have someone calling you Mom or Dad but you can't remember anything about raising that child into an adult. Is this what you meant by wanting to have a child? Probably not. Usually, we want that experience, however difficult, of going through the milestones of raising that child. This highlights the fact that often, although we focus on an outcome, the process itself is what's desired.

As most of us know from experience, larger goals may not actually occur right away. All kinds of things can get in the way. The point is, by walking through the different steps along the way, you are participating in value-driven behavior. At any point during your life, you can know whether or not you are living your values: are you headed west?

While participating in value-driven behavior does not guarantee outcomes, you are much more likely to reach your goals when behaving in valued ways. If I continue heading west, I will probably eventually get closer to San Francisco—assuming similar latitude. Also, by engaging in various value-driven actions you can learn more about what you want in a valued domain. The ultimate question becomes, "What do you want your life to be about?" 🔔[Pay attention to your breathing at this moment.]

Straying from the Path

One of the concerns that we have about discussing values is that this will be just one more way for you to judge yourself as inadequate or not living up to some standard. Although you may be pleased to see the work you've done in some areas of your life, the process of values clarification will inevitably show some areas that you want to change. This may lead to feelings of sadness, fear, and self-judgment. Author E.L. Doctorow said, "writing a novel is like driving a car at night. You can only see as far as your headlights, but you can make the whole trip this way" (Lamott 1994, 18). Just like an author noticing things he or she wants to change while writing, you will probably see things you want in your life that you don't have or ways that you are not living out your values. Can this values clarification exercise be a light to show you the way along your path, one step at a time? See if you can resist the urge to condemn yourself with criticism and self-judgment if you see things about yourself that you don't like. Remember that none of us are *always* living in full accordance with our values. That would be impossible. On occasion, we will all let ourselves and others down. We will lie, be unkind, be irresponsible, let ourselves be walked all over, drink when we said we wouldn't, or generally betray the very values we espouse. However, that's exactly the reason that clarifying values is so useful. Your values can act like a compass, letting you know when you're headed west and when you aren't.

Now, imagine that you value heading west and you find yourself headed east (Hayes, Strosahl, and Wilson 1999; Wilson and Murrell 2004). Let's say you think you're headed toward San Francisco from Reno when you see a sign saying "Interstate 80 East." What should you do then? One temptation might be to continue driving, thinking that you must have read the sign wrong, and then look away when the next sign approaches. Or, you might continue heading east, saying to yourself, "That was so dumb!" or "If I turn around now, how much time will I have wasted going in the wrong direction?" or "What if I get off here and can't find the entrance to I-80 West?" Let's imagine that you have indeed driven 100 miles east AND you want to head west. What's the thing to do? Turn around, right? What if you do turn around, but due to road construction and other issues, you find yourself again heading east? What should you do then? Unless your values have changed, head west again! Have you stopped valuing heading west just because you got turned around once or twice, or even for years? 🔔[Notice what feelings and thoughts are coming up right now.]

Yet, isn't it the case that most of us spend enormous effort chastising ourselves for heading in the wrong direction, not turning around earlier, and "wasting" time and effort? Sometimes we even think we should keep going just because we have already invested time in this direction. From the ACT point of view, it's never too late. There is only this present moment, and you can choose to live it in accordance with your values right now.

How you feel about the direction in which you're headed may not always feel good. Sometimes going west is a painful or uncomfortable experience, like starting or ending a relationship or changing careers. Allowing yourself to get close to another person, for example, may feel scary and difficult. Remember, feelings cannot always be trusted to tell you the truth. Pay attention to them, but hold them lightly. In ACT, we suggest that instead of feeling *good,* the focus be on *feeling* good. That is, being aware and in close contact with what is going on with you, which may be joyful or painful, instead of focusing on having exclusively pleasant experiences. As we discussed in chapter 2, feelings may be the actual scene, or they may very well just be the painting on the canvas. Finding one's true values may feel peaceful, but if the experience is relief instead of peace, look closer. Is your fear driving this "value"?

Another way to look at this issue is that we don't have to have the desired feeling to behave according to our values. You can be experiencing anger toward your partner and still behave lovingly. Someone can be dissatisfied with a job and still go to work. In fact, if we all only went to work when we felt like it, the gross national product would drop considerably. Yet, because we value having the things that work can afford us, such as food, shelter, a sense of accomplishment, connection with others, or making a contribution, most of us go to work even when we don't feel like it. The same applies to other values one might have, such as kindness or honesty. If you only do it when it's easy, when you know people will agree, be proud, and not be upset with you, you're not truly following your values. You're following your feelings. The rest of this chapter will consist of exercises to help you sort out your values and determine how well you're living them.

What Are Your Values?

Below, we will ask you to identify key values in seven major areas of your life: family, work or school, friendships, romantic relationships, leisure, spirituality, and self. (This exercise was adapted from work by Blackledge and Ciarrochi 2006, who built on the work of Sheldon and Elliot 1992, and from work by Wilson and Murrell 2004.) Remember, there is no right or wrong way to do this. 🔔[What is the chatter in your mind right now?] This process is about identifying a direction that *you* want to pursue and not what others would like you to do. You may end up with a description of something that you'd like in your life that you are not yet doing or not yet doing well. That's okay. This work is about your choosing a direction you want to go toward. A shortcut instruction for this exercise is this: If nobody knew what you chose to pursue in your life and there were no internal barriers, such as fear or lack of confidence, what would you really want your life to stand for?

Exercise 8.2: Clarifying and Rating Your Values

1. Read the description of each of the seven areas below and write down a value for each one. Here are a few suggestions that may be helpful:

• If you believe that an area does not pertain to you, such as romantic relationships or spirituality, you may skip it. But remember that just because something is absent from your life right now, it does not mean that you don't value it. Ask yourself whether this is something that you value before you dismiss anything too quickly. On the other hand, you do not have to have something in each area just because we listed them. This is your life and your choice.

• Remember, values are directions, not goals. Here are some examples of values: being honest with a partner, being a good provider for your family, protecting your boundaries, being supportive of friends, continuing to grow emotionally, being kind to all living things, or speaking your truth. These are some life directions we have heard from our clients over the years. However, please choose your own.

• If all you can come up with is an outcome, look for the value behind it. Specific outcomes like having a partner, getting a degree, or belonging to a church, for example, can usually be distilled down to a value. For example, why would having X (a partner, let's say) be important to you? Perhaps you're looking for an emotionally intimate relationship in which you are safe and supported in being who you are. That would be the value.

2. Answer questions 1 through 6 for each value.

3. Calculate Total 1, Total 2, and Total 3 for each value. We will explain how to interpret these numbers at the end of the exercise.

Family

Select an area in your family relations that you would like to explore, or your relationship to a specific family member. This could be about your immediate family, or it could be about your extended family. Examples: behaving kindly, listening to others, having appropriate boundaries, being loyal, or nurturing growth.

When it comes to my family, I want to be about:

[space left intentionally blank in the original book]

Please answer the following questions about the family value you wrote above. The rating scale goes from 1 (not at all for this reason) to 5 (very much for this reason). (Table 8.1)

The reason I identified this family value is because:	
1. I was raised this way, and my parents or other people important to me would be upset if I didn't value this (or pleased to know that I do).	1 2 3 4 5
2. If I didn't value this, I would feel embarrassed, guilty, anxious, or ashamed.	1 2 3 4 5
3. Only a bad or evil person would not value this.	1 2 3 4 5
Total 1 (sum your ratings for the three items above, numbers 1, 2, and 3)	Total 1 = _____

4. This feels important to me from deep inside. Even if nobody knew that I valued this, it would still matter to me.	1 2 3 4 5
5. I experience peace and joy within myself when I behave according to this value.	1 2 3 4 5
6. This lends meaning and vitality to my life.	1 2 3 4 5
Total 2 (sum your ratings for the three items above, numbers 4, 5, 6)	Total 2 = _____
Total 3 (Total 1_____ minus Total 2_____)	Total 3 = _____

Table 8.1

Work or School

This may be about what you value in your work or a career, or going to school. Work for you might be caring for your children, living as part of a religious community, doing volunteer work, or any number of types of endeavors. Feel free to define what work is for you. Find what is consistent with your life and values. Examples: being competent, being reliable, pursuing an area that interests you, enhancing knowledge, helping others, or making a good income.

When it comes to my work, career, or school, what I would like to be about is:

[space left intentionally blank in the original book]

Please answer the following questions about the work value you wrote above. The rating scale goes from 1 (not at all for this reason) to 5 (very much for this reason). (Table 8.2)

The reason I identified this work or school value is because:	
1. I was raised this way and my parents or other people important to me would be upset if I didn't value this (or pleased to know that I do).	1 2 3 4 5
2. If I didn't value this, I would feel embarrassed, guilty, anxious, or ashamed.	1 2 3 4 5
3. Only a bad or evil person would not value this.	1 2 3 4 5
Total 1 (sum your ratings for the three items above, numbers 1, 2, and 3)	Total 1 = _____
4. This feels important to me from deep inside. Even if nobody knew that I valued this, it would still matter to me.	1 2 3 4 5
5. I experience peace and joy within myself when I behave according to this value.	1 2 3 4 5
6. This lends meaning and vitality to my life.	1 2 3 4 5
Total 2 (sum your ratings for the three items above, numbers 4, 5, 6)	Total 2 = _____
Total 3 (Total 1_____ minus Total 2_____)	Total 3 = _____

Table 8.2

Friendships and Other Social Relationships

This area may include friends, coworkers, and others you interact with. It may be about a single relationship you have now or relationships you would like to have. Examples: being a caring person, being reliable, having fun, or being helpful.

When it comes to friendships and other social relationships, what I would like to be about is:

[space left intentionally blank in the original book]

Please answer the following questions about the friendship value you wrote above. The rating scale goes from 1 (not at all for this reason) to 5 (very much for this reason). (Table 8.3)

The reason I identified this friendship or social relationship value is because:	
1. I was raised this way and my parents or other people important to me would be upset if I didn't value this (or pleased to know that I do).	1 2 3 4 5
2. If I didn't value this, I would feel embarrassed, guilty, anxious, or ashamed.	1 2 3 4 5
3. Only a bad or evil person would not value this.	1 2 3 4 5
Total 1 (sum your ratings for the three items above, numbers 1, 2, and 3)	Total 1 = _____
4. This feels important to me from deep inside. Even if nobody knew that I valued this, it would still matter to me.	1 2 3 4 5
5. I experience peace and joy within myself when I behave according to this value.	1 2 3 4 5
6. This lends meaning and vitality to my life.	1 2 3 4 5
Total 2 (sum your ratings for the three items above, numbers 4, 5, 6)	Total 2 = _____
Total 3 (Total 1_____ minus Total 2_____)	Total 3 = _____

Table 8.3

Romantic Relationships

This area may include your relationship to boyfriends, girlfriends, partners, husbands, and wives. It may be about a current relationship or the one you would like to have. Examples: being intimate and honest, sharing similar interests, being trustworthy, experiencing new things, or being physically affectionate.

When it comes to romantic relationships, what I would like to be about is:

[space left intentionally blank in the original book]

Please answer the following questions about the romantic relationship value you wrote above. The rating scale goes from 1 (not at all for this reason) to 5 (very much for this reason). (Table 8.4)

The reason I identified this romantic relationship value is because:	
1. I was raised this way and my parents or other people important to me would be upset if I didn't value this (or pleased to know that I do).	1 2 3 4 5
2. If I didn't value this, I would feel embarrassed, guilty, anxious, or ashamed.	1 2 3 4 5
3. Only a bad or evil person would not value this.	1 2 3 4 5
Total 1 (sum your ratings for the three items above, numbers 1, 2, and 3)	Total 1 = _____

4. This feels important to me from deep in-side. Even if nobody knew that I valued this, it would still matter to me.	1 2 3 4 5
5. I experience peace and joy within myself when I behave according to this value.	1 2 3 4 5
6. This lends meaning and vitality to my life.	1 2 3 4 5
Total 2 (sum your ratings for the three items above, numbers 4, 5, 6)	Total 2 = _____
Total 3 (Total 1_____ minus Total 2_____)	Total 3 = _____

Table 8.4

Leisure Activities

This area may include what you would like to have in the areas of hobbies, having fun, or relaxing. Examples: building in time for me to do nothing, laughing and playing, creating new things, getting exercise, or learning or having hobbies that make my home nicer.

When it comes to leisure activities, what I would like to be about is:

[space left intentionally blank in the original book]

Please answer the following questions about the leisure activity value you wrote above. The rating scale goes from 1 (not at all for this reason) to 5 (very much for this reason). (Table 8.5)

The reason I identified this leisure activities value is because:	
1. I was raised this way and my parents or other people important to me would be upset if I didn't value this (or pleased to know that I do).	1 2 3 4 5
2. If I didn't value this, I would feel embarrassed, guilty, anxious, or ashamed.	1 2 3 4 5
3. Only a bad or evil person would not value this.	1 2 3 4 5
Total 1 (sum your ratings for the three items above, numbers 1, 2, and 3)	Total 1 = _____
4. This feels important to me from deep inside. Even if nobody knew that I valued this, it would still matter to me.	1 2 3 4 5
5. I experience peace and joy within myself when I behave according to this value.	1 2 3 4 5
6. This lends meaning and vitality to my life.	1 2 3 4 5
Total 2 (sum your ratings for the three items above, numbers 4, 5, 6)	Total 2 = _____
Total 3 (Total 1_____ minus Total 2_____)	

Table 8.5

Spirituality

Think broadly in this area. Spirituality may apply to religious affiliations and activities, your own relationship to God or a higher power, or some other area of spirituality for you, such as nature, prayer, or meditation. In our experience, many people have had difficulties in this area and may be quick to write this one off. Give yourself some time to see if there is something here that you haven't yet considered. There might be a new avenue for you that could add meaning to your life. Examples: being true to my religious beliefs, respecting nature, finding time to meditate regularly, being part of a spiritual community, or serving others.

When it comes to spirituality, what I would like to be about is:

[space left intentionally blank in the original book]

Please answer the following questions about the spirituality value you wrote above. The rating scale goes from 1 (not at all for this reason) to 5 (very much for this reason). (Table 8.6)

The reason I identified this spirituality value is because:	
1. I was raised this way and my parents or other people important to me would be upset if I didn't value this (or pleased to know that I do).	1 2 3 4 5

2. If I didn't value this, I would feel embarrassed, guilty, anxious, or ashamed.	1 2 3 4 5
3. Only a bad or evil person would not value this.	1 2 3 4 5
Total 1 (sum your ratings for the three items above, numbers 1, 2, and 3)	Total 1 = _____
4. This feels important to me from deep inside. Even if nobody knew that I valued this, it would still matter to me.	1 2 3 4 5
5. I experience peace and joy within myself when I behave according to this value.	1 2 3 4 5
6. This lends meaning and vitality to my life.	1 2 3 4 5
Total 2 (sum your ratings for the three items above, numbers 4, 5, 6)	Total 2 = _____
Total 3 (Total 1_____ minus Total 2_____)	Total 3 = _____

Table 8.6

Self

This area is about your relationship with yourself. Some survivors of trauma feel that they are damaged at this most basic level. Sometimes even knowing what you want may be difficult. In fact, just this exercise may seem like an impossible task. If that's the case, just do what you can now, and make room for the fact that your values may change as you continue to learn about yourself. Examples: being kind to yourself, respecting the fact that your values are okay even if others disagree with them, being honest with yourself, or setting appropriate boundaries and related issues.

When it comes to my relationship with myself, what I would like to be about is:

[space left intentionally blank in the original book]

Please answer the following questions about the self value you wrote above. The rating scale goes from 1 (not at all for this reason) to 5 (very much for this reason). (Table 8.7)

The reason I identified this self value is because:	
1. I was raised this way and my parents or other people important to me would be upset if I didn't value this (or pleased to know that I do).	1 2 3 4 5
2. If I didn't value this, I would feel embarrassed, guilty, anxious, or ashamed.	1 2 3 4 5
3. Only a bad or evil person would not value this.	1 2 3 4 5
Total 1 (sum your ratings for the three items above, numbers 1, 2, and 3)	Total 1 = _____
4. This feels important to me from deep inside. Even if nobody knew that I valued this, it would still matter to me.	1 2 3 4 5
5. I experience peace and joy within myself when I behave according to this value.	1 2 3 4 5
6. This lends meaning and vitality to my life.	1 2 3 4 5
Total 2 (sum your ratings for the three items above, numbers 4, 5, 6)	Total 2 = _____

Total 3 (Total 1_____ minus Total 2_____)	Total 3 = _____

Table 8.7

The main purpose of this exercise is to give you a chance to clarify what your values are in different domains. Some of these values may change over time. In both this chapter and the next one, we will ask you to come back to your answers to this exercise from time to time. Knowing which direction you want to head toward in life is a crucial aspect of finding life beyond trauma. However, we are not yet done with this exercise.

How Intrinsic Are My Values?

Now that you have completed the first part of this values clarification exercise, let's take a look at what you came up with for Total 3 (Total 1 minus Total 2).

The areas where Total 3 was positive for me were:

[space left intentionally blank in the original book]

The areas where Total 3 was negative for me were:

[space left intentionally blank in the original book]

A positive Total 3 sum suggests that, for that particular value, you are being guided more by following others' wishes or avoiding certain feelings and judgments than you are by your own interests and wishes. The greater the number, the more this is the case for you. 🔔[What is your mind saying about this last sentence? What are the feelings coming up? Can you make room for them as feelings?]

A negative Total 3 sum suggests that for that particular value, you are being guided more by inherent interests or things that lend meaning to your life than by fear or a desire for approval. The greater the number, the more this is the case for you.

At this point, we suggest that you keep in mind the areas where you ended up with a positive Total 3. We hope that the following exercises and discussions will help you understand what might be happening for you in those areas.

***

If you are noticing any self-judgments coming up, see if you can let them go. Remember, this is about clarifying your values and not about beating yourself up. If you feel like defending yourself, arguing, or punishing yourself with criticism, see if you can resist the urge and instead be the sand that accepts the waves coming in and going out. If there is something here that you might need to attend to, listen to it gently.

What If I Don't Know What I Value?

As we discussed in chapter 7, on the self, not knowing oneself or what one wants in life is not unusual for trauma survivors. Sometimes your experience will tell you what you don't want, but that does not always clarify what you *do* want. You may not want to go east, but there are many other choices.

Survivors of trauma have had a great deal of training and incentive to focus on outside factors, away from their inner selves and lives. This is how this process may have unfolded for you:

- If you grew up in an unsafe household, it would not be unusual to focus on what others wanted from you as a way of surviving. Perhaps if you calmed down an alcoholic parent, then things would go more smoothly at the dinner table.

- If you experienced a natural disaster or a car accident, the tendency to focus on trying to predict and control outside events might be really strong. Perhaps the thought is that if you can stay attuned to the weather at all times, you'll know if a hurricane is coming.

- If you have been to war, not focusing so much on what you really wanted but what you needed to do to survive may have helped you stay alive. Perhaps the thought is that if you can tell whether or not a leaf moved in the woods, you might be able to shoot the sniper before he shoots you.

- If you have been attacked or raped, focusing on outside stimuli may seem helpful. Perhaps being able to pick up every nuance of whether an environment is safe might make you feel, if not necessarily be, secure.

- Some of the symptoms of PTSD, like hypervigilance and dissociation, could also contribute to your having less access to how you feel and what you want from life.

🔔 [What is your mind saying right now?] See if you can defuse from emotions like shame or guilt or thoughts like "Look! I don't even know what I want. How can I have a meaningful life?" or "So-and-so really knows what he wants, not like me" or "I'm really broken; I don't even know who I am." Don't push them away, AND remember that they are just passengers on your bus. See if you can bring these thoughts and feelings, as just that, thoughts and feelings, along with you while you continue reading about values clarification.

The next exercises are meant to help you to sort out some of your hidden values by looking more closely at the places you hurt and at what you say you would want if uncomfortable internal experiences were not in your way.

Exercise 8.3: The Quarters of Your Life

If you think about the areas of your life where things hurt, usually you will find something you value on the flip side. If you didn't care about something, it would not hurt. In that sense, as we have said before, pain can be an ally. Put simply: You can follow avoidance to find your pain. You can follow pain to find your values. Here are a couple of examples. (Table 8.8)

Situation/emotion/thought avoided	Avoidance move	The cost
Social gatherings (fear of being evaluated negatively, thought of "What if they don't like me?")	Not attending parties	Not having friends
Being alone with a man on a date (fear I will be attacked or taken advantage of)	Not dating	Not having a romantic relationship and feeling lonely.

Table 8.8

In a way, the pain and the value are two sides of the same coin. The socially phobic person who is terrified of being humiliated and rejected actually cares deeply about human connection. It is like a coin that has on one side "human connection" and on the other the fear and worries about being rejected. Notice that we can perhaps eliminate or reduce the fear of being rejected by avoiding social situations and keeping away from people. However, as we do so, we are throwing the whole coin away, and with it goes the possibility of human connection. This is the coin flip of avoidance. (Image 8.1)

The Coin Flip of Avoidance

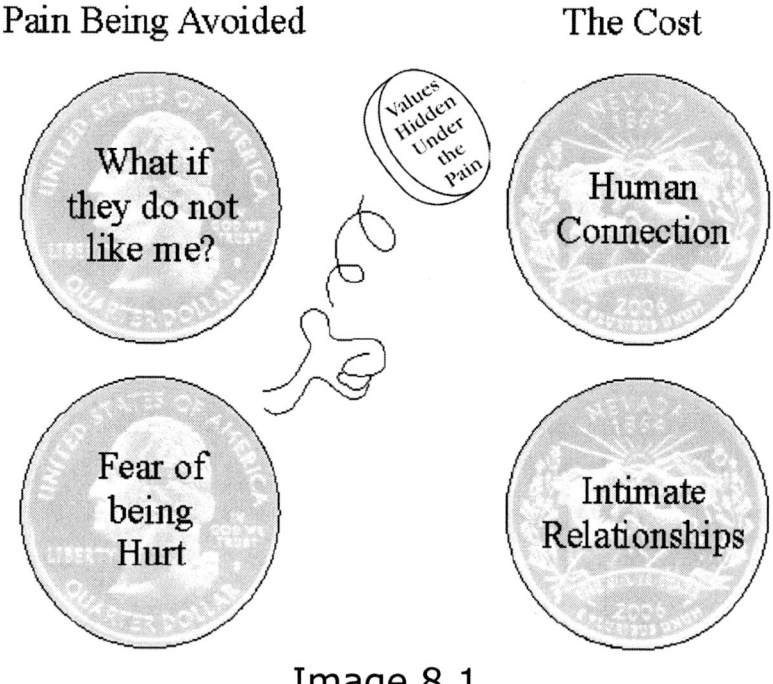

Pain Being Avoided   The Cost

Values Hidden Under the Pain

What if they do not like me?

Human Connection

Fear of being Hurt

Intimate Relationships

Image 8.1

1. Now let's have you try this out. Consider your trauma history and the impact those experiences have had specifically on situations and emotions you avoid. Think about some of the situations, emotions, or thoughts avoided, the avoidance move, and the cost that it has had on your life. Write four of them down below, following the example above. (Table 8.9)

Situation/emotion/thought avoided	Avoidance move	The cost
1.		

Situation/emotion/thought avoided	Avoidance move	The cost
2.		
3.		
4.		

Table 8.9

2. See if you can identify the value underlying each cost, then write it down on the tails side of each quarter of your life in the following graphic. Then, see if you can identify under "Situation/emotion/ thought avoided" what you might need to make room for if you want to live out that value. Write this down on the heads side of the coin. See the examples above.

3. Now, look at each of your four quarters. How much do you care about the value on the tails side of the coin? Are you willing to keep this coin, *with* the pain that will inevitably come with it, the pain you wrote down on the heads side of the coin? Notice that you are already answering this question, in one way or another, by the way you are living your life. If you are keeping the coin, notice that. If you have been

throwing the coin away, ask yourself if that's what you really want to do. (Image 8.2)

The Four Quarters of My Life

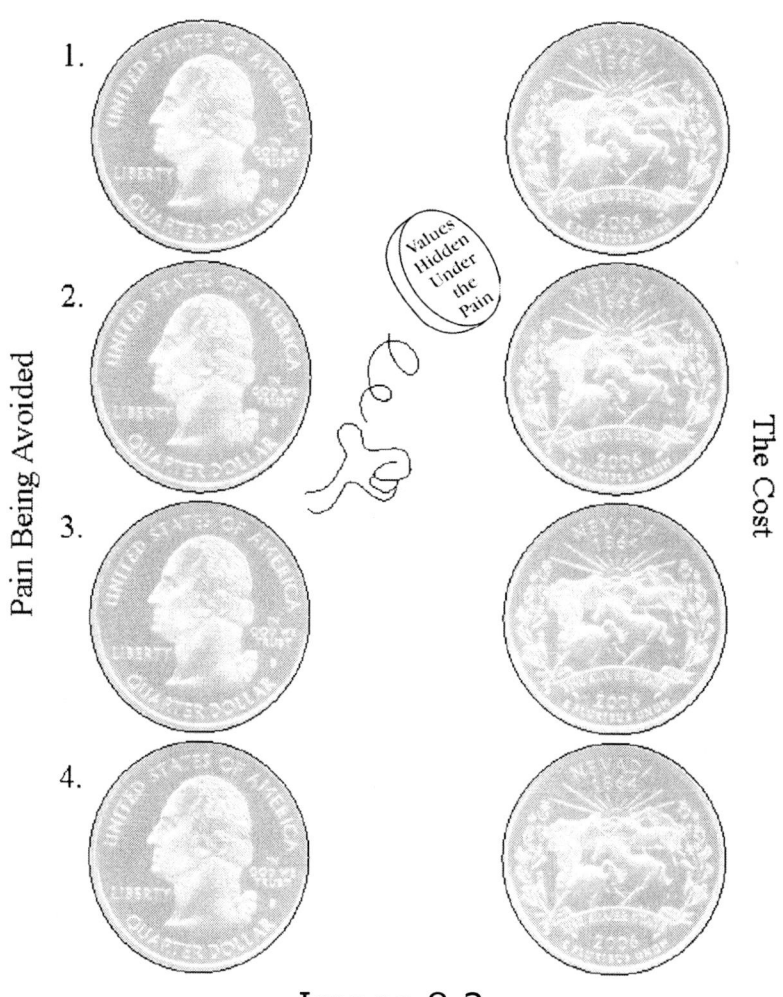

Image 8.2

***

If you have spent many years detached from you self, clarifying your values can be especially important. You can do so not only be following your pain, by also by examining your wishful thinking. The next exercise addresses the latter.

Exercise 8.4: If Only _____, Then _____!

Many times in life you may make the statement "If only _____, then _____." What you say in the first blank is something you imagine isn't possible. Filling the second blank is how your life would change for the better if that "impossible" thing happened. These can refer to past or future events. For example:

1. If only *I could win a million dollars,* then *I would be able to pay for my daughter to go to college.*

2. If only *I had gone to college,* then *I could be my own boss.*

3. If only *I could stop drinking,* then *I wouldn't feel so lousy in the morning.*

4. If only *I hadn't married my husband,* then *I wouldn't have had to go through the abuse.*

---

5. If only *I had the time to exercise,* then *I could lose the weight and feel healthy again.*

6. If only *I had more time,* then *I could volunteer at the local women's shelter.*

7. If only *I could make more friends,* then *I wouldn't be so lonely all the time.*

Take a look at these examples. Some of them may be possible to change, such as making more friends, while some cannot be changed, such as having married a different person. After all, we cannot change the past. Likewise, some are not likely to happen, such as winning a million dollars. Your mind may give you these "if only" statements when you are struggling, creating feelings of hopelessness and additional suffering. 🔔 [Notice what is showing up for you.]

Here's the good news however: There is a value behind each of these "if only/then" statements, because the part after "then" tells you what you may be yearning for in your life—what you value. Here are some values that might be behind the example statements.

1. If only *I could win a million dollars,* then *I would be able to pay for my daughter to go to college.* Value = providing for my family

2. If only *I had gone to college,* then *I could be my own boss.* Value = having freedom and flexibility at work

3. If only *I could stop drinking,* then *I wouldn't feel so lousy in the morning.* Value = having physical health and well-being

4. If only *I hadn't married my husband,* then *I wouldn't have had to go through the abuse.* Value = being respected

5. If only *I had the time to exercise,* then *I could lose the weight and feel healthy again.* Value = having a healthy body

6. If only *I had more time,* then *I could volunteer at the local women's shelter.* Value = giving back to the community

7. If only *I could make more friends,* then *I wouldn't be so lonely all the time.* Value = having personal support

While all of the "if only" statements may not be possible, living the personal values behind these statements is certainly possible. Let's have you give this a try.

For each valued domain, list three "if only/then" statements. For the "if only" statement, we are asking you to think of goals that you may feel are unattainable. We're asking you to think outside the box, let go of limitations, and just write what you wish. The "then" portion (the third column) will be your perceived outcome if the "if only" statement were achieved. In the fourth column, we'd like you to write a personal value that corresponds with the "then" statement. This is the specific value that underlies the ideal outcome.

Here's an example: (Table 8.10)

Domain	"If only"	"Then"	Personal value
1. Family	If I did not have to work two jobs	I would spend more time with my partner	Emotional connection to partner
	I lived in the same state as my parents	I would be able to care for them as they age	Expressing love to parents

Domain	"If only"	"Then"	Personal value
	I was closer with my sister	I could teach my nephew to play baseball	Being a positive influence in my nephew's life as he grows up

Table 8.10

In the table below, go ahead and come up with "if only/then" statements for each domain. (Table 8.11)

Domain	"If only"	"Then"	Personal value
1. Family			
2. Work or School			
3. Friendships			
4. Romantic relationships			
5. Leisure activities			
6. Spirituality			
7. Self			

Table 8.11

🔔 [Notice what is showing up for you right now.]

What was your experience of this exercise? You may have noticed sadness, disappointment, or self-judgment coming up for you when listing your "if only/then" statements. This is not uncommon, because you're writing about meaningful things that are perhaps not present for you in your life right now. There is loss and grief in that. Conversely, you may have also experienced some feelings of hope or clarity in defining your personal value in the fourth column

Trauma, Fear, Avoidance, and Values

Another aspect that may make knowing your values or living them difficult is the fact that for trauma survivors, avoidance can quickly become the standard answer to the experience of fear or any other uncomfortable emotion, thought, bodily sensation, or memory. Because of the prominence of fear as a natural response in traumatic experiences, we will focus on it in this section, but keep in mind that the same concepts apply to other unwanted internal experiences as well.

Fear and avoidance were likely both adaptive and perhaps lifesaving at the time of your traumatic experience(s). In those situations, fear is normal and avoidance is often self-protective. For example, for Hurricane Katrina survivors, fear might have motivated folks to get out of their houses or move food to higher ground right away, before the water came in.

Also, for survivors camped on the rooftops, avoiding looking at each and every body drifting by may have helped them stay focused on their own survival. As we noted, trauma almost always requires a lot of effort to be focused on maintaining safety or surviving. Exploring your feelings is *not* the thing to do when bullets are whizzing an inch above your head. Yet, if after the trauma is over all you can do is avoid when you encounter fear, we know from research that the consequences are likely to be dire (Hayes, Strosahl, and Wilson 1996).

The difficulty arises from the fact that trauma survivors' avoidance behaviors in the face of fear can be either healthy or unhealthy, so a simple rule like "always face your fear" would not be useful, particularly if by "facing" one means staying in the situation. For example, consider the fear you might feel just before a car accident occurs. In this case you would want to respond to fear. It would be lifesaving to turn the wheel of the car to avoid another car about to hit you. Intense fear allows us to escape life-threatening situations such as this one. This is an example of healthy avoidance in the face of fear.

However, if you feel fear and turn the wheel of the car each time you pass that same section of highway, even with no threat of an accident, you literally take yourself off the road of your destination. If all you know how to do in that section of road is swerve the car in fear and that's the road that you need to be on, you cannot move forward. This is an example of unhealthy avoidance in the face of fear.

To help you identify how much fear is guiding your values, we would like to return to the bus metaphor. Another way to think of values clarification is choosing which direction you want your bus to head toward. Which sign do you truly want to go up on the front of your bus?

You can choose to have one of your passengers, say fear, drive the bus, or you can choose to have yourself, based on your values, drive instead.

If the Fear Passenger Drives the Bus

- All situations, people, places, and emotions that you've been afraid to approach will be avoided. You will drive around them.

- The roads you take will be narrow and will be chosen by what is the most comfortable.

- You will need to avoid many obstacles along either side of the road and will often be unable to turn the bus.

- Your destination will be determined by what needs to be avoided.

- You won't be sure where you will end up, because there may be something that needs to be avoided around the next corner.

If Your Values Drive the Bus

- You will choose the destination and all the roads to get you there.

- You will inevitably hit some barriers, AND your desired destination will not change because of these difficulties.

- The road will be wide and will encompass every possible emotion.

- The road may be frightening at times, but you will be driving in meaningful territory.

- Your path and your destination will have meaning to you.

Exercise 8.5: Who Is the Driver of Your Life Right Now, Emotions or Values?

1. Refer back to the values you identified in exercise 8.2. Write a short description of each in the left-hand column of the following table.

2. In the next column, rank each value in order of its importance to you. Use a scale of 1 to 7, with 1 being the most important and 7 being the least important.

3. In the next column, rate the extent to which you've lived by this value during the last month. Use a scale of 0 to 10, with 0 being not at all and 10 being completely.

4. In the next column, rate the extent to which difficult emotions interfered with living that value over the past month. Use a scale of 0 to 10, with 0 being not at all and 10 being completely.

5. Imagine that your bus was never driven by difficult emotions and thoughts. In the right-hand column, describe what you'd be doing in your life with respect to your val-

ues that you aren't currently doing. (Table 8.12)

Value	Importance (1 to 7)	Success in living the value (0 to 10)	Interference from difficult emotions (0 to 10)	What you'd do differently
Family:				
Work or school:				
Friend-ships:				
Romantic relation-ships:				
Leisure:				
Spirituality:				
Self:				

Table 8.12

***

Where Are We Now?

We want to emphasize right now that you *can* create a life that follows your ideal ranking of the valued domains. Beware that this does not mean that you will be reaching all the goals that you have in each valued domain.

Remember, living a valued life is a process, not an achievement. You will fail to live in accordance with your values on and off again all through life. The trick is to notice when you are not headed west and turn around as quickly as possible, unless you truly have changed your values and no longer value heading west.

Sometimes you may not be able to live out your every value because they might be in conflict with one another. A client of ours once noted that he begged someone to give him and his three- and five-year-old kids a ride into town when his car broke down in an isolated area at dusk. As they rode, this father tolerated several under-the-breath insults directed at himself and his kids from their "helper." He noted that this entailed letting go of his value of self-respect in order to get his kids to safety—a value higher in importance for him. Although, at the time, his therapist pointed out that protecting his kids was perhaps exactly what he needed to do to preserve his self-respect!

Living a valued life is following a path that you can create by making small changes and having the willingness to approach a range of feelings and experiences. There can be dignity and meaning in simply living a life in accordance with values, even if the outcomes are not always there.

Take another look at the statements you wrote in "what I would like to be about" for each valued area in exercise 8.2. Do they seem like possibilities? Just like the example list we made for the woman who wanted to start dating, there are likely small steps to be taken toward your value in each domain. If you only had one year to live, would taking even a small step be worth it to you?

What we call values can change as we go through life. In fact, probably most of you noticed some changes even while going through this chapter. That's expected and, from our perspective, even desired—if the new values get you closer to what you want your life to be about. In ACT, we suggest that you let your values be guided by what you truly want in life, and not simply be about being consistent. As we pointed out in chapter 6, there is usually a price to pay for having to remain consistent or "right" in life.

You learned in exercise 8.2 how intrinsic your values are. We know from research that following values that lend meaning, interest, and fun to our lives, as opposed to those we follow to obtain approval from others or to run away from feelings of discomfort, is more closely associated with happiness and reduced stress (Creswell et al. 2005).

Simply put, when it comes to choosing a life direction, we suggest that you move *toward* something meaningful and not simply *away* from something unwanted, such as disapproval or fear (Wilson and Murrell 2004). Now that you have identified the direction you would like to head toward, in the next chapter we will ask you to explore what gets in your way when making a commitment to action.

Journaling

Thoughts

[space left intentionally blank in the original book]

Feelings or Emotions

[space left intentionally blank in the original book]

Self-Judgments

[space left intentionally blank in the original book]

Physical Sensations

[space left intentionally blank in the original book]

Action Urges (What Do You Feel Like Doing?)

[space left intentionally blank in the original book]

CHAPTER 9

Committed Action

with Jennifer Plumb

Our greatest glory is not in never falling, but in rising every time we fall.

—Confucius

As we stated in the introduction, ACT can be summarized in three steps: accept, choose, and take action. Thus far, you have worked on *accepting* your thoughts, feelings, self, and history and *choosing* valued life directions. And now we have come to the point where the rubber meets the road—it is time to *take action.*🔔[Notice what shows up for you right now, as we say this.] As you contemplate the action phase, take a moment to sit with your reaction. Notice any passengers coming up from the back of the bus, perhaps one saying, "I'll read this chapter, but nothing can really work for me." As we encouraged you to do early on, see if you can put judgment aside and just be willing to look at some ideas on how to move forward in your life. You can bring your worries, doubts, and skepticism along with you. They are passengers on your bus, but they need not keep your bus from turning toward a valued direction.

In this chapter, we will focus on setting goals, outlining the steps necessary to engage in those goals, identifying barriers to moving in a valued direction, and suggesting some strategies for dealing with such barriers. This is a particularly interesting area for psychologists because there is actually some data on what can help in making life changes.

What the Research Says

We know quite a bit from research about what helps or doesn't help in making changes in our lives. We will go over some of this information below in order to give you some background for the work you are about to do. AND, with all the knowledge in the world, in the end only *you* can make the decision to move forward. In a sense we are right here, urging you on—AND we can't do it for you. So here is some of what we know helps.

Don't Give Up

The first point we want to make is that taking action is not a one-time choice that goes smoothly from start to finish. Although some people can make changes that they stick to for the long haul, for most of us, taking action can be a winding road, where we go two steps forward and one step back. Commitment, or persistence, appears to be a deciding factor.

As it turns out, Confucius was right: The key issue is rising after we fall instead of never falling at all. For example, we know from research that, when people are working toward achieving a goal, they are more likely to attain it when they persist in *trying* to attain it rather than simply *intending* to attain it (Hinsz and Ployhart 1998).

People who successfully quit smoking have usually tried to quit at least two or three times previously. Persistence matters! (U.S. Department of Health and Human Services, Public Health Service 2000). People who eventually quit using alcohol or drugs generally have several attempts under their belts before they finally quit. Couples who are happiest are not the ones who never fight but, instead, those who fight and are able to resolve their conflicts in a respectful manner (Cramer 2002a; Cramer 2002b).

Make a Public Commitment

Making a public commitment to doing something makes it more likely that you will follow through with the action (Schlenker, Dlugolecki, and Doherty, 1994; Stults and Meesé 1985). This is the principle that many programs, such as 12-step programs, Weight Watchers, and smoking cessation programs, use to encourage behavior change.

A public commitment can mean telling just one other person in your life about it, or it can mean telling several individuals. We know this is difficult from our own real-life experiences. Whether this is right for you depends to a great degree on your support system and your life circumstances.

Pick Goals That Are Small and Easy to Measure

Breaking down goals that are complex, difficult, or long-term makes it more likely that you will succeed. For example, if you want to be a doctor but you're not yet in college, you might want to start out by searching the Web for three potential colleges where you could go to get your undergraduate education. Or you might need to begin by looking for a place to get your GED. As they say, every journey begins with a single step.

If we have no way to gauge whether or not we are accomplishing each goal, it tends to be more difficult to maintain the behavior. So, it's best to come up with behaviors that can be objectively measured. For example, the goal of "having fun" is very difficult to measure. How do we know for sure if we're having the fun we'd hoped for? Whereas, if you have as a goal to go out to the movies with friends every weekend, it's easier to know whether or not you have achieved it. The process of identifying useful new behaviors can be a bit tricky, and sometimes you have to experiment. For example, you may find going to the movies is not fun for you and that you need to adjust the behavior to fit where you really want to be going in your life.

Conversely, research says that selecting challenging goals predicts the most success (Locke et al. 1981) because, as long as we have the ability to engage in them, we tend to work harder toward achieving goals that are not too easy.

Monitor Your Behavior

Sometimes we make assumptions about what is or is not happening in our lives. However, we tend to be inaccurate about our perceptions. Therefore, if you're thinking about changing something, it's not a bad idea to start monitoring what you're actually doing now first. If you're trying to spend less time on the Internet, for example, then start counting how many hours you are currently spending on it first, and then try out different things. This is called establishing a baseline. The simple act of tracking what you are doing may change your behavior (Heidt and Marx 2003).

Establish Larger Patterns of Action

Research has shown that, for people who are struggling with impulsive actions, choosing a larger pattern of action can help them establish different and more workable ways of behaving (Rachlin 1995; Rachlin 2000). What many people do when trying to change something is give up the first time they slip up. On the other hand, if this same person (say, a gambler) has one slip, goes to Gamblers Anonymous that night, and does not continue gambling, the larger pattern of action is "try to change, fail, and then try again." So, it's important to notice not only individual actions but the larger pattern of action we are establishing as we pursue values and goals.

Setting Goals

Remember how, in chapter 8, we distinguished between values and goals? Values are the driving force behind your actions or the areas of life that you find important. But we are never "through" with them. Goals, on the other hand, are activities you choose to engage in as you move in a valued direction.

In a moment, you will write down some different goals you have and the values they're related to. The values you identified from the preceding chapter will help you formulate different goals for yourself. This section will help you practice identifying and clarifying the steps needed to accomplish the goals related to your important values. 🔔[Any thoughts or judgments coming up?] As you complete the next exercise, you may start to notice that your mind has a lot to say about your ability to achieve these goals or that it brings up some emotions for you. Just gently acknowledge those thoughts or feelings at this point; we'll come back to them later.

The next two exercises will help you identify the actions and goals linked with different values. These activities will help you select clear, measurable goals and monitor your progress.

Exercise 9.1: Identifying Valued Actions or Goals

1. If you don't remember them, please look over your answers to exercise 8.2 in the previous chapter prior to proceeding.

2. In the second column in the following table, specify your values in that life area.

3. In the third column, write something that you are currently doing to live that value. It's important to notice the things you are doing well already!

4. In the fourth column, write a goal you can commit to doing to further live this value, starting today. (Table 9.1)

Valued domain	Personal values	Current valued actions	Goals/new valued actions
1. Family			

Valued domain	Personal values	Current valued actions	Goals/new valued actions
2. Work or school			
3. Friendships			
4. Romantic relationships			
5. Leisure			
6. Spirituality			
7. Self			

Table 9.1

Take some time now to notice your responses to this exercise. Any thoughts, feelings, or judgments coming up about the value-based goals you have identified for the future? One of the things ACT has to offer is a way of dealing with internal barriers to action; but first, you will need to know what they are for you.

Exercise 9.2: Goal Clarification

1. Go back to exercise 9.1 and choose four to five goals from the Goals/new valued action column and write them into the table below in the first column. In the second column, write the value that it relates to.

2. Specify whether this is a short- or long-term goal. Rate each goal in terms of how much it is under your control, to what extent this goal can be broken down into smaller steps, and to what extent you will be able to tell that you have accomplished this goal. (Table 9.2)

Goal	Value	Long-term or short-term?	How much under your control? 0, not at all to 10, completely	Do you know the concrete steps to get it done? If not, how can you find out?	Will you be able to know when you have accomplished it?
1.					
2.					
3.					
4.					
5.					

Table 9.2

Now, look back at your answers to exercise 9.2 and examine how feasible each goal is. Then answer the following questions.

Is the Goal in Line with Your Values?

If a goal isn't in line with your value, ask yourself why it's important to you. If the goal and the value seem to not be in alignment, consider the possibility that either the goal needs to be changed, or if the goal feels really important, the value underlying it needs to be identified. This may seem like a no-brainer, but you'd be surprised how often people find themselves doing things that are really not in the service of their values. For example, someone might want to be a really good parent and spend a lot of time at work in order to be a good provider for her family. AND she might come to realize that what she values in parenting is having a close, loving relationship with her children, which involves having more time, not more money.

Can You Recognize What You Can Change?

We have discussed trying to cultivate the wisdom to know what you can change and how to accept the things you can't. There is a lot you can do to make changes, but we don't expect that you are in control of the world—only your own behavior. For example, although you would like to get promoted at work, only some aspects of that goal would be under your control, such as showing up to work on time, improving the system at work, contributing to staff meetings, and applying to your supervisor for a promotion. Other aspects may not be under your control, such as whether or not your supervisor has the authority to give a promotion to anyone, whether there are others in the office with more seniority who would get the promotion first, or whether your company is in a process of making cutbacks. Another example of a goal that would not be under your control would be "to have my daughter like me." You may do certain actions, such as calling her to ask about her life, sending her notes and cards, being emotionally supportive of her during difficult times, or any number of loving behaviors. However, you cannot control whether or not she likes you. She may even love you, but she might not like you all that much. It happens more than we think. Basically, you cannot control how other people feel—that will fall into the realm of acceptance.

What Are the Next Steps to Take to Accomplish This Goal?

If you don't know the steps, finding out about the actual behavior involved in attaining your goal would be your next step. Leaving goals vague can be the downfall of achieving what you want. Not only does this vagueness make it hard to know what to do, but it may also make it impossible to know when it is done. Having concrete steps that are measurable is key in moving toward your goals. Going to the movies with a friend once a month is measurable; being a better friend is not. At the same time, remain open to the data. Our sense of people is that they have an internal compass that provides a sense of when they're moving in a valued direction. And being a better friend will always be a direction—not an end point. So you need to have both: values that provide you with an internal compass AND goals that tell you the next steps to take.

Exercise 9.3: Finding Short-Term Goals Associated with Long-Term Goals

Looking back at your list of goals in exercise 9.2, you will notice that we asked you whether each goal was short- or long-term. Different goals have different timelines. For example, goals such as "Improve my relationship with my mother" may take quite a long time and involve many different steps. One small goal that may be related to the larger goal of improving a relationship may be "Call Mom once a week." It's important to plan goals that are small as well as larger ones. Breaking down each long-term goal into smaller goals makes them more feasible and less overwhelming. Sometimes it may be important to break down a longer-term goal into several shorter-term goals that you can achieve more quickly.

Now make a brief list of the long-term goals you wrote down in exercise 9.2. Next to each long-term goal, write down the steps associated with each. For example, if you want to go back to school, some short-term goals may include getting a list of colleges in the area, looking for child care, applying for financial aid, and completing school applications. These actions can be considered short-term goals that you can accomplish more easily in route to your long-term goal. (Table 9.3)

Long-term goals	Short-term goals associated with long-term goals
1.	[space left intentionally blank in the original book]
2.	[space left intentionally blank in the original book]
3.	[space left intentionally blank in the original book]
4.	[space left intentionally blank in the original book]
5.	[space left intentionally blank in the original book]

Table 9.3

Exercise 9.4: Things You Can Do This Week

Choose a few short-term goals from exercise 9.3 that you can achieve within one week. Ideally, you want to choose activities that you can see from start to finish and that are likely to get accomplished. In completing the chart below, note that each goal may have many actions associated with it. You may need more space, so just put as many activities as you see necessary. You may want to copy the blank form and continue to assign yourself more things to do to accomplish your goals in a stepwise fashion. (Table 9.4)

Value: Continue to learn and improve myself.

Short-term goal	Actions	Date accomplished
Example Take one class from the community college this semester.	1. Go on the Web and get information from the community college on how to register for classes.	June 1
	2. Gather all personal documents needed to register at the community college.	June 15
	3. Go on the Web and get information on which classes are available to take.	July 1
	4. Discuss with my wife how to coordinate babysitting for the night I might be gone every week.	July 3

Value:

Short-term goal	Actions	Date accomplished
	1.	
	2.	
	3.	
	4.	

Value:

Short-term goal	Actions	Date accomplished
	1.	
	2.	
	3.	
	4.	

Table 9.4

Exercise 9.5: No Time Like the Present

1. Look at the actions you listed in exercise 9.4. Before you continue on to the next section, is there a particular action you can do *now?* If not from this list, perhaps something else that you have been postponing but that could be done or started right now, before you go on with the work in this book? Perhaps you can make a phone call, start a conversation, pay a bill, look for something you have

lost, charge the cell phone, do something nice for yourself or someone close to you, or look something up on the Internet. Each moment is an opportunity, and it's possible to live the life you want right now. AND we know that reading this book and doing these exercises is moving in a valued direction for you also.

2. Pick one thing you can do or start to do right now. Choose something that would not take longer than fifteen to twenty minutes, because we want you to come back to the book soon after you complete this action.

What I have selected to do is: [space left intentionally blank in the original book]

3. Put the book down now, and do the task you identified above.

4. What are the thoughts, feelings, and reactions you are experiencing after doing that one action? Write them down below. If you are reading this and didn't attempt to complete the action, gently notice what kept you from doing that, along with your thoughts, feelings, or judgments about not having done the task.

[space left intentionally blank in the original book]

Your responses to step 4 can be very informative. Notice what shows up and see what, if anything, you have to learn from these feelings, thoughts, action urges, and bodily sensations.

Although most people will feel empowered by completing even a small task that perhaps has been avoided, others may experience different types of reactions. For some people, completing one task leads to rumination about all the other tasks that are still to be completed. Either way, noticing what passengers show up for you as you engage in valued action is informative for you. Remember, you are moving in a direction and that means taking action—not being perfect.

As you notice any thoughts, feelings, and other reactions you experienced, ask yourself the following questions:

- Is there anything familiar to you about these thoughts, feelings, and other reactions you had while trying to complete, completing, or perhaps not trying to complete one task?

- Are any of these reactions old passengers on your bus who show up when you try (or don't try) to take action?

- What do you usually do when these passengers come up to the front of the bus?

- Is whatever you do in response to these passengers working for you? If it isn't, would you be 100 percent willing to do something different, even if it means making room for the possibility that several uncomfortable passengers yell at you while you drive the bus?

Noticing your reactions to exercises that involve action will be almost as helpful as completing the exercises themselves. Keep this is mind as you move through the remainder of this chapter.

Exercise 9.6: Tell a Friend

1. As we pointed out earlier in the chapter, making a public commitment about a goal you have can help you get it done. Looking at the actions you identified in exercise 9.4, is there a goal there that you'd be willing to tell someone that you *will* do? Not that you

will *try,* but that you are actually ready to commit to doing? Again, make sure that it is something you are 100 percent willing to commit to doing. Pick something small and doable.

The valued action I have chosen to tell someone about is: _____

2. Tell someone who can be helpful to you in moving forward. Pick someone who will be supportive, but who also is willing to nudge you some. If you have a history of making commitments to a particular person, commitments that you don't keep, pick a different person to tell. Pick someone whom, were you not to complete the commitment, it would matter to.

The person or people I picked to tell: _____

3. Are you willing to make a commitment to tell this person, if not right now (preferable), within the next day, about this goal you've picked to complete? Make the commitment and tell them.

4. Did you tell someone? If you did, notice what showed up for you before, during, and

after making this public commitment. What were your thoughts, feelings, action urges, memories, and bodily sensations? If you didn't go through with the exercise, what happened? Did you think about telling the person but for whatever reason didn't? Did you not even consider going through with the exercise? Whatever happened, notice if it is like you to do what you did, and whether or not that works for you. Is there anything about your response to this exercise that feels like an old move, something you commonly do that doesn't work for you? If you answered yes to this last question, pay close attention to the next section.

Looking for Avoidance

There are several moves that are mired in avoidance that we may engage in when setting goals. We have picked three to discuss in some detail below. Selecting goals that are not truly consistent with one's values may lead to lack of progress and feelings of stagnation. Challenging goals that take time may lead to dismissing the importance of the desired outcome. Similarly, waiting until we can predict an outcome with certainty may lead us to never commit to a course of action at all.

True Colors in Your Goals and Values

If you find yourself starting things but quickly giving up and not finishing, revisiting your values might be a good idea. If you have selected values because others would approve of them or because you'd feel bad if you didn't endorse them, you are less likely to persist in your associated goals. (Notice positive Total 3 areas in chapter 8.) You might quickly run out of energy or feel a sense of purposelessness when attempting to complete the goals related to the value, because they are not really what you want in life. An example might help to illustrate it. One of our clients was the son of a wealthy CEO who was always asking his son what he wanted to do for a living and readily agreeing to give him start-up money for various initiatives. The son, trying to follow in his father's footsteps, went from one unsuccessful business venture to another, feeling like a failure. After drowning his feelings with alcohol for a few years, he went into recovery, where he at first explained to himself and others that his alcoholism was associated with not making enough money. However, after a year of sobriety, he realized that he didn't truly care about making or having money at all. He did care about his father's opinion of him and his own opinion of himself. He had grown up with money and appreciated it, but, unlike his dad, had no joy in the process of making it. Instead, his interests lay in the arts and literature, where the potential for making huge amounts of money is usually low.

True values feel invigorating and empowering (albeit sometimes very challenging), not overwhelming, paralyzing, or stagnant. Your true values give dignity to the steps you take every day, no matter what you're doing at the moment. For our client, being a poor high school art teacher who accepted occasional handouts from his rich father ended up suiting him just fine!

Deciding That You Don't Care

There is a fable by the ancient Greek storyteller Aesop called "The Fox and the Grapes," a story that has been told and retold for centuries. When the fox is unable to reach the grapes, he decides that he doesn't really want them anyway, as they are not ripe yet. This story is the origin of the expression "sour grapes."

Like the fox, it's easy for us to say that we despise what we think we can't have or easily reach. Sometimes we get so fused with thoughts like "I'm not good enough" or feelings of shame and fear that we deny to ourselves a value we really want to pursue. But if we have room for thoughts and feelings like these—if we can accept them and stop fighting with them—then pursuing something we may not get can be much less problematic. For example, one of our clients had convinced herself for years that she didn't want children. After some hard work with us, this woman realized that the real issue wasn't that she didn't want children, but that she was terrified that she'd admit to herself and others that she wanted them—only to be denied them. She remembers the day when she finally said to someone and herself, "I want to have a child" and how her life direction changed from that day forward. All of a sudden, the type of romantic relationship she was seeking became clear to her. Becoming aware of this value brought with it some sadness. What if she really wanted something in her life, walked in that direction, and was unable to ultimately have it? This is not the case with everyone, but sometimes there is pain in identifying a value and goals that may very well not come to fruition. Yet, as we have said before, there is dignity, self-respect, and vitality in living a valued life—even if the outcome is not what we had hoped for.

"I Need to Know Before I Commit"

We all wish we could know how something is going to turn out before we do it. Realistically, we hardly ever have all of the information needed to make a decision, and even when we plan for every possibility we can think of, we can't plan for the unexpected. Sometimes, to deal with the uncertainty of making a decision, we insist that we need to know all potential alternatives or all possible consequences of an action prior to committing to that action. Do you consistently find yourself:

• Using lack of certainty as the reason for not engaging in valued action?

• Not engaging in valued action for fear that things will not come out right or be approved of by others?

• Saying "I'll do that when I know what else is available"?

• Asking over and over again for others' opinions prior to engaging in an action?

If so, see if there aren't thoughts and feelings that you find difficult to sit with, the primary one being uncertainty. Research has shown that intolerance of uncertainty, a concept being studied primarily in anxiety disorders, can have an adaptive function in moderation, but it becomes paralyzing and maladaptive beyond a certain point (Dugas et al. 1998). To be able to engage in valued action, you have to make room for uncertainty about the outcome, whether or not this is the best alternative, and whether or not people will approve. Remember, you don't control outcomes. 🔔 [Are you having any reactions to reading this section? Does it resonate in any way with your own experience of dealing with uncertainty?]

Barriers to Action: Bumps in the Road or Roadblocks?

Now that you've identified some goals, you may start thinking about how difficult it will be to achieve some of these goals. This section of this chapter is about the barriers that keep you from moving in a valued direction.

Exercise 9.7: Identifying Barriers to Actions

The following exercise has been adapted from Hayes and Smith (2005) with permission.

1. Choose some goals that you are having difficulty completing or expect to have difficulty completing, and write them in the left-hand column.

2. In the second column, list the specific action steps associated with each goal.

3. In the third column, note any barriers that might prevent you from completing that particular action. For example, financial responsibilities might interfere with returning to school immediately, or having thoughts like "I don't deserve this" might interfere with having a romantic getaway with your partner.

4. Leave the right-hand column, on strategies to deal with the barrier, blank for now. We'll come back to this in exercise 9.14. (Table 9.5)

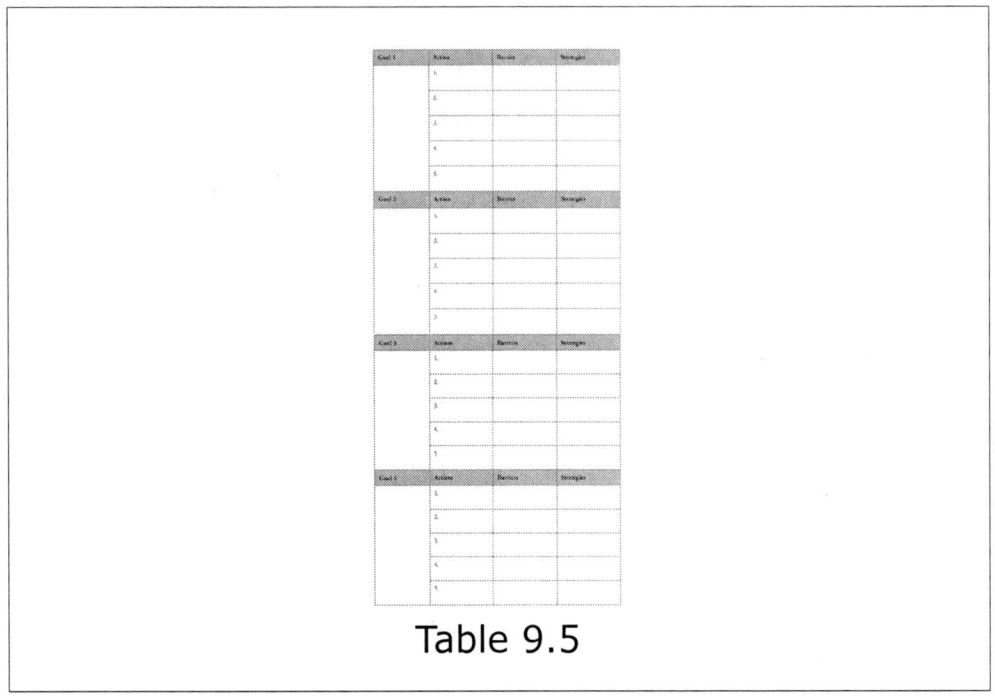

Table 9.5

Barriers Can Be Internal or External

The first thing you will probably notice on your list in exercise 9.7 is that barriers can be either internal or external. Internal barriers are thoughts, feelings, memories, or sensations that get in the way of engaging in a particular action. However, these experiences only *function* as barriers—they are not in and of themselves blocking your ability to move forward. By now, you are familiar with the notion of fusing with your thoughts (believing your thoughts as literal truth), judgments (evaluations), bodily sensations, and memories. You have spent some time examining your mind's tendency to tell you how to feel, think, or act when you experience emotions or engage in life. Now is the time to carefully watch for when internal barriers show up in your journey to commit to valued action.

Exercise 9.8: Your Internal Barriers

Go back to the list of barriers you came up with for exercise 9.7 and list below the internal barriers that you identified.

[space left intentionally blank in the original book]

External barriers can be anything outside of your skin that serves to keep you from doing the things that are important to you. These can relate to your environment, other people, economic and political contexts, and so on.

Exercise 9.9: Your External Barriers

Go back to the list of barriers you came up with for exercise 9.7 and list below the external barriers that you identified.

428

> [space left intentionally blank in the original book]
>
> Some external barriers will more than likely block you from moving forward, but some external barriers are also just *experienced* as barriers. Teasing apart these different types of barriers can be tricky. Let's look at a few examples. (Table 9.6)

Goal	Value	Actions	Internal barriers	External barriers
Go back to college	Personal growth and learning	Complete applications for desired schools.	Feelings of inadequacy show up regarding ability to complete application	No access to Internet to download application from home
		Ask for letters of recommendation.	Thought of "What if I ask and the person says no?"	Person I'd like to ask for a letter has moved and I have no address
		Determine budget for tuition.	Feelings of shame about not having more money	Financial aid decisions have

Table 9.6

In this example, the external barriers are quite concrete issues. The internal barriers are ones that this person could try to approach differently, for example, using mindfulness and willingness to experience uncomfortable thoughts and feelings. These internal barriers may be uncomfortable, but they do not in and of themselves prevent you from moving forward, despite what your mind might say about it!

Let's look at another example that isn't quite as straightforward. (Table 9.7)

Goal	Value	Actions	Internal barriers	External barriers
Get in touch with college roommate, Sally	Maintaining friendships	Call Stan to find out where Sally lives.	Fear that Stan will be upset about my not calling him sooner	Stan travels a lot.
		Call directory assistance to get her phone number.	Thought of "Why bother getting the number when she may not want to speak to me."	Sally's number is unlisted.
		Find out time of day that is best for her.	Worry that she'll think I am needy or controlling	I have a busy schedule all week.

Table 9.7

In this example, the internal barriers are also uncomfortable thoughts and feelings and can also be willingly experienced in the service of something important. The external barriers in this example are a little bit less clear. The first two barriers may require some persistence to overcome. The third, however, may be considered an external barrier that also has internal-barrier components. Simply having a busy schedule does not mean this person doesn't have time to call Sally. But buying into the *thought* about having too busy a schedule could be avoidance of calling Sally because contemplating calling Sally brings up some other uncomfortable thoughts and feelings, such as a thought of "What if we no longer have as much in common and we end up having pregnant pauses on the phone?" or guilt for not having called her sooner.

As much as possible, we suggest that you find the kernel of an internal barrier in the external barrier.

🔔 [Notice any emotions or judgments you may be experiencing about this suggestion.]

Why do we make this suggestion? Because, most likely, this core element is the only thing under your behavioral control. For example, let's imagine that you identified as a barrier having an unkind boss, and you may be able to list several bits of evidence for this evaluation. Those around you even believe you and agree with your assessment. AND this situation is significantly bothering you, you don't want to go to work anymore, you get teary-eyed at work often, and your productivity has suffered. After some initial validation from people about the stickiness of the situation, the question becomes "What now?" In ACT, we suggest looking at potential alternatives for actions, depending on your values, and what might get in the way of your taking action on one or more of those alternatives. For example, given the situation above and the nature of your values, what might keep you from taking action, whether by complaining about your boss to her superior (if that is workable for you and fits with your values), or interacting more effectively with your boss (if this fits with your values), or getting a different job (if this fits with your values), or accepting this situation as it is and not as you wish it to be (if the situation is truly unchangeable and acceptance fits with your values—or perhaps because you need to feed your kids!). This is not to say that there are no external barriers, because there are—poverty, abuse, natural disaster, and war are salient examples. However, it is still helpful to identify ways for you to manage these external barriers, even if, for example, by addressing things at a systemic level, such as joining an organization to combat domestic violence or helping out with a campaign to get an increase on the minimum wage. Not all aspects of external barriers involve internal barriers; that's the reason we are asking you to find the internal kernel if it exists.

Exercise 9.10: Finding the Kernel of Internal Struggle in External Barriers

External barrier	Internal struggles that might interfere with addressing this external barrier
Not enough time	*Worry and thoughts that if I don't overcommit I will not be as "successful." Having to sit with discomfort when coworkers get praised for their successes if I choose to put family first.*

Table 9.8

Go back to the external barriers you identified in exercise 9.9 and see if you can find any internal struggle you may have when addressing external barriers. We provide an example as guidance. (Table 9.8)

Overcoming Barriers to Action

In this section, we will discuss a few additional strategies to overcome internal barriers to action. These build on all the other strategies presented so far in the book, particularly mindfulness and defusion. We chose to cluster these strategies as a section in the commitment chapter because we think they may be particularly useful at times you are feeling stuck in inaction—when you know that you need to do something but have been unable to bring yourself to do it. As we discussed above, we will focus on events happening inside the skin, internally, that may be functioning as barriers to your living a valued life. These will often link back to external barriers, of course, but as we noted above, in ACT we feel that dealing with internal barriers to action is often the most effective way to actually impact your external environment. If you read or listen closely to inspirational leaders who have also been agents of social change, such as Martin Luther King

Jr., Mother Teresa, Gandhi, and the Dalai Lama, you might detect a similar perspective. 🔔[Notice any thoughts or emotions coming up for you.]

By now, you may be very familiar with the particular internal experiences that are difficult for you. You also may have already practiced many skills and techniques that can help you deal with your internal barriers. If you have a favorite mindfulness exercise or defusion technique, continue practicing it. Below, we will attempt to expand your tool bag for dealing with situations where inability to take action is the main problem.

Exercise 9.11: Taking Your Internal Barriers with You

This exercise is inspired by a metaphor in Hayes, Strosahl, and Wilson (1999).

1. On the lines below, list the different internal barriers that are likely to show up for you. There could be many, so it may be useful to put them into categories, such as anxiety, self-evaluation, and so on.

2. Take out the keys that you use on a daily basis. Then write down which key (car key,

house key, mailbox key, etc.) you will associate with each barrier. If you run out of keys, assign a barrier to other things you take with you each day, such as your photo ID, a credit card, a ring, your wallet or purse, or a jacket. We provide an example below. (Table 9.9)

Internal barrier	Item representing it
Thought of "I can't do it."	Photo I.D.

Table 9.9

3. Now you have a list of your common internal barriers, and you have them linked to a set of things that you take with you when you leave your house. These physical items are important for you to be able to function—you need a car key to allow you to drive to work, you need your house key to lock the door when you leave, you need your wallet to be able to purchase things you need to survive. It may seem strange to assign internal experiences to such mundane items, but think about it. Rather than trying to leave behind

each uncomfortable experience, what if it were possible that you could take them with you? Not to necessarily listen to them or act in reaction to them, but have them along for the ride, like passengers on your bus. As you take your keys, wallet, and jacket with you each day, imagine that you are taking with you all of your uncomfortable experiences. Practice some mindfulness around this. Spend a moment each time before you leave the house looking at your keys and belongings. Gently acknowledge each of the experiences they represent, then take them with you to go about your day.

Giving Up Attachment to Outcome

There is one barrier that can get its hooks into all of us: being overly attached to an outcome. Most of us want to be accomplished in some area, owning the house with the white picket fence, having a circle of loving friends and family, or enjoying lots of leisure time. However, life doesn't always oblige. It is often the case that, as we set goals for ourselves, we expect them to work out in the way we envision, and disappointment arises when we don't see that outcome. This is a natural reaction to these types of situations, but buying into thoughts and feelings around this disappointment, such as "Why bother?" or resentment often leads us to becoming stuck. Yet, check your experiences—how often do you get exactly what you want and how often have you been surprised that even though one thing did not work out as you planned, something else further down the line had a positive influence in your life? We can't predict the future. What we can do is set goals for ourselves with the understanding that we can set things up the way we'd like them to go, but watching them succeed or fail does not have to make or break us.

As you read in chapter 8, on values, engaging in activities related to your values is the important part. The way the world responds is another story. You get to choose how to respond to that response: you can try again or choose another goal to engage in. That's why we suggest that if you are feeling disheartened by the impact of your value-driven efforts and this leads to inaction, see if there is a way of letting go of attachment to a specific outcome. Remember, we cannot control much of the world, and the bigger goal is to continue to move in a valued direction. Living your life is a process—not an outcome.

One of our clients' struggle in connecting to his brother might illustrate this point more effectively. Sam hasn't spoken to his brother, Mike, in over ten years. Mike had been using drugs for a long time, and Sam had long objected to it. This conflict came to a head at their mother's funeral, where they got into a bitter argument. They haven't spoken since.

Sam values intimacy and connection and works to maintain close relationships with family and friends. A year ago, Sam decided to try to reconnect with his brother. Mike did not respond well and told Sam to leave him alone. Sam continues to feel extremely sad whenever he thinks about his brother and occasionally sends a card or a letter telling him that he's thinking of him. He has not received any response from Mike.

In this example, Sam is living his value of connection in two ways. The first is that he is emotionally close to his wife and children. The second is that he chose to reach out to his brother, regardless of how his brother responded. Even though his brother has ignored his attempts and Sam hasn't accomplished the goal of connecting with his brother, it has been important to him to continue to behave lovingly toward his brother. Would anyone say that

Sam's value of connection no longer exists because his brother is not reciprocating? On the contrary—despite the outcome, he is living in accordance with that value. He can choose to continue to engage this value in many ways, and he may continue to try to connect with his brother—or not. AND he continues to care about his brother even with the problems between them. That's the only part of the equation Sam has any control over. 🔔[Notice any thoughts, emotions, or memories coming up for you right now. Are there elements of this story that resonate with your own experience?]

Take a moment now and go back to the values you listed in the previous chapter under exercise 8.2. Ask yourself these two questions about each value:

1. Can you make room to live out this value knowing that the outcome you want may not happen? For example, is it possible for you to engage in actions that are about building trust and intimacy in your life, knowing that you may very well get hurt in the process?

2. Would your value change if the outcome you wanted did not occur? For example, would you stop caring about justice if the

world wasn't just 100 percent of the time? Imagine what would have happened if individuals like Martin Luther King Jr., Mother Teresa, Gandhi, and the Dalai Lama made their valued actions contingent on the world being fair and just most of the time!

Letting Yourself Off the Hook

Earlier in the book we stated that, unlike some religious or other cultural traditions, we do not believe that trauma survivors always *have* to forgive other people. We do not see it as a moral mandate. This is still our point of view, but now that we have covered the main concepts in ACT, particularly defusion, we would like to add a caveat to our perspective on forgiveness. In ACT, we do look to forgiveness as a strategy when people seem stuck in inaction. But, before we say more about that, let's clarify just what we mean by forgiveness.

Forgiveness: What It Is, and What It Is Not
Many survivors of trauma believe that forgiveness means that they have to forget the trauma, or that the people involved are no longer responsible for what happened. This is not what we mean by forgiveness. Forgiving is not about forgetting, condoning what hap-

pened, or dishonoring the pain of the trauma. Forgiveness literally means "giving what went before" (Hayes and Smith 2005); therefore, it is a gift to oneself. To forgive is a form of approach, rather than avoidance, and it is not something that is given to someone else or to a wrongdoer. The table below summarizes what forgiveness is, and isn't, from an ACT perspective. (Table 9.10)

Forgiveness is	Forgiveness is not
Letting go of the struggle with trauma	Forgetting about the trauma
Having compassion for painful experiences	Pretending to be okay, dishonoring painful experiences, self-blame
Holding others accountable for their actions resulting in trauma	Condoning other's inappropriate behavior resulting in trauma
Living life in a valued direction	Living life as proof that the trauma occurred
Using pain as empowerment to live life in a valued direction	Using pain as a reason not to engage in valued activity

Table 9.10

As ACT therapists, we explore what is keeping the client stuck and may eventually discuss forgiveness of self, and sometimes of others, as the effective thing to do to live a valued life. ⏏[Notice any thoughts or emotions coming up for you. If you notice yourself having some uncomfortable thoughts and feelings, please see if you can make room for the discomfort AND continue reading this section until we can explain this better.] It is not a coincidence that we are bringing up this topic late in the book. This is a difficult topic to discuss with trauma survivors, as broaching it can so easily become reminiscent of past invalidations and betrayals. Therefore, see if you can use your mindfulness skills (chapter 2) and defusion skills (chapter 6) right now, particularly if you are noticing some anger, resentment, guilt, shame, or judgments of self and others coming up.

In ACT, we view self-forgiveness as the most essential form of forgiveness: forgiveness for what happened, for what you did or didn't do, for what you said or didn't say before, during, and after your traumatic experiences. Ironically, making progress may result in more self-judgments. Sometimes, as people start moving forward in their lives in ways that they didn't think possible, they start having thoughts like "I could have done that all along?" or "What a waste of twenty years!" or feelings of sadness for their loss or anger at themselves for things they did. That's where defusion becomes important: These are just thoughts and feelings. They may well have been the barriers, when taken literally, that kept you from addressing the trauma impact earlier. See if now you can let them simply be passengers on your bus.

Often, self-forgiveness is all that is needed to make our lives work. However, sometimes to live large, we may need to go beyond this self-forgiveness toward forgiveness of others, too (Hayes and Smith 2005). For example, let's imagine that you are a survivor of childhood sexual abuse who for years struggled with substance abuse, chaos, and unemployment. But now, here you are working on ACT skills of mindfulness, defusion, and acceptance, and you realize that you got stuck when you became fused with thoughts such as "You're a liar" (said by the perpetrator) and feelings of guilt and shame. You felt like you had to suffer in your life to prove to yourself and others that you were indeed hurt, you were not a liar, and that it was not your fault. Let's imagine that, along with this realization, you also notice that having a loving family and a successful career (if those are your values) are possible for you, even when the passengers on your bus yell out "Liar" and "It was your fault." In this situation, forgiving your perpetrator is really a gift to yourself, as we said before.

It doesn't mean that you have to spend time with the person who hurt you or put yourself at risk again. But it does mean letting go of the idea that *your suffering must exist because it's the only proof of your trauma.* Realistically, it also means that you need to make room for discomfort, as others around you might conclude that the traumatic experience wasn't so bad if you are doing well now. One of our clients, whose history was very similar to the situation we're describing, heard that after she went back to college and got a degree (despite significant obstacles), her perpetrator had the audacity to take credit for it by saying that the abuse had toughened her up. Would something like that be maddening? Absolutely! However, after venting with friends and loved ones for a while, with defusion, you can come from the perspective that comments like that are just words (milk, milk, milk), the painting on the canvas (not the real scene), passengers on your bus (you are the driver), or pieces on your chessboard (you are the board). A wonderful fishing metaphor to illustrate how forgiving someone else may sometimes be the only route to forgiving yourself is to think of this as one of those instances where you are putting the worm on the hook, but somehow the hook goes through your finger first. In this metaphor, the only way to get your finger unstuck is to let the worm (no pun intended!) "off the hook" first (Hayes and Smith 2005).

Exercise 9.12: Exploring Forgiveness

Compassionately and honestly check in with your experiences as you answer the following questions. In what ways have you kept yourself on the hook with your trauma?

[space left intentionally blank in the original book]

What is your life like when you hold onto your suffering as proof of your trauma?

[space left intentionally blank in the original book]

What would be possible if you let go of the burden of suffering?

[space left intentionally blank in the original book]

🛎[What thoughts and feelings come up as you do this work?] Your mind may have a lot to say about forgiveness. It may say that you aren't strong enough to forgive, that you shouldn't forgive, or that everything will be better once you forgive. In our experience, strong emotions come up when people think about forgiveness. You may feel anxious, sad, tense, relieved, or content. The key to dealing with these reactions is practicing loving-kindness toward your experiences. They are not your enemy—nor is forgiveness. See if you can imagine giving yourself the gift of forgiveness. You may have to give yourself this gift many, many times. Sharing a cup of coffee with a friend is a gift to yourself; drinking, using, or bingeing and purging is not. Saying no and refusing to be taken advantage of is a gift to yourself. Smiling at the cashier and sharing a joke with a coworker is a gift to yourself; spending hours ruminating on the unfairness of it all isn't. Reading this book and allowing yourself to soak it in is a gift to yourself. Life will ask you every day, sometimes many times during that day, whether you choose to let yourself off the hook or not. Isn't that wonderful? Who knew you could be empowered to give yourself a precious gift everyday?

Saying What You'll Do; Doing What You Say

Much of what we do corresponds to what we *say* we will *do*. As a shorthand, we will refer to this sequence of events as *say-do correspondence* (Rogers-Warren and Baer 1976). Say-do correspondence has to do with the relation between what a person says and then does, or does and then re-ports. Yet, at other times, we get stuck in a self-perpetuating cycle of saying that we will be doing something, not doing it, then experiencing a wave of uncomfortable feel-ings of guilt and shame for not having kept our word. These feelings are then pushed away by renewed (but still often unkept) promises. In the field of addictions, individ-uals often talk about the damage done to relationships and self-respect by repeatedly promising to stop drinking, gambling, or drugging without really intending to do so. Fusion and lack of acceptance are often the culprits in this situation. Let's take the situation of someone who promises to stop drinking without intending to stop or without ever truly trying to stop. Many clients tell us that what is often going on in such situa-tions is that they are experiencing some uncomfortable emotions, either because someone is upset with them or because they are in legal or financial trouble, and a quick promise gets people off their back.

In this type of situation, what they say they will do is simply a guideline that comes from some external judgment or rule and has very little to do with contacting experientially what truly matters to them. We are not saying that the person doesn't value sobriety, but that chances are they are not in contact with that value in the moment they make the promise. In such situations, we may say we will do something in order to avoid the bad things that will happen if we don't do it, even if we then end up not doing that thing at all. This can happen even when the stakes are small. For example, you might say that you'll attend a classical music performance with a friend and not really want or intend to go. These are the times when cancellations are backed up by reasons why we can't do something. "I'm feeling sick today" is code for "I didn't really want to do it in the first place; I just said so because it was easier than telling you why I didn't want to do it." 🔔[Notice your thoughts and feelings when you consider this idea.]

The problem with a lack of say-do correspondence is that it tends to lead to inaction because of the snowball effect. Thoughts such as "I've already not done it once; why bother now?" or "I'm a failure" or feelings of shame and guilt are often suppressed, minimized, or defended against with more ineffective behaviors. Rarely do people report feeling good about themselves for engaging in this type of behavior, even when it involves seemingly small white lies like telling a friend that you can't join her at a concert because you're sick, when you really never intended to go in the first place.

What can you do when you get caught in this cycle? What if the rule was shifted in favor of things that were important to you on the level of your personal values? Instead of "I'll say I will do it because bad things will happen if I don't," what if the rule was "I'll say I will do something that is very important to me so that I will actually do it"? This could be a whole new way of accomplishing your goals. Take the classical music concert example from above. You might decide to attend the concert because it would mean a lot to your friend, who is feeling very lonely right now. In this case, promising her that you'll go can help you stick to it when the concert comes around. This is an example of how it is possible to practice saying what you will do and doing what you say.

If you are having the thought that you have burned too many bridges already and people won't trust you, see if you can start there and use your personal values as an internal compass. Whatever you have been doing, see what you can do differently. In the case of addiction, for instance, the person may start out with sharing about how ashamed and embarrassed he or she is not to have done what he or she promised to do, and then make a commitment to be honest, whatever the situation may be. Realistically, though, saying what you do and doing what you say will inevitably require mindfulness, defusion, acceptance, and a strong sense of where your values lie. Say-do correspondence will inevitably entail sitting with uncomfortable emotions, such as fear, sadness, guilt, or thoughts like "I'll be alone for the rest of my life." For example, to reveal to a significant other that you have relapsed again or to tell your best friend that you don't like classical music will result in some responses from the other person, such as disappointment, anger, or even name-calling. Yet, check in with your experience and see how often saying one thing and doing another has worked out for you in the long run. If you are like most people, it may buy some peace in the short term. But realistically, it leads to uncomfortable moments anyhow, and eventually could result in the loss of relationships and a reduction in self-respect, the latter associated with acting in ways that are not in accordance with your values. A very touching therapy moment occurred when one of our clients, who had been very much rejected and criticized by her mother, came in and told her therapist, who was definitely in the mother-figure role, that she had a serious marijuana addiction that she had never talked about and had actively hidden from the thera-pist in the last year of treatment. She said, "Coming in every week with this secret while talking about my values felt way worse than not smoking pot could possibly ever feel."

If this lack of say-do correspondence has been a problem for you and is keeping you stuck, we recommend that you actively practice saying things you will do each day and following through because you *said* you would, confident in the fact that each statement is rooted in your values. Start out with small things like doing the dishes, making a phone call, walking the dog, or taking out the trash. Notice the impact that say-do correspondence has on you and others around you.

In earlier chapters, we mentioned that pretty much everything we do is learned. That's also the case with following our values, such as doing what we say and saying what we do. This type of exercise is a great way to start contacting your experience of what it feels like to follow your values. Sometimes we just don't know how it feels to follow our values, particularly if we have not been very mindful. We may not have had the mindful stance to be able to connect with the experience: "Oh, this is what it's like to follow my values" versus "Oh, this is what it is like not to follow my values." In behavior therapy, we call this *discrimination training*—being able to experientially, not just intellectually, contact the difference between one set of circumstances and another (Skinner 1953). Sometimes we have some minor reactions, like tightness in the stomach or a sudden craving for a drink. But without mindfulness, these experiences get labeled as "coming out of the blue" and do not get registered as reactions associated with behaving in contradiction to our values. Therefore, if this is an area of concern for you, we highly recommend that you try it out and practice, starting with small things, and see what happens.

Making Lemonade: Empowering Your Values

Many of us have heard the phrase, "When life gives you lemons, make lemonade." 🔔[Notice your reactions to this statement and see if you know where these reactions come from.] Often, people talk about harnessing the pain of your experiences and turning the pain into something positive. These statements can be experienced either as empowering or as invalidating and constricting. When we try to avoid pain, we create more suffering. When we honor it and move with it, a wide range of things become possible beyond the pain. When your pain is a source of empowerment, your values can be a source of strength and can give your life direction.

Sometimes, after a difficult or traumatic life experience, people get empowered to act in ways that matter to them. An abuse survivor harnessed her pain to press charges against her perpetrator and sit through his trial. A veteran sought out mental health services after having suffered in silence for many years. An accident victim reconnected with an estranged family member when she got out of the hospital. A grieving mother started a support group for others who have lost a loved one due to violent crimes.

Viktor Frankl wrote a book called *Man's Search for Meaning* (1963), where he discusses the courage and strength of Holocaust survivors amidst a horrific existence. Frankl's discussion of surviving this experience has set an important foundation for understanding life after all types of traumatic experiences. Although we are *not* saying that your trauma should have happened or that those responsible need to be forgiven for their sake, we are saying that there may be ways of being that you value that may have partly come from this trauma. We know for sure that we have worked with many very strong, compassionate, and giving people who have survived terrible traumas. And part of their valued living was to care for others and work in the direction of preventing injustices in the world. In fact, seeing the beauty of the human spirit in the face of adversity and pain is one of gifts we have received in doing this work. Below, we will give you an opportunity to privately explore this concept within your own history.

Exercise 9.13: Finding Meaning in Your Trauma

Please write below a few qualities you have that you value in yourself that may have been related to growth after your trauma:

[space left intentionally blank in the original book]

Take some time right now to jot down your reactions to this exercise. Can you tell which passengers are yelling the loudest right now? Do you know where these passengers have come from?

[space left intentionally blank in the original book]

In your daily life, returning to your values can be extremely helpful. As you set goals and check off smaller actions each day and each week, it can be important to step back and examine the larger pattern. Forgiveness and being mindful do not have to sit in opposition to the source of strength that can come from painful life experiences. You are still standing, and your resilience comes out of surviving and living in the service of what is important to you. Ignoring the strength you have gained from your experiences simply because they were painful or you have forgiven or moved on is like ignoring wisdom because you disagree with its source. Bringing that strength to your actions can be a wonderful source of empowerment, and you do not have to give that up when you build patterns of action in line with your values.

The Final Step: Committing to a Valued Path

Willingness to commit, as we discussed earlier, is an all-or-nothing phenomenon. You can't sort of commit, just like you can't sort of jump. Therefore, making a choice to commit 100 percent to a goal rooted in a value is paramount to making change happen in your life. When you get caught by your very smart mind with good reasons for not doing what you set out to do, ask yourself this question: "If the safety of someone I loved was threatened, could I engage in this action to protect that person?" Can you go to the gym even if you're tired? Not blow up at the salesperson who's denying your request? Give someone a hug when you're mad? Not take that drink when you're craving it?

Now that we have added a few more tools to your bag, let's go back to pinpoint ways to deal with the barriers you identified earlier.

Exercise 9.14: Identifying Strategies to Deal with Barriers

Go back to exercise 9.7. For each barrier you identified, come up with a strategy you will use to deal with this barrier. The strategy can be something from this chapter or from the rest of the book. Try to write down what you can do to deal with that situation, thinking through whether or not that move could work for you under the existing conditions and considering your values. Do not write down something that feels phony or unlikely to work. Mentally put yourself in the actual situation and walk yourself through it, checking to see if what you're suggesting feels real. If something feels rote or like an idea that might work for somebody else but not you, come up with something different. Remember, that's the first step: Do something different than

---

what has gotten you stuck, and then, based on your experience, see if it works or not. Make sure to go back to exercise 9.7 now, before you proceed with reading this page.

🔔[Notice any thoughts, feelings, and judgments that come up while you do this exercise.]

The Big Question

Engaging in life via small steps linked to larger goals, all of which are linked to your values, means that you can build, over time, great things for your life. Great in the sense that you get to live the life you want now, in each moment. Life does not have to live you—you can live it. Setbacks, difficult emotions, uncomfortable memories, old patterns of avoidance, and barriers will show up by the dozen. However, you have the tools to engage in your life *with* these experiences rather than in spite of them. *Trying* to live in accordance with values is not the same as *doing* it. If you are living your life mindfully, with your values and your pain at your side, you will be able to live a meaningful, value-driven life, whether or not specific desired outcomes are attained.

The question is this:

> Given that there is a distinction between you and the things that you are struggling with, such as thoughts and feelings, are you willing to experience all of your thoughts, feelings, bodily responses, and memories, fully and without defense, from a defused perspective, viewing them for what they are (thoughts and feelings) and not what they say they are (intolerable, hopeless), and do what takes you in the direction of your chosen values, at this moment and in this situation?

This is not a question that can be answered permanently—it is one that will be asked of you over and over again by life. Your answer is a free choice each and every time.

Journaling

Thoughts

460

[space left intentionally blank in the original book]

Feelings or Emotions

[space left intentionally blank in the original book]

Self-Judgments

[space left intentionally blank in the original book]

Physical Sensations

[space left intentionally blank in the original book]

Action Urges (What Do You Feel Like Doing?)

[space left intentionally blank in the original book]

CHAPTER 10

Skills in Relationships: Staying Safe and Being True to Yourself

With Karen R. Murphy and Kate M. Iverson

As despair can come to one only from other human beings, hope, too, can be given to one only by other human beings.

—Elie Wiesel

There is a bidirectional association between relationships and trauma: Relationships impact trauma and trauma, in turn, impacts relationships. First, trauma can often occur in the context of relationships (Herman 1992). Second, if you have had a traumatic experience, chances are your relationships have been impacted by it (Polusny and Follette 1995). Third, the more support and connection you have in your life, the faster your recovery from a traumatic experience will be (Herman 1992). Given this mutual influence, we could not have done justice to helping you find a life after trauma without covering ways to improve the quality of your relationships, ways that include keeping yourself safe or perhaps risking connection even when you've been hurt before. Given the breadth and depth of the issues involved, we decided to devote an entire chapter to this topic. Relationships skills relevant to trauma survivors that are based on mindfulness, acceptance, defusion, and values will be the focus of this chapter.

Trauma and Relationships

So far you've learned a lot about the effects of trauma, typical ways you may have reacted to it, and what you can do with your thoughts and feelings about trauma. In the initial chapters, we discussed what has already happened to you and what is happening in your life today. In this chapter, we would first like to take a little time to consider the idea that your past learning often has an influence on current interactions. This is yet another point where we see that the two sides of the coin are connected. On one side is the fact that you are more than your traumatic experiences and on the other side is the probability that you have been influenced by a wide variety of life experiences—including your trauma. The point is *not* that you are to blame for the things that have happened to you or that you are broken in some way. However, understanding the way that your past experiences can influence your present behavior is helpful in assisting you in moving forward in your life.

Everyone who is reading this book is in relationship to a number of people in life. So, when we talk about relationships, we don't just mean the romantic kind. In this chapter we want to discuss some skills that can be helpful in navigating a variety of types of relationships in the context of ongoing chatter by the passengers on your bus. One of the troubling research statistics that comes up over and over again is the finding that those who have experienced a trauma are more vulnerable to being revictimized (Cloitre and Rosenburg 2006; Polusny and Follette 1995). Therefore, we will address retraumatization in detail and move on to some more general skills that can be helpful.

Retraumatization

As you know by now, trauma impacts everyone in some way, from minor distress to more severe mental health and physical health problems. If you are reading this book, you probably have experienced some longer-term problems. However, experiencing trauma can also make you vulnerable to experiencing additional traumas, which is often referred to as *retraumatization* or *revictimization.* The risk of revictimization can be impacted by a number of variables. For example, rescue workers such as police and firefighters and people in military service are likely to experience multiple traumatic events either in the course of everyday duties or while on deployment (Orkutt, Erickson, and Wolfe 2002). In fact, there is significant concern about the relatively new practice in the military of repeated deployment and our lack of knowledge about the impact of this activity. Additionally, women who have experienced childhood abuse are at much greater risk for experiencing adult physical and sexual revictimization (Cloitre and Rosenburg 2006; Smith, White, and Holland 2003).

🔔 [Notice any thoughts, feelings, and judgments coming up for you right now.]

Retraumatization Is Not Uncommon

Much of the scientific research on retraumatization and revictimization has been conducted with survivors of sexual assault. In this chapter we will take a look at some themes from that research that may be helpful for you to know about. First, let's briefly take a look at some statistics:

- After someone has experienced any type of trauma, he or she is at greater risk of experiencing additional traumatic events over the course of his or her life (Polusny and Follette 1995).

- Women who have experienced sexual abuse in childhood are approximately 1.5 to 3 times more likely to experiences a sexual assault in adulthood (Cloitre et al. 1996; Roodman and Clum 2001).

- Men who have experienced sexual or physical abuse in childhood are more likely to be victims and perpetrators of interpersonal violence in adulthood, such as domestic violence (Cloitre et al. 2001).

- Having PTSD can be a risk factor for retraumatization for at least some types of trauma (National Center for Victims of Crime and the Crime Victims Research and Treatment Center 1992).

- Women who are sexually abused in childhood experience more severe and diverse psychological effects, including revictimization, than women who were abused only in adulthood (Cloitre and Rosenberg 2006; Follette et al. 1996).

Some of you will relate very well to the material in this chapter and see the utility in enhancing your awareness and assertiveness skills in relationships. Some of you may find that you already have a good grasp of the ideas presented below. In that case, we hope that this chapter will help you strengthen your skills and find new and empowering ways to live your life fully. We are in no way implying that everyone who experienced a trauma has problems with these skills. However, we cannot ignore the statistics that tell us that you may be at risk for further trauma. Therefore, we decided to include this information for your consideration. You can decide which part or parts will be most useful to you.

Safety and Revictimization Issues

Given the statistics that we presented above, you may find yourself having thoughts such as "What if I experience another trauma?" or "Is the current relationship I am in an abusive one?" One thing we can take away from the above research is that trauma happens to people and trauma can happen more than once.

That is to say, you may have already experienced more than one traumatic event in your life or you may be at risk for experiencing another traumatic event in the future.

🔔 [Notice any reactions you may be having to this discussion. You may be having thoughts that we are painting a rather bleak picture. You may also notice that you are experiencing some nervousness and anxiety.]

Before we move forward, let's simply take a moment to notice some of the thoughts and feelings you are having about retraumatization right now.

Exercise 10.1: Noticing Thoughts and Feelings About Retraumatization

What are some of the thoughts you have when you hear about retraumatization rates?

Example: *Bad things aren't supposed to happen to good people.*

[space left intentionally blank in the original book]

What are some of the feelings you have when hearing that you might be at risk for experiencing another trauma?

Example: *Nervousness and anxiety*

[space left intentionally blank in the original book]

What are some of your action urges right now? Is there any thing you want to do in response to your thoughts and feelings?

Example: *Stay at home where it is safe.*

[space left intentionally blank in the original book]

So, part of you may be feeling uncomfortable and part of you may be feeling curious about what you can do to help yourself or someone you know. As we have discussed throughout this book, we know that spending a lot of time worrying about the possibility of experiencing another trauma does not actually make us any safer in the long run. Instead, being immersed in our thoughts and out of contact with our environment may actually increase our risk. Additionally, living a very restricted life in the service of safety may keep us from pursing valued goals. For example, getting fused with a thought such as "If I never get into another relationship, I can never be hurt" can keep us isolated, as we may try to hide out or avoid life in an attempt to avoid getting hurt again. In an effort to stay safe from emotional or physical harm, we may stop calling our friends, stop doing things we used to enjoy, or attempt to escape through alcohol or other drugs. Despite our best intentions, many of these behaviors prevent us from fully engaging in our lives, AND these measures do not actually increase our safety and satisfaction. In the previous chapters you've learned a lot about engaging fully in your life and living in the present moment. Now we will give you some ideas that are designed to help you to live your life in a safer and more empowering way.

Avoidance and Revictimization

It is important that we come back to the idea of avoidance again and how it can sometimes lead to more problems. If you have experienced a traumatic event, you may have a thought like "There must be something wrong with me; these things don't happen to other people that I know." In ACT, we take the approach that:

- There is nothing wrong with you.

- You are a complete person who has every-thing you need to lead a complete and full life.

- You are not broken.

- You do not need to be fixed.

What you may need is to learn or *relearn* skills that can help keep you safe, with mindfulness as a foundation. We choose to call the strate-gies discussed in this chapter skills because we believe that they are not things that most of us are simply born with but instead things that we learn over the course of our development. As we pointed out in chapter 2, some of us may never have had the opportunity to learn these skills for reasons that were out of our control. For example, if you grew up in a home where you were neglected, ignored, or abused, you may not have learned some of these skills. Or, you may have grown up in a family that simply didn't emphasize or teach you these skills. Or, you may have been in family or social environ-ments that taught you other behaviors that took their place, such as ignoring your feelings, substance use, isolation, or some other form of avoidance. This latter situation is often the case in abusive or alcoholic families, but it happens in other families as well. While you are not to blame for things that happened to you in the past, you have the ability to respond (response-ability) *now* in the most effective way to help empower you to live your life fully. 🔔[Notice any bodily sensations you may be experiencing right now.]

As mentioned earlier in this book, mindlessly following our feelings about events is not always useful. Some of the behaviors you do because they help you *feel* safe might actually put you in more danger. Let's talk about that for a bit. Avoidance, in certain situations, actually does two things:

1. Puts you at risk for traumatic events to occur

2. Reduces your ability to cope with those events if they do occur

Many people have trouble identifying danger cues and responding to these cues effectively. This could be a function of not having learned effective strategies for noticing abuse or not having the necessary skills for responding in high-risk situations. Understanding the factors that put people at risk for revictimization continues to be an important area of research. Clinical researchers have developed some interesting insights into why avoidance and other factors might be related to early victimization experiences (for an excellent description read Cloitre, Cohen, and Koenen's 2006 book *Treating Survivors of Childhood Abuse).* The bottom line is that it actually makes a lot of sense that you may have trouble coping with risky situations. Think about it like burning your hand on a stove.

Metaphor: Burning Your Hand on a Hot Stove

If you accidentally set your hand on a hot stove, you immediately pull your hand away. You felt pain, and this signaled you to react. You probably didn't take the time to think this through, "Hmm, my hand is on the stove, and my hand is starting to hurt. I have two options here: I could leave my hand on the stove, or I could take it off. If I take it off, the pain will probably go away. Therefore I will remove my hand." You simply acted out of the feeling of pain. Unfortunately, when we feel pain a lot, or the pain feels too overwhelming, we may find ways to avoid those painful feelings. We engage in behaviors to get away from the pain (at this point, you probably are well acquainted with your old moves), which can happen with or without our awareness at the moment. Attempting to avoid pain makes sense; no one wants to spend their life constantly feeling afraid, sad, or generally in pain. Or, in the case where we are constantly feeling the sensation of being burned, such as when we experience certain PTSD symptoms (flashbacks, hyper-arousal), then our danger cues can be constantly activated, to no avail. We may then learn to ignore them over time because we are unsure if there is real danger or just our PTSD symptoms flaring up when we are actually safe. Either way, the problem is that when you no longer allow yourself to feel or notice your pain, you also stop taking your hand off the stove—and you get burned. The message is that if you stop paying attention to the cues your body and the world gives you, such as pain from contact with a hot burner, you are likely to get burned even more severely from leaving your hand on the burner. Now remember, there are always two sides to the coin. So, if you have been revictimized, that does not mean it is your fault. Life can throw some dangerous things at us, and what's important is to recognize what is in our control and what is not. 🧘[Notice your breathing right now.]

Of course, the above metaphor is a simple example of a very complex process that generally works on a much subtler level. However, the point is that avoidance of emotional pain and discomfort may have a similar impact on your life. If you organize your life around avoidance, you may miss important cues and even danger signals in your body and in the world. Additionally, if you go through another traumatic event and respond to it with more avoidance, isolation, and so on, you are simply turning up the gas on the burner.

The message here is that many survivors learn to disconnect from the internal mechanisms that help promote awareness of potential danger. When these fight-or-flight mechanisms are ignored or unavailable to you, they are unable to help keep you safe. By now you've learned how many survivors learn to shut down awareness of emotions to protect themselves from overwhelming emotional pain and betrayal. Unfortunately, shutting down awareness of emotions also puts us at risk for more pain and betrayal. As discussed throughout the book, mindfulness and defusion are key skills to bring to bear on these situations.

Another key form of avoidance for many trauma survivors occurs in the context of relationships.

Some people report avoiding close relationships, and others report finding ways to avoid intimacy within relationships. Either form of avoidance can lead to suffering and isolation. The next exercise is designed to identify your own patterns in relationships.

Exercise 10.2: Identifying Triggers for Avoidance Behaviors in Relationships

Typically, when something is hurting us, we pull away from it to prevent ourselves from being burned. When you consider burning your hand on a stove, the trigger for moving your hand away would be the heat felt on your fingers and hand. Over the next few days, see if you can identify three examples of triggers for avoidance behaviors that you notice in your interactions with other people (from family, friends, and coworkers to the cashier at the supermarket). Some of these examples may not feel like a big event in your life; in fact, they may be so automatic that you hardly notice them at first. Often, the whole pattern will occur fairly quickly, in a matter of seconds or minutes. Other patterns may be more obvious. For each example of triggers for avoidance behaviors, use the

476

worksheet to fill in the trigger, the response, and what you are avoiding.

1. For "Circumstance," write down the
environment or situation you were in and
what happened.

2. For "Trigger," describe what caused you
to react.

3. For "Response," describe what thoughts,
feelings, bodily sensations, memories, or
action urges you felt in reaction to the
trigger.

4. For "Avoidance pattern," describe what
avoidance behavior you actually engaged
in, and consider whether this is an old
move for you.

5. For "Consequences," describe how the
avoidance pattern worked for you—how
you felt or other consequences it had over
the next few hours or days. How did it
impact you or your relationship with others
involved in the situation?

Before you begin, you can take a look at
the following worksheet completed by a

client. This exercise was adapted from one by Addis and Martell (2004).

Example 1

Circumstance: *Visiting my parents, who physically abused me as a child, at their house on Sunday afternoon.*

Trigger: *My mother mentioned something about my being a "sensitive" child.*

Response: *I felt hurt and misunderstood, as well as angry at my mother. I was also upset with my father for not saying anything to defend me.*

Avoidance pattern: *I disengaged from the conversation and stopped paying attention to what they were talking about. I left shortly after that.*

Consequences: *Felt depressed and numb for the rest of the day.*

Trigger Example 2

Circumstance: *I ran into my Army buddy's widow at the market. I started having more flashbacks of the war later this week.*

Trigger: *I had a flashback of seeing my friend killed.*

Response: *I experienced feelings of terror and helplessness.*

Avoidance pattern: *I was going to have one drink to calm down yesterday and ended up drinking all night.*

Consequences: *I passed out and forgot that I had a dinner date scheduled with my girl-friend. Now she won't talk to me. I had a thought of "I'm such a loser."*

Note: Before you complete this worksheet, make extra copies for future use.

Situation 1

Circumstance: _____

Trigger: _____

Response: _____

Avoidance pattern: _____

Consequences: _____

Situation 2

Circumstance: _____

Trigger: _____

Response: _____

Avoidance pattern: _____

Situation 3

Circumstance: _____

Trigger: _____

Response: _____

Avoidance pattern: _____

Consequences:

Now look closely at the avoidance patterns you have identified. How do these fit with the values you identified in exercise 8.2? List three things you can do to help change these avoidance patterns.

[space left intentionally blank in the original book]

Trusting Your Instincts

As we noted earlier, there are always two sides to a coin. While we have been discussing the problems of avoidance in relationships, sometimes it may be useful for you to pay attention to your gut feeling that something is wrong or not safe.

🔔 [Notice any thoughts, feelings, and judgments coming up for you right now.]

We recently worked with a young man who was seeking treatment due to a recent physical assault he experienced at the store where he works. Here are some of the internal cues that he reported experiencing immediately before he was attacked:

- My instincts told me "something is wrong here."

- The look on my attacker's face made me uncomfortable from the beginning.

- I didn't like him coming closer to me.

- Something told me to stay away from him, but I didn't want to be rude.

In therapy, it became evident that the client blamed himself for not trusting his instincts. However, this is what many of us do in these types of situations. Many trauma survivors will state that they second-guessed themselves with thoughts and feelings such as these:

- "I must be overreacting."

- Fear of hurting the guy's feelings by blowing him off or even running away.

- "I must be getting paranoid because of what my dad did to me when I was growing up."

- "I don't want to be mean."

- Desire to be polite.

You may find some of these passengers familiar. Many of us second-guess our internal instincts, particularly if they have gone off in the past for seemingly no reason. You may have been raised to be polite and do not want to hurt another person's feelings or make them mad. In the case of our client, his assault was certainly not his fault, nor did he do anything to promote the assault. However, one goal of treatment was to help him learn to trust his instincts again. In other words, trust your experience—what are your emotions telling you when you are mindful of what is going on with you? Paying attention to the wisdom within our experiences allows us to notice our emotions and decide how to behave.

There is a tightrope to walk here, and we are aware of the challenge. Elsewhere in the book we warned you not to become fused with your emotions and not to let fear drive your bus. AND here we are asking you to trust your instincts and emotions. Although this may seem contradictory, it isn't. If you recall from our discussion of values in chapter 8, sometimes fear is adaptive and sometimes it isn't. The key issue is workability: Are you still driving your bus in the value-driven direction? Are you veering left to avoid hitting a car, or are you veering left because your passengers tell you to, even when there is no imminent danger? The key factors are mindfulness, workability, and reliance on your experience. To help you hone these skills, we will present several exercises in this chapter to help you learn how to engage in this type of discrimination training—an important element in keeping yourself safe and making relationships work.

Exercise 10.3: Listening to Your Warning Receptors

This exercise will have two parts: the first will be about someone else and the second will be about yourself. First, we'd like you to read the example given below about Jane. While you're reading the example, circle all of the potential cues that Jane may have ignored or minimized.

Jane was shopping at a local grocery store one evening. She was picking out some ingredients for tacos when a man looked at her, walked toward her, and stood very close to her in the aisle. She felt uncomfortable and she stiffened, but she told herself that he was probably just looking at the same items she was. Then he started asking her questions, and she felt more uncomfortable. She thought about walking away, but she decided that he was probably harmless, and she didn't want to hurt his feelings because he was probably just lonely. Yet, she still sensed that there was something "off" about him—she especially didn't like the way he was looking at her and how close he stood to her. He then said something sexually explicit to her. At that point she gave him a dirty look and walked away. She felt unsettled for the rest of the day. This incident happened within the course of a couple of minutes.

🔔 [Notice any thoughts, feelings, and judgments coming up for you.]

Now that you identified these cues with someone else, we will ask you to bring this exercise closer to home. This issue will make more sense if you can link it to something in your own life. Take some time to think about a time when not paying attention to, minimizing, or avoiding your emotions and physical instincts may have actually put you in more danger.

We would like you to write about a time when you may have ignored or missed your internal cues. For example, this could be a time you refused help when you may have needed it, when you used substances and found yourself in unsafe settings, or when you told yourself you were overreacting when later events suggested otherwise. Once you think of the event, describe it in the space below.

[space left intentionally blank in the original book]

Now, take some time to think about how allowing yourself to pay more attention to your internal responses may have improved your safety. Write about it in the space below. If any passengers on your bus come up, see if you can make room for them simply as thoughts, emotions, and self-judgments without the need to control them.

[space left intentionally blank in the original book]

Emotional Awareness Skills

Researchers have found that there are certain aspects of awareness, or lack thereof, that are associated with revictimization (Cloitre, Cohen, and Koenen 2006; Najavits 2006). Therefore, we would like now to build on mindfulness skills we covered earlier in the book with an exploration of mindfulness of emotions in particular. Identifying and labeling emotions more readily and precisely may help you stay safe.

Difficulty Feeling: Identifying and Labeling Emotions

- Do you ever have the experience of not being sure what you really feel about a certain situation?

- Do you get your thoughts confused with emotions?

- Do you regularly have the thought "I'm better off just ignoring my emotions"?

- Do you hold the belief that you only feel one thing at a time?

- Do you wonder if you even have feelings?

If you answered yes to any of the above questions, then congratulations! You're human. But seriously, many of us have difficulty knowing and understanding what we are feeling, especially if the emotion is intense or the feeling of numbness is coming up. And, we know that trauma survivors often have even more difficulties with identifying and labeling their emotions. This difficulty may be a direct result of experiencing trauma or it may be more a reflection of your attempts to deal with emotions after your trauma. Whatever the reason may be, don't worry. There are things you can do to enhance your understanding of emotions and how they can actually help you be fully present and safe.

Learning what you are feeling and labeling your feelings is just like any other skill. It takes practice. Just as we are constantly having thoughts, we are also constantly having feelings. If you have ignored your feelings for a long time, then it may take a little bit of work to get back in touch with them. Or, if you grew up in a household that didn't talk about feelings, you may have to learn what feelings are and what they feel like. Feelings are what they sound like—they are sensations we feel inside of us that we learn to label in certain ways. Emotions are often discussed as having physical, cognitive, and behavioral components—as complex phenomena that result from the interplay of all these areas (Frijda 2007; Linehan 1993a). Therefore, all these elements are important in being able to become mindful of your emotions and will be included in the next exercise.

Noticing What Is Going On Inside of You

[Pay attention to what is happening in your mind right now. Listen to what the sensations in your body are telling you. Be mindful of your experiences.]

Sometimes it's easier to label other people's feelings than our own. If you're not sure what you are feeling, ask yourself: "What might someone else be feeling in this situation?"

Exercise 10.4: Understanding Your Emotions

The following exercise is designed to help you become more aware of the components of emotional responding. Take a few minutes and think about how you experience each of the following emotions. Also, list what you tend to do when you feel each of these emotions.

Example: When I feel *excited* I notice:

In my body **increased heart rate, more energy**

In my thoughts **This is fantastic.**

In my body language **wider eyes, moving around, smiling**

With my actions **talking more, telling people I'm excited, working toward my goal**

When I am feeling excited I tend to **go after my goal**

1. When I feel *happy* I notice:

In my body _____

In my body language _____

In my thoughts _____

With my actions _____

When I am feeling happy I tend to _____

2. When I feel *sad* I notice:

In my body _____

In my body language _____

In my thoughts _____

With my actions _____

When I am feeling sad I tend to _____

3. When I feel *mad or angry* I notice:

In my body _____

In my body language _____

In my thoughts _____

With my actions _____

When I am feeling mad or angry I tend to _____

4. When I feel *afraid* I notice:

In my body _____

In my body language _____

In my thoughts _____

With my actions _____

When I am feeling afraid I tend to _____

5. When I feel *disappointed* I notice:

In my body _____

In my body language _____

In my thoughts _____

With my actions _____

When I am feeling disappointed I tend to _____

6. When I feel *loving* I notice:

In my body _____

In my body language _____

In my thoughts _____

With my actions _____

When I am feeling loving I tend to _____

7. When I feel *embarrassment* I notice:

In my body _____

In my body language _____

In my thoughts _____

With my actions _____

> When I am feeling embarrassed I tend to
> _____

Some tips to help you become more aware of your feelings are:

- Frequently ask yourself: "What am I feeling right now?" or "What sensations do I notice in my body?"

- Check in with what you're feeling every hour of the day for practice.

- Imagine what somebody else might be feeling in the situation.

- Watch a movie and try to label what each of the characters might be feeling in each scene and why.

- Take notice of other peoples' feelings.

- Listen to a favorite song and label the emotions it evokes.

Difficulties Being Present: Dissociation

🔔 [Name one bodily sensation you are experiencing this moment.]

As discussed in chapter 1, dissociation is a common experience among trauma survivors. Dissociation refers to a lack of awareness about what is going on around you and in your body. The term also refers to times when you feel as if you are cognitively and emotionally distanced from the current situation—as if you are "here, but not really here." As a review of what you learned in chapter 1, here are a few key points about dissociation:

- It's often an automatic response to overwhelming emotions.

- It's sometimes referred to as shutting down or going blank.

- It is the experience of going from a feeling state to a numb state.

- In its most extreme forms, dissociation may feel as if you have left your body or lost time.

- In more mild to moderate forms, dissociation is most frequently a response to fear and anxiety.

- Dissociation typically leads you to feel less present in the current moment.

As discussed in chapter 1, dissociation usually serves to help you during a trauma, but it is not as useful after the trauma has ended. *Dissociation can be problematic from a safety standpoint because it can delay your awareness or reaction time to danger.* As noted before, mindfulness, remaining fully aware and awake, is the most effective strategy for dealing with dissociation. However, if you find yourself dissociating, don't judge it—notice it. The discussion and exercise below will attempt to help you increase mindfulness of dissociation itself.

Three Steps to Help Prevent Dissociation

1. *Recognize your triggers for dissociation.* Typical triggers include strong emotions, such as fear, anxiety, or shame.

2. *Become more aware of when you are beginning to dissociate.* Try checking in with yourself to prevent dissociation. You could

try checking in with yourself every hour or so. Dissociation, even in milder forms, can have a seductive quality (for instance, when you are in a meeting and you tune out), and resisting it may involve a strong commitment.

3. *Overcome dissociation with mindfulness.* Redirect your attention to the present moment. Focus on what you are doing and remember that it is okay to feel what you feel.

Exercise 10.5: How Present Are You?

Just as you did in chapter 1, rate yourself in terms of where you are right now in regard to being aware of and present with your life experiences. Use a scale of 0 to 10, with 0 being really checked out and 10 being very aware of the present moment: (Image 10.1)

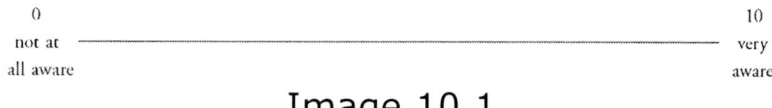

Image 10.1

How does this compare to where you were when you first started this book? Where do you want to be?

> [space left intentionally blank in the original book]
>
> As discussed in chapter 9, what are the internal and external barriers for you in stopping dissociation?
>
> [space left intentionally blank in the original book]

Recognizing Risky Situations

When you engage in less dissociation and more mindfulness skills, it becomes much easier to recognize safety and danger cues in your environment. First of all, you have to pay a good amount of attention to your environment and your own intuition.

Potentially Risky Situations

1. *Physical force or coercion to pressure you to do something that you do not want to do.* Physical coercion is a pretty straightforward concept. By this we mean that someone else is using physical force to get you to be involved in something that you don't want to be involved in. Examples may include sexual acts, unsafe sex, drinking

and driving, drug use, cheating, or criminal activity.

2. *Verbal force or coercion to convince you to do something you do not want to do.* Verbal coercion is a little more difficult to define than physical coercion. By verbal coercion, we mean that someone convinces you to do something by using threats or other manipulation. Examples include threatening to harm you, threatening your reputation if you don't comply ("I will tell everyone that you are a tease") or promising to support you in some way if you acquiesce ("I will be in a relationship with you if you have sex with me").

3. *Isolated situations.* Being in an isolated place, like someone else's apartment, makes it more difficult to get help or leave a situation if you feel you are in danger.

4. *Difficulty being assertive.* Difficulties setting boundaries or saying no can lead to being involved in activities in which you don't feel comfortable, such as criminal activities, drug use, or sexual activities.

Now that we've spelled out some potentially risky situations, you might wonder just what you're supposed to do about it if you find yourself approaching one of these situations. Well, for the first three instances, try to know your environment and pay attention to where you are and what's going on around you. Try to avoid isolated places, particularly if you are with someone you don't know very well. And always keep your cell phone handy in case you need it.

As for trying to be more assertive, this can be a difficult strategy for some trauma survivors. Remember that you have a right to your feelings and your personal space. Be clear if you do not want to do something (see "Assertiveness," below). And again, trust your instincts. If something is telling you to walk away, trust your intuition and leave the situation.

🔔 [What is your mind saying right now about this topic?]

Drugs and Alcohol and Revictimization

As discussed briefly in chapter 1, it is not unusual for survivors of trauma to use drugs and alcohol as a way to cope with uncomfortable emotions and memories. Remember, this is not about blame or judgment—in fact, our culture actively teaches us that substances are great to help you cope. AND it seems that trauma survivors are at especially high risk. Many men and women in substance-abuse treatment report current PTSD, and an even larger percentage of them report having experienced one or more traumatic events (Najavits 2006). In fact, substance-use disorders are far more common in trauma survivors than the general public (Kessler et al. 1995). And, we have found that many trauma survivors tend to minimize their own substance use. Research indicates that the following groups of trauma survivors have particularly high rates of substance use:

- Veterans

- Sexual-assault survivors

- Childhood sexual and physical abuse survivors

- Victims of domestic violence

- Rescue workers

We think it's important for you to be aware of the correlation between substance use and revictimization. This is not to point fingers or to place blame if you have already been revictimized but to help promote your own awareness of risky situations and staying safe. Additionally, drugs and alcohol are commonly used by perpetrators of trauma, such as rapists, batterers, and murderers, who may be under the influence at the time of the assault or use substances to help sedate the victim (Bureau of Justice Statistics, 2002). If you find that your drinking or drug use may be putting you at greater risk for more trauma, then access some of the resources given in chapter 11, including a number of self-help programs that are offered at no cost.

Exercise 10.6: Passengers on Your Bus During High-Risk Situations

It is likely the case that you have all the skills you need but have a hard time using them in certain situations. Sometimes just feeling overwhelmed and aroused can cloud our ability to notice what we are feeling and keep us from knowing how to act in a situation.

Think about some situations in which you're likely to feel overwhelmed. This will vary a lot from person to person, but some situations that our clients have told us about include asking a partner to wear a condom, telling someone to stop touching you, leaving a bar when thinking you've been drugged, or telling someone not to call you. Pick one situation where you feared your safety might have been threatened in the past, or one that you could foresee happening in the future and write it down below.

[space left intentionally blank in the original book]

Next, we want you to notice what could get in the way of you acting in an effective manner in the above situation. Remember the passengers on your bus? Take a moment to look at which ones are likely to show up in the front of the bus when you fear for your safety.

What thoughts come up front?

[space left intentionally blank in the original book]

What emotions come up front?

[space left intentionally blank in the original book]

After noticing these passengers, the issue is where to head the bus. What can you do to give yourself time to decide the effective thing to do? Here are some examples: take a bathroom break, excuse yourself from the table, or call a friend and get a second opinion. What else can you think of to help you when you get overwhelmed? Next time, try to notice the passengers on your bus who are talking to you right in that moment. We will talk a whole lot more about *how* you can drive your bus in the direction of effective behavior in the following section.

Interpersonal Skills: Helping You Stay in the Driver's Seat

Frequently, traumatic events happen in the context of interacting with other people. It can become easy to blame ourselves for these events ("I shouldn't have said that," "I shouldn't have been wearing that," "I should have known better," and so on). While what happened to you is not your fault, there are things you can do to help keep yourself safe in the future, and a lot of these things have to do with how you communicate with other people.

Similarly, regardless of the nature of your traumatic experience, your relationships with people are likely to have been affected in many different ways, including feeling misunderstood, having difficulty trusting others, feeling disconnected because of the physical distance (in the case of war), or having a reduced sex drive. The bottom line is that relationships may have been the context for trauma, or were likely impacted by your trauma, or can definitely help you in the process of finding life after your trauma. Therefore, this portion of the chapter is about interpersonal skills. 🔔[Any thoughts or judgments coming up?] This simply means skills you can use in relationships with other people, including family and significant others, coworkers and bosses, and even strangers. So, when we say relationships, we don't necessarily mean romantic relationships. As noted above, relationships include every person you know, whether it is a romantic partner, a friend, a family member, or the cashier at the grocery store.

We've spent most of our time in this book talking about approaching instead of avoiding. After reading the first part of this chapter, now you may be thinking, "I know when I'm in danger, but I don't know what to do about it." Now we're going to take some time to learn how to interact with people in ways that keep you safe, and how to react when you think you are in danger.

Do you ever have moments when you know you don't like something or when you suspect you might be in danger but feel helpless to do anything to change the situation? This may be because you, like many of us, have difficulty knowing what to do or say, or it may be because you have the skills but can't seem to use them in that particular situation ("I know what I should do, but I just can't seem to do it").

We're going to start by talking about things that prevent us from using the skills we already have when interacting with people. You may have already become aware of some these barriers in earlier chapters. Now we want to specifically address these in terms of relationships and safety. Then we'll present some new skills that you can add to what you already know.

Thoughts That Can Get in the Way

As discussed throughout the book, our internal experiences, when taken literally, can prevent us from achieving value-driven, long-term goals. We have looked at emotions specifically above; now we want to turn to thoughts. These may be thoughts such as "They won't like me if I say no" or "I don't want people to think I'm mean" or "I'll look weak if I ask for help" and so on. The first step in developing willingness to move forward *with* some of these thoughts is being able to recognize them when they do show up.

Exercise 10.7: Noticing Thought Passengers That Interfere with Safety

Write down five thoughts that, taken literally, may prevent you from doing what works in risky situations.

Examples: *I should know what to do. I'm going to screw things up again. I'm probably just overreacting again.*

1. _____

2. _____

3. _____

4. _____

---

5. _____

Now, take a second to look at the thoughts you listed above. In the spaces below, write ways in which you could have that thought and still do what works for you. In other words, write a response to that thought. For example, if you wrote above, "They won't like me if I say no," you may write here, "My mind is telling me this, but my experience has been that this isn't always true" or "My mind is telling me this, and even if it means they won't like me, I value my safety" or "Thank you, Mind, for that thought."

Defusion, appeal to experience, and a focus on value-driven action are all ACT strategies that may help you approach these old thoughts in new ways, in order to keep you safe and in healthy relationships. These are just a few suggestions. Only experience can reveal which strategy will work when and for whom. As we discuss in the next section, context is crucial.

1. _____

2. _____

3. _____

4. _____

5. _____

Context Is Everything

We believe that you probably have many of the skills you need to stay safe in the future. It may just be the case that some situations make it more difficult to use the skills than others. Sometimes it can be very easy to say no or ask for what we need in low-stakes situations. This may mean we can ask for help in the grocery store, but we can't ask for help within our personal lives. Or maybe we can say no when we're feeling calm and are not upset but find it more difficult when we are hurt or angry. (Remember exercise "How Full Is Your Tank" in chapter 2?) For these reasons, it can be helpful to practice asking for what we need and saying no in low-stakes situations. This can allow us to be better prepared to use interpersonal skills in difficult situations.

The first step when practicing using skills is identifying situations in which it would be easy for you to do what works and situations in which it is hard to use your skills. What makes a situation easy or hard may depend on lots of things, such as:

- Your relationship to the person (How well do you know him or her? Is this person in a position of power, such as a boss?)

- Similar past experiences (Have you had practice with the skill? For instance, if you have never asked for a raise before, it might feel more scary.)

- Believability of the thoughts you have when in the situation or imagining the situation

- The emotions that a situation invokes

Let's see if an example can help illustrate this point.

Case Story: Monica
Monica is very successful in her career. She is a manager in her company and is directly responsible for four other employees. She finds it easy to ask her employees to complete work-related tasks. She thinks, "I am their direct boss, therefore I have a right to ask them to complete this task. It shows that I am a competent leader in this company." Monica has

been feeling stressed lately due to an increasing workload, parenting difficulties, financial strain, and coping with a traumatic event. She has considered various things, including asking for some time off from work, requesting a raise, and asking for emotional support from a friend. Monica is encountering barriers to asking for these things and has thoughts such as "If I ask for time off, they may think I'm irresponsible" and "My friends have enough problems of their own; they don't need to worry about mine as well." When Monica makes a list of things that are easy to ask for and things that are difficult to ask for, it looks like this (going from easiest to most difficult):

1. Asking employees to complete work-related tasks

2. Asking my direct boss for help (additional people) to complete the work

3. Asking a friend to babysit so I can have some time to myself

4. Asking a friend for a loan to help pay a bill

5. Asking a friend if I can talk to her about some things I am struggling with

Now, we'll bring this exercise closer to home and ask you to identify what is easy or difficult for you to do as far as making requests of others.

Exercise 10.8: What Is So Hard About Asking for What You Want?

In the space provided below, create your own list of things that are easy and difficult for you to ask for (ranging from easiest to most difficult). Are there thoughts, feelings, bodily sensations, or memories that serve as barriers for you with each item?

1. _____

What makes this easy or difficult? [space left intentionally blank in the original book]

2. _____

What makes this easy or difficult? [space left intentionally blank in the original book]

3. _____

What makes this easy or difficult? [space left intentionally blank in the original book]

---

4. _____

What makes this easy or difficult? [space left intentionally blank in the original book]

5. _____

What makes this easy or difficult? [space left intentionally blank in the original book]

Now that you have your list, it's time to start practicing using your skills to ask for things that you need. Check your willingness level. Go back to your list and pick actions that you would be 100 percent willing to commit to doing this week. Start with the easiest thing on your list and work your way toward the most difficult. Preferably, put the book down right now and go call someone, or e-mail, or ask in person.

Whenever you complete each of the tasks, write in the spaces below any any observations you made about practicing asking for things you need.

1. When I _____, I noticed that [space left intentionally blank in the original book]

2. When I _____, I noticed that [space left intentionally blank in the original book]

3. When I _____, I noticed that [space left intentionally blank in the original book]

4. When I _____, I noticed that [space left intentionally blank in the original book]

5. When I _____, I noticed that [space left intentionally blank in the original book]

For each of the above examples, take a minute to think about how asking for help worked for you. Did it give you a little more free time? Did it help reduce your stress or help you feel connected to someone else? Remember, sometimes these requests will be denied. That is a normal part of the process for all of us. Notice the passengers that show up and see if you can continue driving in your valued direction.

Assertiveness: Saying No and Asking for What You Need

You've probably heard the phrase "just say no" or some equivalent of that. People who hear about your situation may say, "I don't know why you put up with it" or "I'd never let someone treat me that way." If we find ourselves in hurtful or dangerous situations, it does not mean that we like it that way or that we don't want to get out of them. Often we simply don't know how to make those changes. Learning to say no and ask for what we need is the first part of establishing boundaries and limits in relationships with other people.

When to Say No or Ask for Help
The two most frequent factors in saying no or asking for help are learning when it is appropriate to do so (discrimination training) and willingness to sit with some uncomfortable feelings and thoughts. Everything we have discussed so far in this book pertains to the second factor; for now, we would like to talk about the first: knowing when to say no. There is no easy way to know when it is the right or wrong time to say no. It all depends on your own limits and values. 🔔[Notice any bodily sensations coming up right now. Breathe.]

When we talk about limits, we are talking about how much you can take on before you start to feel overwhelmed. Sometimes we find that we say yes to everything and soon are so overwhelmed that we become paralyzed and can no longer do anything. Think about the old phrase "the straw that broke the camel's back." We put a straw on the camel's back, and it carries it easily. If the camel can carry one straw, it seems logical that it could carry two. So we add another straw, and the camel still carries the load easily. Then we add another one, and another, and so on, until instead of easily carrying the load, the camel's back breaks. We may have a tendency to continuously say yes to things until we cannot move at all. Becoming mindful of your limits means noticing your bodily reactions, your emotions, your thoughts, and your action urges so that you can know how many "straws" you can carry and still move around well in your life.

Exercise 10.9: The Straw That Broke the Camel's Back

Take a minute to think about the "straws" you carry on your back. These are things we do because our mind tells us we should do them or because we can't see a way to live our lives without doing them. They may be things we enjoy, or they may be things we dislike doing. They are all the things we have said yes to in our lives. These may be things such as taking on an extra shift at work, being there for a friend, or staying in a relationship. Write some of your straws below.

1. _____

2. _____

3. _____

4. _____

5. _____

6. _____

7. _____

8. _____

9. _____

10. _____

In the space below, pick five of the above straws that might be your "back breakers" and brainstorm ways in which you could say no or ask for help with that item. When thinking about how you might say no, consider what internal barriers you might need to address in order to be able to say no.

1. Straw: _____

New response: _____

2. Straw: _____

New response: _____

3. Straw: _____

New response: _____

4. Straw: _____

New response: _____

5. Straw: _____

New response: _____

Respecting Your Values

We won't spend much time talking about identifying values in this section, as we covered that in chapter 8. But saying no and asking for what you need becomes important when you are compromising the things you value in your life. This could be because you are saying yes to things that compete with your values. For example, you may value spending time with your children but agree to work extra shifts. Saying no requires an ability to identify when your values are being compromised, AND things are not always black or white. You may have to make compromises or delay certain goals. However, you can always remember your values and take small steps in those directions.

🔔 [Notice any emotions coming up.]

Exercise 10.10: Respecting Your Values in Relationships Even When It's Uncomfortable

This exercise is intended to help you identify relationship areas in your life in which your values are being compromised. Fill in the following spaces with the first thought your mind gives you. It's possible that some of this may not apply to you currently, AND it might still be useful to write down a situation where that value *could* be compromised.

1. In friendships I value _____

This value is not respected when [space left intentionally blank in the original book]

I could respect this value if I said no to or asked for [space left intentionally blank in the original book]

2. In romantic relationships I value_____

This value is not respected when [space left intentionally blank in the original book]

I could respect this value if I said no to or asked for [space left intentionally blank in the original book]

3. In my relationships at work I value _____

This value is not respected when [space left intentionally blank in the original book]

I could respect this value if I said no to or asked for [space left intentionally blank in the original book]

4. In my family relationships I value _____

This value is not respected when [space left intentionally blank in the original book]

I could respect this value if I said no to or asked for [space left intentionally blank in the original book]

5. In my interactions with acquaintances or strangers (for example, a repair person or cashier) I value

This value is not respected when [space left intentionally blank in the original book]

I could respect this value if I said no to or asked for [space left intentionally blank in the original book]

The above exercise is meant to bring a mindful perspective to your values in relationship areas and how these values could be compromised. Again, as discussed earlier in the book, sometimes we have to work hard at discrimination training—knowing what is a value violation and what isn't. Otherwise, it would be easy to ignore cues and turn them off. This could be another situation of leaving our hand on a hot stove.

Talking About Your Trauma

Talking about traumatic events can be a very *difficult* AND *positive* experience. We have spent the majority of this book explaining how avoiding thoughts and feelings surrounding your trauma can actually make your suffering worse. It makes sense, then, that talking about your trauma to others could be a healthy and adaptive means of coping. Unfortunately, some people have negative experiences when talking about their trauma. Sometimes the people we tell have negative reactions, such as telling us we deserved it, as in the case of sexual abuse or assault, or asking us not to talk about it because it's too upsetting to them, as in the case of terror attacks, natural disasters, or war. Sometimes our own minds give us thoughts such as "I shouldn't have said that" or "No one else needs to be pulled into this." Deciding what to tell, when to tell, and who to tell can be difficult decisions. We've put together some guidelines that can help make talking about your trauma a positive and healthy experience.

Who to Tell

There are no right or wrong people to talk about your trauma with. The important thing is to pick people that you trust and feel comfortable with, and whom you have found to be supportive in the past. It's not uncommon for people to tell others about their trauma only to feel ashamed and embarrassed later. This doesn't mean you shouldn't talk about your trauma, but it does mean that you should treat your story with respect. You will get the most benefit from telling your story by sharing it with someone who you feel will value having heard it. 🔔[Where is your mind right now?]

Relationship to the Person
When you are deciding who to share your story with, it's important to consider your relationship to this person. This includes the context in which you know them. Is the person a friend? A coworker? A family member? Is there a power differential (is the person your boss or a subordinate)? While the context in itself need not dictate whether or not you share you story with this person, it can help you gauge the workability of your decision, particularly relative to your values. For example, you may decide not to share with a coworker if you value keeping your professional and personal lives separate. People tend to have more positive experiences when they share their stories with those in their personal lives, as opposed to those in their professional lives. This does not mean you cannot share with coworkers or col-

leagues, especially since we often form friendships with coworkers and other professional colleagues. Ultimately, how the relationship type influences what you decide to share is up to you.

Intimacy of the Relationship

As we mentioned earlier, sometimes people have feelings of shame or regret after talking about their trauma. You can make this less likely by choosing to talk with someone you're fairly intimate with. Intimacy here is not necessarily romantic or sexual intimacy but rather a feeling of closeness. So, a question you can ask yourself is "How close do I feel to this person?" Of course, sharing your trauma may actually add intimacy to a relationship, but there normally needs to be a foundation in place before you talk about your trauma. Intimate relationships are generally relationships in which you can talk about your emotions, thoughts, and opinions and receive a supportive and caring response. You will probably have a better experience if you share your trauma with someone you already feel close to.

What to Tell and How to Tell It

Even if you can identify people in your life you would feel comfortable sharing your trauma with, it can be difficult to know exactly what to say or how to start that conversation. The following section can help you determine what you're willing to share and will give you some suggestions on how to ensure you get the most from the experience.

Choose What to Share

We may tell ourselves, "If I'm going to share this, I need to tell everything." This doesn't have to be the case—what you share is a choice. Sometimes we are only willing to share parts of a story or would prefer to share things one piece at a time. For example, you may decide that you would like a coworker to know that you're struggling with a trauma, but you may not feel comfortable sharing the details with that person. What you tell is entirely up to you. However, many people have difficulty hearing about the details of a traumatic experience. It can be helpful to tell people what happened in a general way. Some people may ask for more information, depending on their relationship to you and how much they know they can handle. It doesn't mean that they don't care about you or your experiences if there are things they don't want to know.

It's important to take time to think through what you're willing to share. If you find it helpful, write down the things you would like to disclose. Spend some time thinking about what it will be like to talk to this person, including how he or she might react and how you will feel. Remember, no matter how much you prepare for a conversation, it will never go quite as planned. This means you may end up sharing more or less than you originally intended, or the person's reaction may not be what you expected. Part of making this experience a positive one is being open to what happens in the moment. [Any reactions to this sentence?]

Prepare the Listener
Part of making this an effective experience is picking an appropriate time and giving the person you are sharing with a chance to prepare. This doesn't mean you have to schedule this conversation in advance. Actually, sharing these events is often easier when it comes as a natural part of a conversation. Preparing the listener simply means giving a heads-up on what you are about to share. This may only require you to say something like "I'd really

like to share something with you about my life. This is something that can be difficult for me to talk about, and it will mean a lot to me to be able to talk to you about it." By preparing the listener, you are also making it more likely that the experience will go well. The listener will then know that this conversation is important to you and that it may be difficult for you to share some things. Introducing the topic in this way makes it more likely that the listener will recognize the value in what you are sharing.

Time. Part of preparing the listener also includes picking an appropriate time to share. This means picking a time when the other person is available, both physically and emotionally. So, if you know that the person has several other tasks that require attention or is not emotionally present (he or she may be upset, using substances, distracted, and so on), pick another time to share your trauma. You will get more out of the experience if the person is available. In addition, make sure you have the time to tell your story. For example, don't tell your story if you only have five minutes before you go to work. Make sure you have time not only to tell your story but also to spend some time on the emotions and reactions that follow the telling.

Location. Where you decide to have the conversation can be as important as what you decide to say. Since you're sharing a very personal event, the location should reflect this. This isn't to say that you can't have the conversation in a public place, but the location should be a place where you can talk freely and comfortably. If you're worried other people may hear or are otherwise distracted by the environment, it will detract from your experience.

Tell the person what you need. Of course, you cannot dictate how a person should react or what the right response is, but you can help your listener along by explaining what you need from them. Although people may genuinely care and want to express this to you, sometimes people lack the skills to do so. Similarly, people may jump into problem-solving mode and try to "fix" your trauma. This can leave you feeling misunderstood or as though you didn't get the response you wanted or needed. Unfortunately, such disappointing responses can even insert distance into a relationship instead of intimacy. You can help people help you by telling them up front what it is that you want or need. Simple statements such as "It's really helpful just to have someone listen to me" or "What helps me the most is just being able to talk about this" can go a long way toward making sharing your trauma a better experience.

Exercise 10.11: Sharing Your Experience with Another Person

Take some time to think about who you might choose to share your trauma experience with. The questions below will help guide you through the different factors to consider.

1. What is your relationship to this person?

_____

2. How is sharing about your trauma with this person in the service of your values?

[space left intentionally blank in the original book]

3. How close do you feel to the person? Will sharing this increase your sense of closeness?

[space left intentionally blank in the original book]

528

4. How has this person reacted when you have shared emotions, thoughts, and opinions in the past?

[space left intentionally blank in the original book]

5. Which passengers on your bus might show up when you are actually talking about your trauma with this person? What would be an effective way of responding to them?

[space left intentionally blank in the original book]

6. Which passengers on your bus might show up after you talk to the person, regardless of the person's response? What would be an effective way of responding to them?

[space left intentionally blank in the original book]

7. If the person responds in a way that is disappointing to you, what can you do to take care of yourself?

[space left intentionally blank in the original book]

Your Valued Life Choices

The bottom line is that we want this work to be about your life choices. Many of our clients have come from situations where all their choices were made by someone else and they were always told what to do. This treatment is different. We hope we've offered you guidelines, ideas, and suggestions that will help *you* to choose your valued directions in relationships.

Journaling

Thoughts

[space left intentionally blank in the original book]

Feelings or Emotions

[space left intentionally blank in the original book]

Self-Judgments

530

[space left intentionally blank in the original book]

Physical Sensations

[space left intentionally blank in the original book]

Action Urges (What Do You Feel Like Doing?)

[space left intentionally blank in the original book]

CHAPTER 11

Moving Forward in Your Life: Additional Resources

with Kate Iverson

We must learn to be still in the midst of activity and to be vibrantly alive in repose.

—Indira Ghandi

You're Not Alone

Although the effects of trauma are often painful, it has been part of our goal to bring you to a point of understanding that the traumatic experience that you have endured does not define who you are as a person. Many people who experience trauma will recover naturally or find that they are able to live a vital life even while experiencing some trauma-related symptoms. However, if you find that, despite your efforts reading this book and doing the exercises, you are still experiencing distressing symptoms or you can't get past other obstacles in moving toward your values, then don't worry—you're not alone.

After going through one or more traumatic events, many people find that they need some additional help and support to live valued lives. The take-home message of this book is that trauma impacts everyone differently, and it is normal to struggle with the impacts of trauma. AND you do not have to spend the rest of your life in struggle mode. As discussed in the chapter 1, some factors that may be impacting you are:

- The severity or nature of the trauma you survived, such as interpersonal violence

- The who, what, when, and where aspects in which the trauma occurred, including social and cultural contexts

- Whether you have endured more than one traumatic event and whether the trauma continued over long periods of time, such as in war situations, child or partner abuse, or torture

- Your relationship to any perpetrator

- The length of time you've experienced post-traumatic stress disorder

- Individual factors, such as aspects of your individual genetic makeup (for instance, your temperament)

- The number of resources available to you, including social support, money, stable housing, and so on

- The coping strategies you know and can use effectively

- The amount of shame and guilt associated with the trauma

We believe that there are definitely situations that call for a therapeutic intervention from a trained professional. Needing this kind of intervention certainly doesn't mean that something is wrong with you. If you find that your symptoms do not go away with time or that you experience symptoms that are very severe, then you may want to consider seeking additional help through therapy. After all, about one-third of individuals who develop PTSD do not recover from the trauma on their own (Kessler et al. 1995). The good news is that there are effective interventions available to you.

When to Seek Help

Many trauma survivors seek therapy not only to address their struggles with PTSD symptoms, but also to address important aspects of their lives that aren't working—such as relationships, substance abuse, parenting, and work-related problems. Seeking therapy is not a sign of weakness but instead a sign that you take your life seriously enough to make an effort to have it work the way you would like.

Let's take a look at some signs that may indicate you might benefit from therapy. Do remember that this is not an in-depth list by any means:

- Ongoing nightmares related to the trauma

- Extreme distress reactions to reminders of the trauma, such as dissociation or substance use

- Suicidal thoughts or threats

- Self-harm behaviors, such as cutting, burning, or overmedicating

- Doing something that is against your values repeatedly

- Extreme irritability and anger outbursts that are interfering with intimate relationships or work productivity

- Being abused

- Abusing or neglecting someone else

- Feeling stuck in some or all aspects of your life

What You Should Expect from Therapy

The first thing you need to know is that therapy is confidential, meaning your therapist will not share any information with anyone unless you ask him or her to do so. Your therapist will discuss limits to confidentiality with you in your first appointment (reporting laws, ensuring safety, and legal involvement). Make sure you ask as many questions as you would like. Typically, you will first meet with a therapist for an "intake appointment" or evaluation so that the therapist can get a sense of some of the problems you are currently experiencing. The intake evaluation may involve completing paper-and-pencil measures and/or going through an interview. The therapist will work with you to develop goals for treatment that address your unique needs. If you are currently in a crisis situation, such as ongoing domestic violence, extreme suicidal thoughts, danger of harming someone else, or extreme substance abuse, your therapist will likely work with you to guarantee your safety before beginning therapy for PTSD. Once you begin therapy for PTSD, you will typically meet with a therapist once a week for approximately fifty minutes. The length of time that people need therapy varies.

Most individual therapists are sensitive to issues that are especially important when working with survivors of trauma, such as the following:

- The importance of providing a trusting and safe environment for the person seeking help. Many individuals with PTSD have trouble trusting others, particularly if the trauma they experienced involved other people (like abuse or assault).

- Paying attention to safety issues, such as those related to the need to give survivors control over the intensity of treatment or a person's safety after leaving a violent or abusive relationship.

- Providing adequate education and reassurance regarding PTSD symptoms and other symptoms, such as depression, over the course of treatment.

Additionally, your therapist should not ignore related problems that you may be experiencing, such as substance abuse or couple relationship problems.

What If You Feel Skeptical or Too Anxious to Try Therapy?

Many of us experience some doubt or worry about therapy or talking to a therapist. We live in a society that tells us to be tough or that only really messed-up people need therapy. The fact of the matter is, many successful people have gone to therapy and report that it has been helpful to them.

You may also worry about whether or not the therapist will be able to truly understand you if he or she has not gone through a traumatic experience. We believe that skilled therapists can help you regardless of their history. A metaphor to illustrate this point is presented below.

Recovering from trauma is like being in the process of climbing up a steep mountain that has lots of dimly lit places. It is the therapist's task to look at the places where people often struggle or slip while climbing the mountain, watching out for you and shouting out directions if he or she can see places you might slip or hurt yourself. A therapist would not be able to do this by standing at the top of your mountain and looking down at you. That is why you sought help from someone who is on a separate mountain, across the valley from you. That way, the therapist does not need to know exactly what it feels like to climb your mountain to see where you're about to step, and what might be a better path for you to take (adapted from Hayes, Strosahl, and Wilson 1999).

Effective Treatments for PTSD

If you have read this book and done all the exercises, you have probably gained quite a bit of insight into your struggles, including the factors in your life that may be keeping you in a continuous struggle. The purpose of this self-help book was to provide a starting point in the journey toward healing and recovery, an opportunity for compassion, healing, and growth.

Fortunately, there has been quite a bit of science and research aimed at understanding and treating PTSD. If you are experiencing PTSD, several treatment options are available for you including:

- Individual psychotherapy

- Group therapy

- Pharmacotherapy (medicines)

- Some combination of these

All of these treatments have demonstrated helpfulness for many people experiencing PTSD. Much of the information about these treatments is derived from practices recommended by the PTSD Treatment Guidelines Task Force established by the board of directors of the International Society for Traumatic Stress Studies (ISTSS) in 1997 and now published in *Effective Treatments for PTSD*, by Foa, Keane, and Friedman (2000). Psychologists and other appropriate mental health providers can help provide further education about reactions to trauma and ways of dealing with the emotional impact so that you can move forward in your life.

Electronic Resources

To find an ACT therapist or to learn more about ACT, visit the Web site for the Association for Contextual Behavioral Science (www.contextua lpsychology.org/therapist_referrals).

- The American Psychological Association (APA) Web site provides steps to help you locate a psychologist in your area. Simply go to http://locator.apahelpcenter.org/ and type in your zip code or city.

- The Association for the Advancement for Behavioral and Cognitive Therapies (ABCT) Web site provides an excellent computerized system for finding a cognitive-behavioral therapist in your area. Simply go to "Find a Therapist" (www.abct.org/members/Directo ry/Find_A_Therapist.cfm) and type in the city where you live, the format of therapy you are looking for (individual, group, couples therapy), and the problem(s) for which you are seeking help. The ABCT Web site also provides other helpful resources, such as a section designed to provide information and help for trauma and Disaster (www.aab t.org/091101%20Folder/091101/index.html). This Web site also includes helpful tips for finding a therapist.

- International Society for Traumatic Stress Studies (www.istss.org/) may also be helpful.

- The National Center for PTSD (www.ncptsd. va.gov) includes numerous helpful fact sheets associated with trauma, PTSD, and related problems.

You can find other ACT workbooks to help with depression, anxiety, and a variety of life issues at the New Harbinger online bookstore: www.n ewharbinger.com. There is also an ACT and trauma book for professionals published by New Harbinger.

We want you to know that we respect what you have survived and your efforts to move forward in your valued directions. We wrote this book because we have seen so much growth in people who have done this work. Our goal was to share some of that with you.

In peace,

Victoria and Jacque

References

Addis, M., and C. Martell. 2004. *Overcoming Depression One Step at a Time.* Oakland, CA: New Harbinger.

American Psychiatric Association. 1994. *Diagnostic and Statistical Manual of Mental Disorders.* 4th ed. Washington, D.C.: American Psychiatric Press.

Blackledge, J.T., and J. Ciarrochi. 2006. Assessing values in Acceptance and Commitment Therapy. Paper presented at the 2006 conference of the Association for Behavior Analysis in Atlanta, Georgia.

Brach, T. 2003. *Radical Acceptance: Embracing Your Life with the Heart of a Buddha.* New York: Bantam.

Brenner, N.D., P.M. McMahon, C.W. Warren, and K.A. Douglas. 1999. Forced sexual intercourse and associated health-risk behaviors among female college students in the United States. *Journal of Consulting and Clinical Psychology* 67:252–259.

Breslau, N. 2002. Epidemiologic studies of trauma, posttraumatic stress disorder, and other psychiatric disorders. *Canadian Journal of Psychiatry* 47:923–929.

Breslau, N., and R.C. Kessler. 2001. The stressor criterion in DSM-IV posttraumatic stress disorder: An empirical investigation. *Biological Psychiatry* 50:699–704.

Breslau, N., R.C. Kessler, H.D. Chilcoat, L.R. Schultz, G.C. Davis, and P. Andreski. 1998. Trauma and posttraumatic stress disorder in the community: The 1996 Detroit area survey of trauma. *Archives of General Psychiatry* 55:626–632.

Brewin, C.R. 2003. *Posttraumatic Stress Disorder: Malady or Myth?* New Haven, MA: Yale University Press.

Bryant, R.A. 2006. Cognitive behavioral therapy for acute stress disorder. In *Cognitive Behavioral Therapies for Trauma,* 2nd ed., 201–227, edited by V.M. Follette and J. Ruzek. New York: Guilford Press.

Bureau of Justice Statistics. 1992. Drugs and Crime Facts, 1991. Washington, DC. September 19.

Chiles, J.A., and K.D. Strosahl. 2004. *Clinical Manual for Assessment and Treatment of Suicidal Patients.* Washington, DC: American Psychiatric Association.

Chodron, P. 2001. *The Places That Scare You: A Guide to Fearlessness in Difficult Times.* Boston: Shambala.

Cloitre, M., L.R. Cohen, and K.C. Koenen. 2006. *Treating Survivors of Childhood Abuse: Psychotherapy for the Interrupted Life.* New York: Guilford Press.

Cloitre, M., and A. Rosenberg. 2006. Sexual revictimization: Risk factors and prevention. In *Cognitive Behavioral Therapies for Trauma,* 2nd ed., 321–361, edited by V.M. Follette and J. Ruzek. New York: Guilford Press.

Cloitre, M., K. Tardiff, P.M. Marzuk, A.C. Leon, and L. Potera. 1996. Childhood abuse and subsequent sexual assault among female inpatients. *Journal of Traumatic Stress* 9:473–482.

Cloitre, M.K., K. Tardiff, P.M. Marzuk, A.C. Leon, and L. Portera. 2001. Consequences of childhood abuse among male psychiatric inpatients: Dual roles as victims and perpetrators. *Journal of Traumatic Stress* 14:47–61.

546

Cramer, D. 2002a. Relationship satisfaction and conflict over minor and major issues in romantic relationships. *Journal of Psychology: Interdisciplinary and Applied* 136:75–81.

Cramer, D. 2002b. Satisfaction with romantic relationships and a four-component model of conflict resolution. In *Advances in Psychology Research,* 129–137, edited by S.P. Shohov. Hauppauge, NY: Nova Science Publishers.

Creswell, J.D., W. Welch, S.E. Taylor, D.K. Sherman, T. Grunewald, and T. Mann. 2005. Affirmation of personal values buffers neuroendocrine and psychological stress response. *Psychological Science* 16:846–851.

DePrince, A.P., and J.J. Freyd. 2004. Forgetting trauma stimuli. *Psychological Science* 15:488–492.

Dong, M., R.F. Anda, S.R. Dube, W.H. Giles, and V.J. Filetti. 2003. The relationship of exposure to childhood sexual abuse to other forms of abuse, neglect, and household dysfunction during childhood. *Child Abuse and Neglect* 27:625–639.

Dugas, M.J., F. Gagnon, R. Ladouceur, and M.H. Freeston 1998. Generalized anxiety disorder:

A preliminary test of a conceptual model. *Behaviour Research and Therapy* 36:215–226.

Foa, E.B., T.M. Keane, and M.J. Friedman. 2000. *Effective Treatments for PTSD.* New York: Guilford Press.

Follette, V.M., M.A. Polusny, A.E. Bechtle, and A.E. Naugle. 1996. Cumulative trauma: The impact of child sexual abuse, adult sexual assault, and spouse abuse. *Journal of Traumatic Stress* 9:25–35.

Follette, V.M., and J.I. Ruzek. 2006. *Cognitive-Behavioral Therapies for Trauma.* 2nd ed. New York: Guilford Press.

Forest, H. 1996. *Wisdom Tales from Around the World.* Little Rock, AR: August House.

Frankl, V.E. 1963. *Man's Search for Meaning.* New York: Washington Square Press.

Friedman, M.J. 2006. Posttraumatic stress disorder among military returnees from Afghanistan and Iraq. *American Journal of Psychiatry* 163:586–593.

Frijda, N.H. 2007. *The Laws of Emotion.* Mahwah, NJ: Lawrence Erlbaum Associates.

Hawking, S. 1988. *A Brief History of Time.* New York: Bantam.

Hayes, S.C., D. Barnes-Holmes, and B. Roche, eds. 2001. *Relational Frame Theory: A Post-Skinnerian Account of Human Language and Cognition.* New York: Plenum Press.

Hayes, S.C., V.M. Follette, and M. Linehan, eds. 2004. *Mindfulness and Acceptance: Expanding the Cognitive Behavioral Tradition.* New York: Guilford Press.

Hayes, S.C., J. Luoma, F. Bond, A. Masuda, and J. Lillis. 2006. Acceptance and commitment therapy: Model, processes, and outcomes. *Behaviour Research and Therapy* 44:1–25.

Hayes, S.C., and S. Smith. 2005. *Get Out of Your Mind and Into Your Life.* Oakland, CA: New Harbinger.

Hayes, S.C., and K.D. Strosahl, eds. 2004. *A Practical Guide to Acceptance and Commitment Therapy.* New York: Springer.

Hayes, S.C., K.D. Strosahl, and K.G. Wilson. 1999. *Acceptance and Commitment Therapy:*

An Experiential Approach to Behavior Change. New York: Guilford Press.

Hayes, S.C., K.G. Wilson, E.V. Gifford, V.M. Follette, and K.D. Strosahl. 1996. Emotional avoidance and behavioral disorders: A functional dimensional approach to diagnosis and treatment. *Journal of Consulting and Clinical Psychology* 64:1152–1168.

Heffner, M., and G. Eifert. 2004. *The Anorexia Workbook: How to Accept Yourself, Heal Your Suffering, and Reclaim Your Life.* Oakland, CA: New Harbinger.

Heidt, J.M., and B.P. Marx. 2003. Self-monitoring as a treatment vehicle. In *Cognitive Behavior Therapy: Applying Empirically Supported Techniques in Your Practice,* edited by W.T. O'Donohue, J.E. Fisher, and S.C. Hayes. Hoboken, NJ: John Wiley & Sons.

Herman, J.L. 1981. *Father-Daughter Incest.* Cambridge, MA: Harvard University Press.

Herman, J. 1992. *Trauma and Recovery: The Aftermath of Violence—From Domestic Abuse to Political Terror.* New York: Basic Books.

Hinsz, V.B., and R. Ployhart. 1998. Trying, intentions, and the processes by which goals influence performance: An empirical test of the theory of goal pursuit. *Journal of Applied Social Psychology* 28:1051–1066.

Hoge, C.W., C.A. Castro, S.C. Messer, D. McGurk, D.I. Cotting, and R.L. Koffman. 2004. Combat duty in Iraq and Afghanistan, mental health problems, and barriers to care. *New England Journal of Medicine* 351:13–22.

Kabat-Zinn, J. 1994. *Wherever You Go, There You Are: Mindfulness Meditation in Everyday Life.* New York: Hyperion.

Kabat-Zinn, J. 2005. *Coming to Our Senses: Healing Ourselves and the World Through Mindfulness.* New York: Hyperion.

Kelley, H.H. 1973. The processes of causal attribution. *American Psychologist* 28:107–128.

Kessler R.C., A. Sonnega, E. Bromet, M. Hughes, and C. Nelson. 1995. Posttraumatic stress disorder in the National Comorbidity Survey. *Archives of General Psychiatry* 52:1048–1060.

Kiser, L.J., and M.M. Black. 2005. Family processes in the midst of urban poverty: What does the trauma literature tell us? *Aggression and Violent Behavior* 10:715–750.

Kulka, R.A., W.E. Schlenger, J.A. Fairbank, et al. 1988. *Contractual Report of Findings from the National Vietnam Veterans Readjustment Study.* Research Triangle Park, NC: Research Triangle Institute.

Lamott, A. 1994. *Bird by Bird.* New York: Pantheon Books.

Linehan, M.M. 1993a. *Cognitive-Behavioral Treatment of Borderline Personality Disorder.* New York: Guilford Press.

Linehan, M.M. 1993b. *Skills Training Manual for Treating Borderline Personality Disorder.* New York: Guilford Press.

Locke, E.A., K.N. Shaw, L.M. Saari, and G.P. Latham. 1981. Goal setting and task performance: 1969–1980. *Psychological Bulletin* 90:125–152.

Loftus, E.F. 1993. The reality of repressed memories. *American Psychologist* 48:518–537.

552

Masuda, A., S.C. Hayes, C.F. Sackett, and M.P. Twohig. 2004. Cognitive defusion and self-relevant negative thoughts: Examining the impact of a ninety-year-old technique. *Behaviour Research and Therapy* 42:477–485.

Merrill, L.L., C.J. Thomsen, S.R. Gold, and J.S. Milner. 2001. Childhood abuse and premilitary sexual assault in male navy recruits. *Journal of Consulting and Clinical Psychology* 69:252–261.

Najavits, L.M. 2006. Seeking safety: Therapy for posttraumatic stress disorder and substance use disorder. In *Cognitive-Behavioral Therapies for Trauma,* 2nd ed., 228–257, edited by V.M. Follette and J.I. Ruzek. New York: Guilford Press.

National Center for Victims of Crime and the Crime Victims Research and Treatment Center. 1992. *Rape in America: A Report to the Nation.* Arlington, VA: National Center for Victims of Crime.

Nhat Hanh, T. 1987. *The Miracle of Mindfulness: A Manual on Meditation.* Boston: Beacon.

Orkutt, H.K., D.J. Erickson, and J. Wolfe. 2002. A prospective analysis of trauma exposure: The mediating role of PTSD symptomatology. *Journal of Traumatic Stress* 15:259–266.

Orth, U., and E. Wieland. 2006. Anger, hostility, and posttraumatic stress disorder in trauma-exposed adults: A meta-analysis. *Journal of Consulting and Clinical Psychology* 74(4):698–706.

Pennebaker, J.W. 2004. *Writing to Heal.* Oakland, CA: New Harbinger.

Pistorello, J., and V.M. Follette. 1998. Childhood sexual abuse and couples' relationships: Female survivors' reports in therapy groups. *Journal of Marital and Family Therapy* 24: 473–485.

Polusny, M., and V.M. Follette. 1995. Long-term correlates of child sexual abuse: Theory and review of the empirical literature. *Applied and Preventive Psychology: Current Scientific Perspectives* 4:143–166.

Rachlin, H. 2000. *The Science of Self-Control.* Cambridge, MA: Harvard University Press.

Rachlin, H. 1995. The value of temporal patterns in behavior. *Current Directions in Psychological Science* 4:188–192.

554

Rahe, R.H. 1978. Life change measurement clarification. *Psychosomatic Medicine* 40:95–98.

Resnick, H.S., D.G. Kilpatrick, B.S. Dansky, B.E. Saunders, and C.L. Best. 1993. Prevalence of civilian trauma and posttraumatic stress disorder in a representative national sample of women. *Journal of Consulting and Clinical Psychology* 61:984–991.

Riggs, D.S., S.P. Cahill, and E.B. Foa. 2006. Prolonged exposure treatment of posttraumatic stress. In *Cognitive-Behavioral Therapies for Trauma,* 2nd ed., 65–95, edited by V.M. Follette and J.I. Ruzek. New York: Guilford Press.

Roberts, L.J., C.F. Roberts, and K.E. Leonard. 1999. Alcohol, drugs, and interpersonal violence. In *Handbook of Psychological Approaches with Violent Criminal Offenders: Contemporary Strategies and Issues,* 493–519, edited by V.B. Van Hasselt and M. Hersen. New York: Plenum Press.

Rogers-Warren, A., and D.M. Baer. 1976. Correspondence between saying and doing: Teaching children to share and praise. *Journal of Applied Behavior Analysis* 9:335–354.

Roodman, A.A., and G.A. Clum. 2001. Revictimization rates and method variance: A meta-analysis. *Clinical Psychology Review* 21:183–204.

Salkovskis, P.M., and P. Campbell. 1994. Thought suppression induces intrusion in naturally occurring negative intrusive thoughts. *Behaviour Research Therapy* 32:1–8.

Schlenker, B.R., D.W. Dlugolecki, and K. Doherty. 1994. The impact of self-presentations on self-appraisals and behavior: The power of public commitment. *Personality and Social Psychology Bulletin* 20:20–33.

Sheldon, K., and A. Elliot. 1992. Goal striving, need satisfaction, and longitudinal well-being: The self-concordance model. *Journal of Personality and Social Psychology* 76:482–497.

Skinner, B.F. 1953. *Science and Human Behavior.* New York: The Free Press.

Smith, P.H., J.W. White, and L.J. Holland. 2003. A longitudinal perspective on dating violence among adolescent and college-age women. *American Journal of Public Health* 93:1104–1109.

Solso, R.L. 1991. *Cognitive Psychology.* Needham Heights, MA: Allyn and Bacon.

Stretch, R.H. 1991. Psychosocial readjustment of Canadian Vietnam veterans. *Journal of Consulting and Clinical Psychology* 59:188–189.

Stults, D.M., and L.A. Meesé. 1985. Behavioral consistency: The impact of public versus private statements of intentions. *Journal of Social Psychology* 125:277–278.

Tichener, E.B. 1916. *A Text-Book of Psychology.* New York: MacMillan.

Tjaden, P., and N. Thoennes. 1998. Full report of prevalence, incidence, and consequences of violence against women: Findings from the National Violence Against Women Survey. *Research in Brief* pp. 2 & 5. Washington, DC: National Institute of Justice, U.S. Department of Justice. November.

Tjaden, P., and N. Thoennes. 2000. Prevalence and consequences of male-to-female and female-to-male intimate partner violence as measured by the National Violence Against Women Survey. *Violence Against Women* 6:142–161.

U.S. Department of Health and Human Services, Public Health Service. 2000. *You Can Quit Smoking: Consumer Guide.* Washington, DC: U.S. Department of Health and Human Services, Public Health Service.

Walser, R. 2004. Stress, trauma, and alcohol and drug use. A National Center for PTSD fact sheet. *Iraq War Clinician Guide,* 2nd ed., edited by P.P. Schnurr and S.J. Cozza. Palo Alto, CA: Department of Veterans Affairs, National Center for PTSD.

Wegner, D.M. 1994. *White Bear and Other Unwanted Thoughts: Suppression, Obsession, and the Psychology of Mental Control.* New York: Guilford.

Wegner, D.M., R. Erber, and S. Zanakos. 1993. Ironic processes in the mental control of mood and mood-related thought. *Journal of Personality and Social Psychology* 65:1093–1104.

Wilson, K., and A. Murrell. 2004. Values work in acceptance and commitment therapy: Setting a course for behavioral treatment. In *Mindfulness and Acceptance: Expanding the Cognitive-Behavioral Tradition,* edited by S.C. Hayes, V.M. Follette, and M.M. Linehan. New York: Guilford.

Zindel, V., M.G. Williams, and J.D. Teasdale. 2002. *Mindfulness-Based Cognitive Therapy for Depression: A New Approach to Preventing Relapse.* New York: Guilford Press.

Victoria M. Follette, Ph.D., is a clinical scientist with a special interest in the etiology and treatment of trauma-related problems. She is professor of psychology and chair of the Department of Psychology at the University of Nevada, Reno. She was named Distinguished Alumna by the Department of Psychology at the University of Memphis, Tennessee, where she received her doctoral degree. Follette's clinical work is focused on survivors of interpersonal violence, and she examines the use of acceptance-based behavioral therapies in the treatment of this population.

Jacqueline Pistorello, Ph.D., is a psychologist with Counseling Services at University of Nevada, Reno (UNR). She earned her doctorate in clinical psychology at UNR and completed her clinical internship at Brown University Consortium. She specializes in two behavioral approaches, acceptance and commitment therapy (ACT) and dialectical behavior therapy (DBT), both of which have been gaining national and international acclaim. She has pioneered the conduct of these approaches to college counseling center settings, and currently has a grant from the National Institute of Mental Health (NIMH) to adapt DBT to college students and is writing another grant to implement ACT in the prevention of mental health problems among college students. In collaboration with Victoria Follette, she has been applying ACT and ACT-informed approaches to the treatment of trauma survivors, particularly child sexual abuse survivors, since 1989.

Image I

Books For ALL Kinds of Readers

At ReadHowYouWant we understand that one size does not fit all types of readers. Our innovative, patent pending technology allows us to design new formats to make reading easier and more enjoyable for you. This helps improve your speed of reading and your comprehension. Our EasyRead printed books have been optimized to improve word recognition, ease eye tracking by adjusting word and line spacing as well as minimizing hyphenation. Our EasyRead SuperLarge editions have been developed to make reading easier and more accessible for vision-impaired readers. We offer Braille and DAISY formats of our books and all popular E-Book formats.

We are continually introducing new formats based upon research and reader preferences. Visit our web-site to see all of our formats and learn how you can Personalize our books for yourself or as gifts. Sign up to Become A RHYW Registered Reader.

www.readhowyouwant.com

CPSIA information can be obtained at www.ICGtesting.com
Printed in the USA
LVOW070154021111

253045LV00017B/20/P